Withdrawn

THE KINGS & QUEENS OF
SCOTLAND

THE KINGS & QUEENS OF
SCOTLAND

EDITED BY

RICHARD ORAM

TEMPUS

First published 2001

PUBLISHED IN THE UNITED KINGDOM BY:

Tempus Publishing Ltd
The Mill, Brimscombe Port
Stroud, Gloucestershire GL5 2QG
Tel: 01453 883300
www.tempus-publishing.com

PUBLISHED IN THE UNITED STATES OF AMERICA BY:

Tempus Publishing Inc.
2 Cumberland Street
Charleston, SC 29401
Tel: 1-888-313-2665
www.arcadiapublishing.com

Tempus books are available in France and Germany from the following addresses:

Tempus Publishing Group   Tempus Publishing Group
21 Avenue de la République   Gustav-Adolf-Straße 3
37300 Joué-lès-Tours   99084 Erfurt
FRANCE   GERMANY

British Library Cataloguing in Publication Data.
A catalogue record for this book is available from the British Library.

ISBN 0 7524 1991 9

Typesetting and origination by Tempus Publishing.
PRINTED AND BOUND IN GREAT BRITAIN.

Front Cover, left to right: Mary Queen of Scots; David I; Seal of David I; Charles I

CONTENTS

INTRODUCTION

The kingship of the Scots, as a component of the modern British crown, is one of the oldest monarchies in the world. Its origins can be traced with a fair degree of confidence to the early sixth century AD and the kingship of the migrant Scots of Dál Riata in Ulster, who established a kingdom, also named Dál Riata, in the peninsulas and islands of the south-western Highlands of the country we know as Scotland. While the main purpose of this book is to trace the lives of the men and women, descendants of these first colonist kings, who occupied the throne of Scotland from the mid-eleventh to early eighteenth centuries, it will also explore the processes that brought mastery of the Scottish mainland to these heirs of piratical Irish warlords. In addition, however, it will also chart the histories of the other kingdoms and peoples with whom the Scots shared the north of Britain – Britons and Picts – who made their own unique contribution to the character and culture of the later kingdom. The first part of the book focuses on the usually violent processes by which the early rulers of the Scots gradually extended their mastery over the northern British mainland. It is a bloody – and in places bewildering – catalogue of heroes and villains, who almost literally carved their path to the throne and strove to extend their power over the land. From the violence and mayhem of these formative years, however, emerged a powerful monarchy that succeeded in projecting its authority over what we would now recognise as Scotland.

By the thirteenth century, the kings of Scots had emerged as one of the two most powerful rulers in the British Isles, controlling a kingdom that dominated the north of these islands. Having eliminated the last domestic challenges to their position, the later Canmore kings turned their energies towards welding what was still a disunited kingdom into a unified realm. It is testimony to their achievement that when their dynasty died out, the kingdom did not die with them but hung on to its new-found unity and growing sense of national identity in the face of seemingly insuperable threats to its independent status. Scotland's kings provided the nation with a focus that ensured its survival in the face of the ambitions of England's powerful Plantagenet rulers.

The traumas of the Wars of Independence and the civil wars between the supporters of Balliol and Bruce served to underpin the nation's identity in the fourteenth century. The legacy of these events was a fierce chauvinism that took as its focus the Stewart kings. The drive and ambition of that remarkable family saw Scotland emerge as a powerful player on the European stage, re-establishing contacts that led to a cultural cross-fertilisation from which grew the distinctive Scottish cultural identity of the later Middle Ages and Renaissance. The strident nationalism of the fifteenth century, however, gave way to a hard-headed realism in the sixteenth century as Scotland again moved closer politically to its neighbour and 'Auld inimie', England. It was perhaps the supreme irony of British history that, after centuries of struggle by kings of England to impose their mastery over the northern kingdom, it was a Scottish king who came south to rule as the first monarch of a united realm. It was not, however, a marriage made in heaven and there were several occasions when it seemed that the union would end in acrimonious divorce. In the end, however, it was the very threat of separation that forced both Scotland and England to reconsider their mutual interests, the result being the 1707 Act of Union. 1707 is not, of course, the end of the tale, which is still growing and evolving, but it marked a significant new departure in the history of Scotland's rulers as they moved towards a British and Imperial future. Thus, with the death of Anne, the last of the direct Stuart line to rule in these islands, we come to the end of a story that spans over one thousand years. The words of the earl of Seafield when Scotland's old parliament voted itself out of existence in 1707 are equally appropriate here. 'There's ane end of ane auld sang'.

A NOTE ON NAMES

In the first chapter, many of the names of the kings and great lords will be unfamiliar to most readers. The forms of the names used are, as close as possible, the Gaelic or Brittonic (the language of the Britons and Picts, akin to modern Welsh) versions by which these individuals would have been known. From the emergence of the Picto-Scottish kingdom of Alba, the names of the rulers are given in Gaelic with the modern anglicised form in brackets afterwards. From the mid-eleventh century onwards, the names are given in their most common modern forms. Place-names are generally given in their modern form, but occasionally older forms are used.

GENEALOGIES

The Kings of Alba

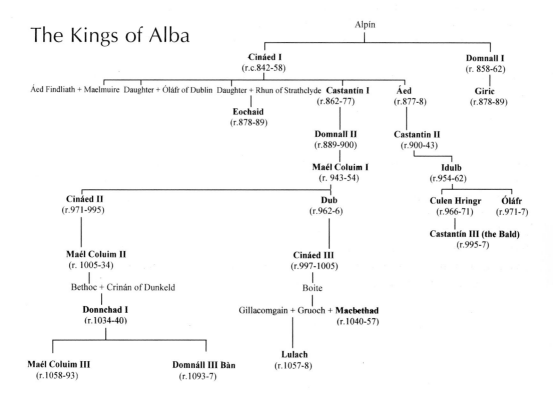

Alpín

Cináed I
(r.c.842-58)

Domnall I
(r. 858-62)

Áed Findliath + Maelmuire Daughter + Óláfr of Dublin Daughter + Rhun of Strathclyde **Castantín I**
(r.862-77)

Áed
(r.877-8)

Giric
(r.878-89)

Eochaid
(r.878-89)

Domnall II
(r.889-900)

Castantin II
(r.900-43)

Maél Coluim I
(r. 943-54)

Idulb
(r.954-62)

Cináed II
(r.971-995)

Dub
(r.962-6)

Culen Hringr
(r.966-71)

Óláfr
(r.971-7)

Castantín III (the Bald)
(r.995-7)

Maél Coluim II
(r. 1005-34)

Cináed III
(r.997-1005)

Bethoc + Crinán of Dunkeld

Boite

Donnchad I
(r.1034-40)

Gillacomgain + Gruoch + **Macbethad**
(r.1040-57)

Maél Coluim III
(r.1058-93)

Domnáll III Bàn
(r.1093-7)

Lulach
(r.1057-8)

The Canmore Dynasty

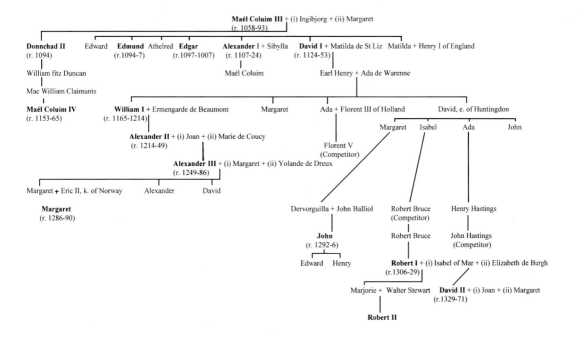

Maél Coluim III + (i) Ingibjorg + (ii) Margaret
(r. 1058-93)

Donnchad II
(r. 1094)

Edward **Edmund** Athelred **Edgar**
(r.1094-7) (r.1097-1007)

Alexander I + Sibylla
(r. 1107-24)

David I + Matilda de St Liz Matilda + Henry I of England
(r. 1124-53)

William fitz Duncan

Maél Coluim

Earl Henry + Ada de Warenne

Mac William Claimants

Maél Coluim IV
(r. 1153-65)

William I + Ermengarde de Beaumont
(r. 1165-1214)

Margaret

Ada + Florent III of Holland

David, e. of Huntingdon

Margaret Isabel Ada John

Alexander II + (i) Joan + (ii) Marie de Coucy
(r. 1214-49)

Florent V
(Competitor)

Alexander III + (i) Margaret + (ii) Yolande de Dreux
(r. 1249-86)

Margaret + Eric II, k. of Norway Alexander David

Dervorguilla + John Balliol

Robert Bruce
(Competitor)

Henry Hastings

Margaret
(r. 1286-90)

John
(r. 1292-6)

Robert Bruce

John Hastings
(Competitor)

Edward Henry

Robert I + (i) Isabel of Mar + (ii) Elizabeth de Burgh
(r.1306-29)

Marjorie + Walter Stewart

David II + (i) Joan + (ii) Margaret
(r.1329-71)

Robert II

The Stewarts

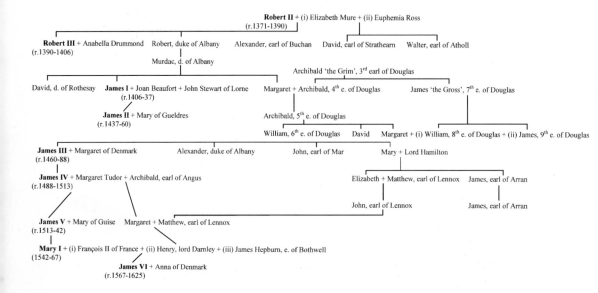

The British Stewarts

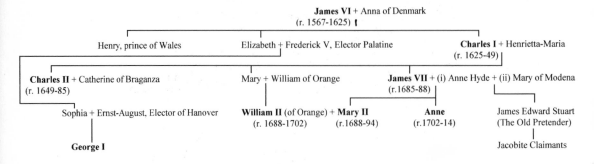

Key to genealogies

Monarchs in bold
Dates of reign ()
e. denotes earl
A broken line denotes illegitmacy
(i) denotes first husband/wife
(ii) denotes second husband/wife
(iii) denotes third husband/wife

MAPS

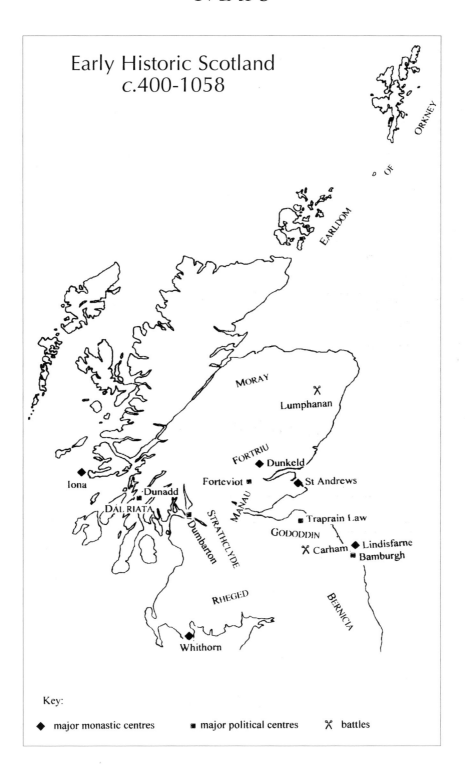

Early Historic Scotland
c.400-1058

ORKNEY

EARLDOM

MORAY

✗ Lumphanan

FORTRIU

◆ Dunkeld

Forteviot ■

◆ St Andrews

Iona ◆

■ Dunadd

DÁL RIATA

MANAU

■ Traprain Law

GODODDIN

STRATHCLYDE

Dumbarton

✗ Carham ◆ Lindisfarne

■ Bamburgh

RHEGED

BERNICIA

◆ Whithorn

Key:

◆ major monastic centres   ■ major political centres   ✗ battles

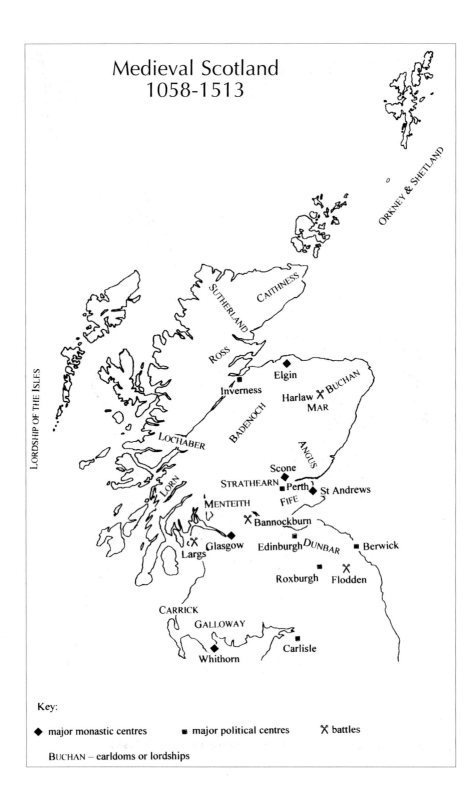

Medieval Scotland
1058-1513

ORKNEY & SHETLAND

LORDSHIP OF THE ISLES

SUTHERLAND

CAITHNESS

ROSS

Elgin

Inverness

Harlaw ✗ BUCHAN

MAR

BADENOCH

LOCHABER

ANGUS

Scone

LORN

STRATHEARN ■ Perth ◆ St Andrews

MENTEITH

FIFE

✗ Bannockburn

Glasgow   Edinburgh DUNBAR   ■ Berwick

Largs ✗

Roxburgh ■ ✗ Flodden

CARRICK

GALLOWAY

Carlisle ■

Whithorn ◆

Key:

◆ major monastic centres   ■ major political centres   ✗ battles

BUCHAN – earldoms or lordships

Early Modern Scotland
1513-1714

■ Inverness

Aberdeen ■

✗ Glencoe   ✗ Killiecrankie

Dundee

Perth   ◆ St Andrews

Stirling   Dunfermline

Linlithgow ■

Leith ✗ Dunbar

Edinburgh

Glasgow ◆

Key:

◆ major monastic centres   ■ major political centres   ✗ battles

THE EDITOR & CONTRIBUTORS

RO   Dr Richard Oram, University of Aberdeen

MP   Dr Michael Penman, University of Stirling

CM   Dr Christine McGladdery, University of St Andrews

MM   Dr Maureen Meikle, University of Sunderland

The Editor

Richard Oram is Honorary Lecturer in History at the University of Aberdeen and has written extensively on Scottish history. His other books include *Lordship of Galloway* and *Scottish Prehistory* and he is the editor of the new Scottish history magazine, *History Scotland*.

The Contributors

Christine McGladdery is Honorary Lecturer at the University of St. Andrews, her other books include *James II*.

Maureen M. Meikle is Senior Lecturer in History in the School of Humanities and Social Sciences at the University of Sunderland. She was co-editor, with Elizabeth Ewan, of *Women in Scotland c.1100-c.1750*. She is currently writing *Renaissance and Reformation: The Long Sixteenth Century in Scotland*, forthcoming in *The Birlinn History of Scotland* series.

Michael Penman is Lecturer in History at the University of Stirling. His first book *The Bruce Dynasty: David II* is out in 2002. He is currently researching a new biography of Robert the Bruce and a new interpretation of the battle of Bannockburn, also for Tempus.

ONE

THE EARLY KINGS
IN SCOTLAND, c.84-1058

THE EARLIEST KINGS, c.84 – 600 AD

The kingship of the Scots was one of the most ancient monarchies in the British Isles even in the Middle Ages, but it was a comparative newcomer in the ranks of rulers who emerge from the darkness of prehistory in the early centuries AD. The first chiefs or kings who appear are little more than names in the histories and records of the Roman campaigns in northern Britain in the late first century AD. They were the rulers of Celtic tribes whose territories lay in the path of the advancing legions. Of course, these were not kings as we would understand them today, rulers of well-ordered states whose governments were run by ministers and bureaucrats supported by a fiscal system, dispensers of justice and formulators of law for the good of their subjects generally. Early kingship was something quite different. It was, in the first place, much simpler. There were no bureaucracies, no government, no 'policy'. Justice was not yet the preserve of the king and his advisors, but lay in the hands – or, more exactly, the minds – of what became a hereditary class of lawyers and judges. Kings upheld the law, they did not yet formulate or dispense it. The king, however, was more than just a symbolic cipher; he did exercise real leadership, especially in times of war. Above all, he was the head of a hierarchical society.

The first Celtic chieftain to whom we can give a name is Calgacus (the 'Swordsman'), warlord of the tribe that we know as the Caledonians, who lived north of the river Tay. He led a confederation of tribes which opposed the Roman general Gnaeus Julius Agricola's invasion of this region in the 80s AD. In the writings of Agricola's son-in-law, the Roman historian Cornelius Tacitus, Calgacus appears as the civilized Romans' stereotypical image of the noble savage. There is nothing in Tacitus's account of Calgacus's resistance to Agricola's campaign, which culminated in the Caledonians' defeat at *Mons Graupius*, that can be accepted as representing the 'real' man. His great speech before the battle, memorable for its ringing description of the Caledonians as 'the last men on earth, the last of the free', is pure invention, laden with imperial propaganda. While Calgacus's supposed reference to the fate in store for his people under Roman rule, 'they create a desolation and they call it peace', is probably an accurate reflection of what did lie ahead, it was nothing more than a member of the Roman intelligentsia's criticism of what he considered the moral degeneracy of his supposedly superior state in comparison to the purity and simplicity of the barbarian. Indeed, when shorn of all the noble sentiments for which Tacitius made him the mouthpiece, all that survives of Calgacus is his name.

Over a century later, the next Celtic ruler to be mentioned in Roman records of northern Britain is an equally faceless name: Argentocoxos ('Silver Leg'). He appears in the Roman writer Dio Cassius's account of the early third-century campaigns in northern Britain of the Emperor Septimius Severus as the leader of a confederation of tribes from which probably emerged the later kingdom of the Picts. In this account, he is presented as more than just a war-leader, conducting negotiations for peace with the emperor in 210 and breaking his word and the treaty soon afterwards. Again, however, Dio Cassius's image of Argentocoxos is a stereotype in which probably only the name is real.

These chance survivals of Celtic names in Roman sources have become straws at which generations of historians have clutched in an effort to explain the emergence of the earliest kingdoms. These were kingdoms of the people we refer to as *Britons*, the descendants of the tribesmen who had opposed the legions in the first and second centuries AD. They were the Celtic people who occupied most of the mainland of Britain until the arrival of the Angles and the Saxons from what is now modern Germany. Although they had acquired a veneer of Roman civilization, their culture and art was the direct descendant of that of pre-Roman Britain and, rather than the Latin used in the Empire, they spoke a language akin to modern Welsh.

Some historians have argued that several early royal dynasties of these Britons within what is now Scotland owed their power and position to the imperial authorities. The Romans, it has been said, set them over peoples living on the northern fringes of the imperial province of Britannia (roughly equivalent to modern England and Wales) to provide stability and a buffer against more hostile territories beyond the effective reach of Roman power. For example, the genealogies of the sixth-century kings of Rheged, whose territory wrapped round the head of the Solway Firth, traced their descent to Magnus Maximus. He was a late fourth-century general who used Britain as the springboard for a bid for the imperial throne. It has been suggested that this supposed descent from Magnus Maximus probably represented his appointment of a trusted agent to rule over a strategic frontier zone, from whom the later kings were descended, rather than an actual ancestral link. Similar arguments have been advanced for Padarn Pesrut, a ruler over the district known as Manau in the area now repre-

2. The defences of the Iron Age fort on the Mither Tap o' Bennachie, Aberdeenshire. The low ground on the northern side of the hill has been identified as a possible site of the great battle of *Mons Graupius*.

3. Inscribed Roman tablet from the Castlehill Station, Antonine Wall.

4. The Antonine Wall at Rough Castle, Bonnybridge, Stirlingshire. Beyond this line lay the territory of the *Maeatae*.
5. Dumyat, Stirlingshire, the 'Fort of the Maeatae', one of the peoples from whom the early kingdoms emerged.

sented by Clackmannan, eastern Stirlingshire and western West Lothian, whose style 'Pesrut' has been interpreted as 'of the red cloak' or 'red tunic'. His red cloak has been viewed as evidence that he held some official status in Roman frontier society, with the giving of the cloak marking his appointment to political authority. Recent re-analysis, however, has suggested that he did not have a red cloak but a red shirt, and in any case purple was the imperial colour, not red. Much, too, has been based on the presence of the names Cinhils and Cluim in the pedigree of the kings of the Britons of Strathclyde, representing the Celticized forms of the Roman names Quintilius and Clemens. But names alone are not sufficient evidence for Roman origins for these men, and it must be remembered that in the sixth and seventh centuries, when many of these genealogies were constructed, the Britons were seeking to present themselves as the heirs of Rome in the struggle against the new barbarians, the Germanic Angles and Saxons who were steadily encroaching on Celtic territory.

One of the early kingdoms of the Britons for which a direct descent from a Celtic tribe of the Roman period into a post-Roman power can be confirmed is that of the Gododdin. Here, the name alone shows a succession from the *Votadini* tribe recorded in Roman writings, whose territory stretched from the Tweed into the Forth valley, to the sixth-century Gododdin. While the tribe, whose territory appears largely to have avoided a military garrison system during the various phases of Roman military occupation of southern Scotland, must have existed in some kind of friendly client relationship with Rome for most of the period down to the late fourth century, Roman influence over its culture appears slight. Indeed, when the ruling elite of Gododdin can first be glimpsed, striding boldly through the words of the early Welsh poem *Y Gododdin*, there is nothing Romanized in their behaviour and attitudes other than their Christianity, and they epitomize everything that is Celtic and barbarian, like some echo from late Greek and early Roman descriptions of the continental Celts.

Gododdin was just one of a series of Christian British kingdoms to evolve in the country beyond the old imperial frontier in the Southern Uplands of Scotland. In the central Borders' valleys of Ettrick and Yarrow a shadowy dynasty ruled the territory of another tribe first recorded in the Roman period, the *Selgovae*. They are the most elusive of these early rulers, their presence recorded only in such monuments as the Yarrow Stone, a monolith raised in commemoration of 'Nudus and Dumnogenus, the sons of Liberalis', as its worn inscription proclaims. The rulers of the neighbouring kingdom of Rheged emerge as far more substantial figures from verses attributed to the poet Taliesin and from the fragmentary historical account known as *Historia Brittonum*. Rheged was one of the more substantial and powerful kingdoms of the Britons. Centred most probably on the old Roman *civitas* at Carlisle, its territory stretched south down the western side of the Pennines and north and west into Galloway. In the earlier sixth century, it had also extended east of the Pennines to Catterick in Swaledale, but by the time of Urien or Urbgen, perhaps the greatest of its kings, that eastern enclave had already fallen to the spreading power of the pagan Angles. *Historia Brittonum* tells us of wars waged by Urien in an effort to regain this strategic outpost that controlled the eastern end of the trans-Pennine routes, and in poetic tradition he appears as leader of a powerful cavalry war-band that drove the Anglian foot-soldiers back to their stronghold at Bamburgh. Urien seems to have been a man of ability and foresight, who understood the threat that Anglian power posed to all the northern kingdoms, not just his own. In the late 580s, he succeeded in assembling a coalition of British kings which in 590 managed to storm Bamburgh and trap the fleeing Anglian king and his warriors on the tidal island of *Medcaut*,

6. Traprain Law, East Lothian. The hillfort was the chief centre of the *Votadini* during the Roman period.

7. Edinburgh Castle, identified as the *Din Eidyn* of Mynyddog, king of Gododdin.

the modern Lindisfarne. With victory within sight, however, the jealous rivalry of the Britons surfaced and, in an act of treachery, Urien was murdered by one of his 'allies', Morcant, ruler of an unidentified kingdom. To Taliesin and later writers, Urien's death was a disaster from which Rheged – and the rest of the Britons – never recovered, for the collapse of his coalition allowed the Angles a respite in which they consolidated their power and returned to pick off the divided Britons one by one.

Rumours of Rheged's demise were greatly exaggerated. Urien's successors may never have regained the power and authority that he had held, but Ywain map Urbgen was remembered in Welsh poetic tradition as a mighty warrior, while his younger brother, Rhun, established more friendly ties with the Angles and may have stood sponsor for Edwin, king of Northumbria, at his baptism. Rhun's son, Royth, however, appears to have been the last of his line and with him the kingdom of Rheged vanishes from history. Royth's daughter, Riemmelth, was one of the two wives of Oswiu, king of Northumbria from 641 to 670, and it is possible that through this tie some part of Rheged passed into Anglian control. Arguments for a peaceful union, however, should be discounted, for it is unlikely that the male members of the wider royal kin in Rheged would have allowed their 'inheritance' to fall to a stranger simply because his wife was daughter of the last king. Friendship or alliance between Rheged and Northumbria did not extend to unopposed absorption and political extinction of one by the other. When the Northumbrians occupied the territory of Rheged, it was as conquerors and colonists, not as heirs by marriage.

Rheged was not the first of the northern British kingdoms to fall in the face of the Northumbrian advance. *Y Gododdin*, the poem attributed to the Welsh poet Aneirin, describes preparations made by Mynyddog, king of Gododdin, for a campaign in about the year 600. The poem describes his entertainment in his hall at *Din Eidyn*, probably underlying the present Edinburgh Castle, of a select force of heroic warriors drawn from all the kingdoms of the Britons and even from among their cousins the Picts, the Celtic people who lived to the north of the Firth of Forth. It was a riotous, drunken assembly of boastful braggarts, each determined to outdo the others in acts of reckless bravery. Aneirin concentrates on the 300 chieftains that formed the core of the expedition, but doubtless they were accompanied by their retinues for the attack on Catterick that followed. It is ironic to a modern reader that Aneirin's epic tale ended in the bloody slaughter of the Gododdin warriors, not the expected victory, but this is a celebration of glorious, if ultimately futile, deeds not a commemoration of triumph. Defeat at Catterick broke the power of Gododdin, for in the early 600s the Angles were spreading into the Lothian plain, while the Scots of Dál Riata also sought to fill the vacuum left by the collapse of the British kingdom. By the middle of the seventh century, the only British power of any consequence to survive was the Dumbarton-based kingdom of Strathclyde.

RO

THE KINGS OF STRATHCLYDE c.450-1018

Of the people that traced their descent as successors of the Celtic tribes that had emerged by the time that the Romans stamped their mark on what is now Scotland, the Britons of Strathclyde, the heirs of the *Damnonii* of the lower Clyde valley, were ultimately the most successful and longest lived. As the other kingdoms of the Britons slowly fell before the advancing power of the Northumbrians, Strathclyde rose to pre-eminence and in Scottish sources her kings were referred to not just as *a* king but *the* king of the Britons. To add to the confusion, their kingdom was sometimes referred to as Cumbria (the 'Land of the Fellow Countrymen), a name that is now used to describe only the region of north-western England that was for a time the southernmost part of Strathclyde. In later Scottish minds, the only Britons were the Britons of Strathclyde. Their tribal kingdom, with its chief centre at *Ail Cluaide* ('The Rock of the Clyde'), known to the later Gaelic-speaking Scots as Dumbarton ('The Fort of the Britons'), emerged from the shadows of fifth-century Roman Britain in a letter from the British missionary in Ireland, St Patrick. This letter lambasted the war-band of a king named Ceretic, identified in later genealogies as a founding figure in the Strathclyde dynasty, branding them as slave-takers and allies of the Picts and Scots, not fellow citizens of Romans and Christians. The implication is that Ceretic and his men liked to think of themselves as Roman, and one of the titles used by his grandson, Dyfnwal Hen, suggests that the Strathclyde kings saw themselves as *protectores* or rulers of a Roman federate people. Little more is known of either him or his descendants down to the middle of the sixth century, other than that they were leaders of a powerful war-band that played an important role in the internecine rivalry among the galaxy of petty kingdoms that emerged from the ruins of the Roman province of Britannia.

By the mid-sixth century, Strathclyde's rulers rise from the still confused and confusing documentary records as firm historical figures rather than the semi-mythical characters of the early genealogies. Tudwal, grandson of Dyfnwal Hen, for example, appears in an eighth-century poem about the miracles of St Ninian as a tyrannical persecutor of the saint and his mission, while his son Rhydderch Hael was a contemporary and friend of St Columba and participated in the great confederation of northern British kings assembled by Urien, king of Rheged, against the growing power of the Angles of Bernicia. In the mayhem and confusion of this turbulent period, Strathclyde's rulers sought allies amongst the other emergent powers of the northern British mainland, forging ties through marriage. It appears, for example, that Tudwal's aunt married a prince of the Scots, a people from the north of Ireland who had begun to settle in the area now known as Argyll. This was Gabrán, whose son, Áedán mac Gabráin, established his kingdom of Dál Riata as the military powerbroker in the north in the late sixth century. Tudwal's nephew, Beli, who ruled as king in the 620s, forged links with the dominant Pictish kingdom of Fortriu, and one of his sons, Bridei, became one of the Picts' most successful kings. The general impression from these alliances is of a minor power, surrounded by bigger players, seeking security through ties with its more powerful neighbours. All of this changed, however, from the middle of the seventh century.

Strathclyde emerges unexpectedly as a significant power in the 640s, indeed, it became the most powerful of the northern kingdoms. Its location was highly strategic, as it controlled several of the major routes providing access to and from the south-west Highlands – via Loch Lomond and Strathcarron – into the central Lowlands and the Southern Uplands. For the Scots of Dál Riata in particular, who had long cherished ambitions to expand eastwards into the fertile lowlands, Strathclyde was a major obstacle. In 642, Domnall Brecc, king of Dál Riata, was defeated and slain in Strathcarron by his kinsman Ywain map Beli, king of Strathclyde. The Britons' poets exulted in the triumph. 'And the head of Dyfnwal Frych [Domnall Brecc],' one gloated, 'ravens gnawed it'. This new-found power continued through the seventh century, with Strathclyde dominating both the Picts and the Scots. Ywain's son Elffin, for example, seems to have played a signif-icant part in the triumph of his uncle Bridei mac Beli, king of the Picts, over the

8. Dumbarton, citadel of the Britons of Strathclyde.
9. Loch Lomond, Dumbartonshire. The strategic routes through the kingdom of Strathclyde radiated from the southern end of this inland waterway.

Northumbrians in 685. But in a world of shifting loyalties and alliances, the Britons of Strathclyde soon found themselves confronted by their former allies. In 750, at Mugdock to the north-west of Glasgow, Ywain's great-grandson Tewdwr fought against, defeated and slew Talorgen, brother of the powerful Pictish king Unuist son of Uurguist. His defeat of what was at that time the most powerful war-band in the north was a setback for Pictish power, but victory had evidently come at a cost. In the same year, Tewdwr was clearly unable to prevent Eadberht, king of Northumbria, from conquering and annexing the district of Kyle in what is now central Ayrshire, a region that had probably fallen within Strathclyde's orbit. In 756, Unuist gained his revenge for the death of his brother when, in alliance with Eadberht and the Northumbrians, the Picts invaded Strathclyde, sacked Dumbarton, and forced Tewdwr's son, Dyfnwal, into a humiliating submission.

Strathclyde remained under Pictish domination into the early ninth century but enjoyed a brief renaissance of its power during the period when the Scot Cináed mac Alpín (Kenneth mac Alpin) and his successors were consolidating their hold over the former Pictish kingdom (see below pp 36-39). By the mid-ninth century, however, Strathclyde was facing new and more powerful enemies in the shape of the Norse of Dublin and the emergent hybrid kingdom of the Picts and the Scots. In 871, after a four-month siege, the Norse stormed and sacked Dumbarton, carrying off shiploads of prisoners, possibly including Strathclyde's king, Arthgal, to the slave-markets of Dublin. The following year, apparently with the connivance of the king of Scots, Castantin mac Cináeda (Constantine I mac Kenneth), whose sister was married to Arthgal's son Rhun, Arthgal was put to death by his captors. The influence of the Scots was now dominant in Strathclyde, underscored by the Gaelic name Eochaid given to Rhun's son. Eochaid's Gaelic blood ensured him a place in the turbulent succession to the Scottish kingship and from 878 to 889 he ruled jointly with his cousin Giric. It is probable that Eochaid was very much the junior partner in this arrangement, possibly little more than Giric's client-king over Strathclyde, but the association ensured that when Giric was deposed in 889 Eochaid, too, was overthrown.

Tradition states that from the time of Eochaid Strathclyde was simply a satellite of the rapidly expanding kingdom of the Scots. In support of this, it has been suggested that Castantin mac Áeda (Constantine II mac Aed), king of the Scots, imposed his brother, Domnall mac Áeda (Donald mac Aed), as king over the Britons, and that henceforth Strathclyde served as a training-ground for future Scottish rulers. That interpretation, however, has always been difficult to reconcile with the evidence for a continuing line of British-named kings, possibly descended from Eochaid's brother, Dyfnwal, and the supposed implanting of Domnall mac Áeda has been shown to be based on a flawed reading of an early chronicle. While Strathclyde may have become a client of Scottish kings, it survived as a recognizably independent entity.

The upheavals of the ninth century had a profound impact on the kingdom. There is little sign that Dumbarton was reoccupied as the chief seat of Strathclyde power after 871, with new centres at Cadzow and Lanark in Clydesdale emerging in its place. This south-eastwards drift also saw a significant expansion of Strathclyde power into the territory of the crumbling Northumbrian kingdom. In the tenth century, Strathclyde influence stretched into the Solway plain, and Carlisle and Cumberland fell within its boundaries. At the height of this expansion, the River Eamont at Penrith and the Rey Cross on Stainmore marked the southern limits of Strathclyde's power. This expanded authority appears to have been achieved in alliance with the Scots. In 934, Ywain, king of Strathclyde, and Castantin, king of the Scots, were put to flight by Athelstan, king of Wessex, and in 937 the two were again active in the field against the English, this time in alliance with Oláfr Gothfrithsson, king of Dublin. In 945, an English army ravaged Strathclyde in retaliation for the Britons' support of the Dublin Norse, and King Edmund of Wessex is said to have given the kingdom to Máel Coluim mac Domnaill (Malcolm I), king of the Scots. Arch-survivors, the native dynasty still maintained its grip on its kingdom in the person of Ywain's son, Dyfnwal. But in 973, Dyfnwal is recorded to have submitted to the English king, Edgar, and may have resigned his kingdom to his son, Máel Coluim. Certainly, Dyfnwal is reported to have travelled to Rome, where he became a priest and died in 975. The background to his resignation in 973 may have been the killing in 971 of Culen, king of the Scots, by Rhydderch, who has been identified as a son of King Dyfnwal. The killing, reported as Rhydderch's response to the abduction and rape of his daughter by Culen, was followed by the devastation of Strathclyde by the warriors of Culen's successor and a bloody battle in which the Britons were victorious. Despite this show of defiance, however, Strathclyde was being drawn increasingly under the domination of the Scots and the extinction of its independent existence loomed. Máel Coluim's brother and successor, Ywain, known to history as Owen the Bald, was to be its last independent king. In 1018, Ywain joined the army of his overlord, Máel Coluim mac Cináeda (Malcolm II), king of the Scots, for an invasion of Northumbria. Although the campaign ended in a victory at Carham, Ywain appears to have been one of the battle's casualties. There is no evidence that he had any family, and the next ruler of Strathclyde appears to have been Donnchad, grandson of the Scottish king. This time, the takeover was final.

RO

THE KINGS OF DÁL RIATA c.500-843

Strathclyde's western neighbour, Dál Riata, was a comparative newcomer on the political map of Britain in the sixth century. This was the original kingdom of the Scots, the core from which the medieval kingdom eventually grew, and its rulers are often referred to in early annals simply as 'king of the Scots'. Occupying much of what is now Argyll, the kingdom, according to the traditional accounts, was the result of a steady migration of Gaelic-speaking Irish colonists – known as *Scotti* – from the eastern Ulster kingdom of Dál Riata, over which a semi-mythical king, Fergus Mór mac Erc, had extended his unifying rule. Both portions of the kingdom were known as Dál Riata, distinguished geographically as either 'Scottish' or 'Irish', but the name here is used to refer to the 'Scottish' element alone. The extent of any migration from Ireland is subject currently to question, but it is clear that by the sixth century the islands and penin-sulas of Argyll were inhabited by a people who, although they shared much in common with their neighbours, the Britons and Picts, spoke the Gaelic language of the Irish and looked to Ireland for political, cultural and spiritual leadership. Little else about them is certain, and it is practically impossible to disentangle fact from fiction in the various origin legends that were developed to explain the process of state-building involved in the formation of Dál Riata.

The best known of these origin legends identifies the three *cenéla*, or kinship groups, into which the people of Dál Riata were later divided, as being descended from the three sons of Fergus Mór. In northern Argyll, occupying the district now known as Lorn, was the *Cenél Loairn*. Islay and its associated islands were the territory of the *Cenél nOengusa*, while Kintyre and the Cowal peninsula were controlled by the *Cenél nGabráin*. The traditional account identifies Gabrán, from whom the *Cenél nGabráin* supposedly took their name, as the eldest of the three brothers, hence his *cenéla*'s control of the kingship over all three kindreds. This model, however, is no longer accepted at face value, and Gabrán and his kin and dependents are seen instead as later arrivals in Argyll who imposed their mastery over two earlier groups of colonists. Whatever the processes involved, by the middle of the sixth century the Scottish kingdom of Dál Riata had achieved a measure of unity and had emerged as a powerful force in relations with its neighbours, the Picts and the Britons of Strathclyde. Indeed, there are some suggestions that Gabrán's family had already begun to intermarry with the Picts – a development that foreshadowed the ninth-century fusion of the Picts and Scots under a single king. The relationship, however, was not entirely peaceful, and when the Irish missionary and politician St Columba arrived in Argyll in 563 he entered a recently defeated kingdom whose ruler, Conall mac Comgaill, was possibly subject to Pictish overlordship.

Columba was a prince of the all-powerful Irish Uí Neill kindred and was a key figure in the Church in north Ireland. His role in Dál Riata was as much political as religious, for he was deeply involved in the appointment of Conall's first cousin Áedán mac Gabráin as king there in 574. Áedán may have been exiled from Argyll in the 560s and had returned to claim the kingship at the head of a large war-band, forcing the Scots to select him over Conall's son. In terms of re-establishing Dál Riata as a major power, it was a wise choice, for Áedán quickly proved to be an aggressive and ambitious warrior-king. By 575, he had redefined the relationship between his kingdom and its nominal overlord back in Ireland, the king of the northern Uí Neill, in an agreement that revealed the naval and military strength of Dál Riata. By the 580s, that strength was being projected around the northern maritime world, with Áedán's fleet raiding Orkney and Man, while his war-band penetrated deeply on plundering raids into Pictland. In the 590s, he was without question the dominant power in the northern British Isles, exerting influence over his mother's kin in Strathclyde and expanding his domain into Pictish territory. The emergence of an aggressive new power in the Angles of Bernicia – the northern half of Northumbria centred on Bamburgh in Northumberland – presented him with fresh opportunities and challenges. Raids into Bernician territory, both of which ended in defeat, on the second time in the landmark battle of Degsastan in 603, have in the past been presented as his part in a 'pan-Celtic' response to the threat of the growing strength of the Germanic Angles, but should probably be seen as little other than opportunistic predatory raids. Their consequences, however, were far-reaching, for Degsastan confirmed Bernician control over the Solway plain, while also signalling a dramatic decline in Dál Riata power that accelerated after Áedán's death in 608. This image of Áedán as a ruthless predator is at odds with that of the pious and wise ruler offered in some sources. This gentler presentation derives from the writings of Abbot Adamnán of Iona, in whose *Life of St Columba* the king appears as a devout and obedient devotee of the saint, on whose counsels he depended. Columba may indeed have exercised some influence over Áedán, for the king's disastrous military decisions followed the saint's death in 597, but it is recognized widely by historians that Adamnán's stress on Áedán's deference to Columba was part of the late seventh-century abbot's efforts to establish his right to political infuence over Dál Riata kings of his own day. Behind Adamnán's portrayal still lurks the violent warlord of the earlier records.

While Degsastan had been a serious check to Dál Riata power, expansion and aggression remained the chief characteristics of its kings – as recorded in the annals – after Aedán's death. His son and successor, Eochaid Buide, continued to project his authority over neighbouring

10. Dunadd, Argyll and Bute, citadel of the Scots of Dál Riata.

11. Dunollie Castle, Oban. The medieval ruins occupy the site of the fortress of the Cenél Loairn segment of the Dál Riata kings.

12. Iona Abbey. The restored medieval monastery buildings occupy the site of Columba's sixth-century monastery.

territories, against which he launched a succession of predatory raids aimed at the securing of plunder with which he could maintain his position as a 'good king' to his warriors. The bubble, however, burst in the reign of Eochaid's son, Domnall Brecc ('Freckled' or 'Spotty' Donald). Although he possessed the drive and ambition of his forebears, he had none of their luck. His reign is recorded in a catalogue of five battles between 622 and 642, two in Ireland, in which he lost control over his family's homeland, and three on the Scottish mainland, in the last of which, against the Strathclyde Britons, he was defeated and killed. Domnall's death brought the aggressive expansionism of the *Cenél nGabráin* to an abrupt end. It also ended the *Cenél nGabráin*'s monopoly on power, for over the next century they were challenged for the kingship by successive heads of *Cenél Loairn* and by a rival segment of their own kindred, the *Cenél Comgaill*. It is hard to avoid the impression from this period that Dál Riata had dissolved into a series of petty and rival kingdoms, one or other of which, from time to time, succeeded in imposing its domination over the rest. In the 670s and 680s, the dominant force were the *Cenél Loairn*, whose ruler, Ferchar Fota, is recorded as 'king of Dál Riata'. His war-band, however, was routed by the men of Strathclyde in 678 and it seems improbable that he maintained control over all of Argyll down to his death in 697. This ebb and flow of power continued into the eighth century, with the *Cenél Loairn*, under their king, Selbach, again achieving a brief mastery in the early 720s. By this date, Scottish divisions and weakness had attracted the attention of Dál Riata's powerful neighbours, and from the 720s the kingdom was drawn increasingly into the orbit of the Picts.

In 741, Unuist mac Uurguist, or Óengus I mac Fergusa, to give him the Gaelic form of his name, the all-powerful Pictish king, sent his war-bands into Dál Riata and, having defeated its rival kings, imposed his overlordship over the Scots. As Unuist's name indicates, the boundaries between Pict and Scot were already blurred, and there are strong arguments in favour of the ruling elite of Pictland already having been essentially Gaelic and Gaelicized in character, but this should not hide the fact that the Scots had been defeated and subjugated by a hostile foreign power. Periods of independence were intermittent and brief. In the 770s, Áed Find, who in 768 had won a victory over the Picts in Strathearn, restored some kind of unity to the Scots, but after his death in 778 it appears that Pictish overlordship was restored, albeit in the form of a dynasty of Dál Riata origin. Indeed, it seems that these half-Pictish half-Gaelic kings also held the kingship of Dál Riata into the ninth century, with the heads of the Dál Riata *cenéla* reduced to the status of subordinate clients. By the 830s, it appeared certain that Dál Riata would be absorbed wholly as a province into the increasingly powerful Pictish kingdom, but in 839 the Pictish ruling line was eliminated in a single battle against the Danes. Out of the wreckage stepped Cináed mac Alpín, an obscure *Cenél nGabráin* dynast, who in the 840s succeeded in imposing his lordship over Pictland and began the creation of the Picto-Scottish kingdom that we know as *Alba*.

RO

THE PICTISH KINGS c.550-c.848

Despite several decades of research, the Picts – the inhabitants of most of what we now call Scotland north of the Firth of Forth – are still a problematic people. The problems do not surround the origins, culture and society of the Picts: much of the old mythology built on the idea of a mysterious people who appear from nowhere and then equally mysteriously vanish into the mists of history, leaving only a legacy of inscrutable carvings and indeci-pherable inscriptions, has been swept away in the light of more recent archaeological discoveries. Instead, they centre on the difficulties of establishing a coherent narrative history for the Pictish kings before the later eighth century. Part of this difficulty lies in the bewildering labyrinth of the succession to the Pictish kingship, with usually no clear links evident between the holder of that kingship, his predecessors or successors. To some scholars, this characteristic has been seen as evidence for a system of matrilinear succession, where the kingship was transmitted through the female line to sons of women of the ruling kindred, but for others it is simply a sign of the political fragmentation of Pictland, with a variety of territorial kindreds vying for control of an over-kingship. It is, as yet, an unre-solved dispute.

In the past, the possibility of a unique succession system and other seemingly exotic charac-teristics led to the suggestion that Pictish society contained a significant element of a much older culture, pre-Celtic and possibly representing the survival of traditions that dated back to the Bronze Age or earlier. We can, however, now say with confidence that the Picts were cultur-ally a Celtic people, whose language was related to that of the Britons of southern Scotland and whose material culture was largely indistinguishable from that of their neighbours. In short, they are the descendants of the tribesmen who opposed Agricola's legions in the 80s AD and Septimius Severus in the early third century. By the 190s, the earlier patchwork of rival tribes had coalesced into larger confederations. Two of these, known in Roman records as the *Mæatae* and *Caledonii*, fought against Rome in the period 196-211, while in the fourth century we hear of two groups of Picts named *Verturiones* and *Dicalydones*. It has often been assumed that these groups are largely interchangeable, with *Verturiones* being and alternative name for the *Mæatae* and so forth, but this is far from certain. Place-names suggests that the *Mæatae* were located in the Stirling area – Myot Hill near Denny and Dumyat, the westernmost summit of the Ochil Hills, representing modern forms of *Mæatae* – while the *Verturiones*, whose name may later be represented by the Pictish *Fortriu*, a kingdom centred on lower Strathearn, can be positioned to their north and east, beyond the Ochils. Roman sources simply locate the *Caledonii* or *Dicalydones* 'beyond' the *Mæatae*, a hopelessly vague description that has seen them being labelled as the inhabitants of the mainland north of the mountain massif of the Cairngorms and the Mounth. Yet, what place-name evidence we have, such as Dunkeld and Schiehallion – the fort and the *sidhe* or 'fairy hill' of the Caledonians – would locate them in Strathtay and the river valleys feeding in to it. Such a location, too, is 'beyond' the *Mæatae* and *Verturiones*. The issue, however, is further clouded by the writings of an early eighth-century Northumbrian monk, Bede, who described the Picts as being divided into two groups, those who lived 'on this side of the mountains' and those who lived beyond them. This bipartite division, usually presented as northern and southern divisions, has been seized upon as evidence for the continuation of the earlier groupings represented by *Verturiones* and *Dicalydones* in particular, and has been built into an elaborate theory of kingdoms of Northern and Southern Picts. Beyond the naming of one king, Bridei mac Máelchú, whose stronghold near Inverness was visited by Columba, however, there is no evidence that such a northern kingship ever existed. Indeed, from the later sixth century onwards, it is clear that the heart of the Pictish kingdom lay in the area repre-sented by the later counties of Angus, Perthshire and Fife, and it is here that the men known to history as 'king of the Picts' were based.

The earliest recorded Pictish kings are little more than names in lists. The first to appear as something more is Bridei mac Máelchú, who flourished between *c.*555 and *c.*584. He occurs in Adamnán's *Life of Columba* as the king to whose court the saint travelled in the early 560s on what seems to have been primarily a diplomatic mission. Bridei is recorded to have inflicted a crushing defeat on the Scots of Dál Riata in c.559, a defeat that may have resulted in the death of their king, Gabrán mac Domangart, the exile of his son, Áedán, and the subjection of the Scots to Pictish overlordship. Bridei's success won him the title *rex potentissimus*, 'most powerful king', from Adamnán, writing over a century after the king's death. Little more is known of his acts, but Adamnán provides some important information concerning his lifestyle and court. Bridei, and most of his people, were pagan, and one of Columba's objectives was to win his protection for Christian missionaries within his domain. His power reached to Orkney, for a sub-king of *Orcc* is recorded as being present at Bridei's court. The king's main adviser was a druidic priest named Broichán, who exercised great influence over Bridei and his nobles, and who remained an implacable foe of Columba's. The king's court was in a strongly fortified hillfort, at the heart of which stood the royal 'house' or hall, where Bridei met with his counsellors and where ceremonial feasting would have taken place. Bridei, however, did not meet with Columba in the hall, but went to meet him in the open, for it was believed that the saint was a powerful wizard and that it was more difficult for magic to work in open sunlight than in a closed chamber. When all this is put together, we are provided with an image of a powerful warrior king, whose authority, based on his position as the head of a society dominated by a pagan priesthood on one hand and a warrior aristocracy on the other, stretched from Argyll to Orkney.

After Bridei, the picture descends once again into confusion. There is some evidence that kings such as the Scot Áedán mac Gabráin of Dál Riata and Neiton and Beli, kings of Strathclyde, established some kind of overlordship over the Picts and that some may, indeed, have ruled as joint kings. From the 650s, the dominant power in the British Isles was Northumbria – which consisted of all of what is now England north of a line from the Humber to the Mersey and a large part of Scotland south of the Forth-Clyde line – and the Northumbrian king, Oswiu, succeeded in establishing his mastery over the Picts. From 653 to 657 he imposed his nephew Talorgen, son of Eanfrith, as king over the Picts and, after a military offensive in the 660s to reconfirm his control over them, established a second puppet, Drest. In 672, however, following Oswiu's death, Drest was expelled by the Picts and a new king, Bridei mac Beli, the uncle of Dyfnwal, king of Strathclyde, took the throne. This reversal brought a savage response from the new Northumbrian king, Ecgfrith, who in 672 inflicted a crushing defeat on the Picts, slaughtering their army and forcing Bridei to acknowledge his overlordship. In 685, however, Bridei gained his revenge when his army annihilated Ecgfrith and the cream of his warriors at Dunnichen or Nechtansmere at Letham near Forfar. For an all too brief period, now, the Britons and their Pictish satellites dominated the north.

After Bridei mac Beli's death in 693, there was a fresh Northumbrian challenge for the mastery of Pictland, but that was halted in its tracks by the victory of the new king, Bridei mac Derile, in battle in 698. Bridei was succeeded in 706 by his brother Nechtan mac Derile, but the Pictish successes of the previous twenty years did not continue. Nechtan's reign did not progress auspiciously. In 711 his army suffered a crushing defeat at the hands of the Northumbrians, and the Picts again submitted to some degree of Northumbrian overlordship. The defeat may have opened up the fault lines within the Pictish kingdom, for two years later Nechtan's brother Cináed was killed in an internal power struggle, and in the same year Nechtan imprisoned his kinsman Talorgen mac Drostan, who may already have been

13. Craig Phadraig, Inverness. The hillfort overlooking the confluence of the River Ness
with the Beauly Firth may have been the site of Bridei mac Máelchú's stronghold, visited
by St Columba.

14. Burghead Bull, Moray. A frieze of bull sculptures may have adorned the walls of the
Pictish fortress.

15. 'The Battle Stone', Aberlemno, Angus. The battle scene on the rear of this Pictish Class II sculptured stone has been interpreted by some as a representation of the Pictish victory over the Northumbrians in 685 at nearby Dunnichen or Nechtansmere.

sub-king of Atholl. One factor in these disputes was the attempt by one dynastic segment to monopolize power in its hands, a move resented bitterly by other leading kindreds who considered that they had a right to seek the kingship. These crises drove Nechtan into a deeper dependence on Northumbria, whose ecclesiastical influence was reasserted over the Pictish Church by 717 when the king expelled the clergy linked to Columba's monastery at Iona from his kingdom. The crisis within Pictland, however, deepened rather than eased and in 724 Nechtan was driven from his throne and forced into a monastery by Drest, the head of one of the rival lineages. That, however, was just the beginning of the struggle, for in 726 full blown civil war erupted when Nechtan came out of his 'retirement' and attempted to regain his throne. Drest defeated and captured Nechtan, but later in the year was himself defeated and deposed by a third contender, Alpín. A further complication was added the following year when Unuist mac Uurguist, or Óengus mac Fergusa, a man evidently of Gaelic ancestry but described as king of Fortriu, entered the contest and inflicted three defeats on Drest; in 728 he triumphed over Alpín too. Unuist's victory may have persuaded Nechtan mac Derile to make another bid for power, and later in 728 he totally defeated the weakened Alpín and resumed the kingship of the Picts. In 729, however, Nechtan was challenged by Unuist, defeated and driven for a final time into monastic life, where he died c.732. Having dealt with Nechtan, Unuist now turned to Drest, who still controlled a war-band, and defeated and slew him in battle. This victory marked the beginning of a Golden Age of Pictish power, albeit under a man of apparently Dál Riata background.

The reign of Unuist mac Uurguist marked a new high tide of Pictish might, charted in the records by a catalogue of battles and acts of violence. Having thoroughly crushed all opposition to him from rival potentates, he embarked on an aggressive policy of extending his authority beyond the bounds of Pictland. His first ambitions in the direction of Dál Riata, led by his son Talorgen, were defeated heavily in 731. In 736, as the internal disputes within the kingdom of the Scots escalated, Unuist himself led an invasion of Dál Riata that resulted in the capture and sack of the citadel of Dunadd, the capture of two of King Selbach's sons and the devastation of the land. His next victim was Talorgen mac Drostan, the ruler of Atholl, who had been an opponent of Nechtan mac Derile's as long ago as 713. His kingdom was an area of Gaelic settlement that bordered to the north Unuist's own power centre in Fortriu. The annals record laconically in 739 the drowning of Talorgen by Unuist. Two years later, Unuist's power reached a new high point when he again invaded Dál Riata, defeating and slaying its king, Indrechtach, in a battle that the annals described as the 'smiting' or 'overthrow' of Dál Riata. All the evidence suggests that the Scots were reduced to the status of tributary vassals.

This spread of Pictish power was of major concern to the Britons of Strathclyde, who must have felt threatened by the extension of Unuist's might around their northern and western borders. In 744 there was the first in a series of wars between the Britons and Picts, culminating in 750 in a crushing defeat for the latter at the hands of Tewdwr, king of Strathclyde, which saw the death of Unuist's brother Talorgen mac Uurguist. We know little about the consequences of this battle, but it seems that for the two years until his death in 752 Tewdwr succeeded in imposing his overlordship over the Picts, and Unuist's over-kingship may successfully have been challenged from within Pictland. The annals link the death of Tewdwr in 752 to a brief civil war in Pictland which saw Unuist defeat a certain Bridei mac Máelchú, a link which implies that Bridei was dependent on Strathclyde. Unuist regained the over-kingship and in 756 sought to take his revenge on Strathclyde. In alliance with

Eadberht of Northumbria, the Picts invaded Strathclyde, captured and sacked Dumbarton and forced Dyfnwal map Tewdwr into a humiliating submission. The Britons won a quick revenge, cutting to pieces the booty-laden Pictish army as it returned to Fortriu, but this stinging reprisal did not seriously undermine Unuist's power. When he died in 761, probably aged over seventy, he was still the greatest power in the north.

Pictish power declined abruptly after Unuist's death and by 768 Dal Riata, under Áed Find, had shaken off their mastery and succeeded in defeating the Pictish king, Cináed, in Fortriu itself. Again, the decline resulted in a succession of challenges for power between rival kindreds within Pictland. In 789, the then reigning king, Conall mac Tadc, was defeated by a certain Castantin mac Uurguist, a man of probably Dál Riata origin and possibly the nephew of Áed Find. Conall escaped and succeeded in holding on to some semblance of power until about 807, when he was killed in Kintyre and Castantin's reign was considered to have begun. Castantin represented something new, a Gaelic kindred that was determined to keep power within its own hands and freeze the other major Pictish kindreds out of any contention for the throne. Furthermore, whereas past rulers of Pictland had ruled Dál Riata through vassals or dependent kinsmen, Castantin clearly ruled both territories as king. It seems then that around forty years before the traditional date at which Cináed mac Alpín (Kenneth mac Alpin), king of Dál Riata, took the kingship of the Picts, the major migration east of the Scots had already begun and that from soon after 800 Pictland was ruled by a succession of Gaelic-speaking Scots.

The migration of the Scots appears to have been linked to the intensification of Viking raids on the western coast and islands of Scotland, raids that had seen the burning of Iona in 795, 802 and 806. The eastward shift in Scottish power was intended to be more than just a foreign warlord imposing his over-kingship on a defeated people, for Castantin was clearly building a firm base for his new regime. From 807 until his death in 820, Castantin fostered ties with the Church in Pictland, especially the monastery at St Andrews, which was developed as the major cult centre of the new monarchy that was being constructed. The mac Fergus lineage may have been working closely with the Church to develop its image and authority. Castantin's name, the Gaelic form of the Latin *Constantinus*, may have been part of this process. It is perhaps no accident that this, the name of the first Christian emperor of Rome, was adopted into a lineage that was to display remarkable pretensions as a renewer of Christian life in its kingdom and which had a considerably exalted view of its own status. The process continued under his brother and successor, Óengus II mac Fergusa, who appears to have been responsible for the foundation of a new monastery at Dunkeld, to which relics of the great saint of Dál Riata, Columba, were eventually brought following the abandonment of Iona in the face of increasing Viking attack. Óengus, in co-operation with the senior clerics of his kingdom, who were in regular contact with the Europe of the Frankish empire of Charlemagne and his sons, developed an increasingly sophisticated view of his kingship. The principal symbol of this was his palace complex at Forteviot in Strathearn, south of Perth, from which only a few fragments of sculpture remain, which may have been modelled on the Carolingian palaces at Aachen and Maastricht. Placed in the heart of Fortriu in lower Strathearn, amongst the richest farmland in his kingdom, the palace was at the core of a 'ritual' landscape that incorporated already ancient prehistoric remains – now only visible from the air as cropmarks – along with new monuments such as the Dupplin Cross, richly carved with the symbols of Biblical royal power. At the time of his death in 834, Óengus had established his kingdom as the premier force in the northern British Isles.

16. Strathearn, the heartland of the Pictish kingdom of Fortriu.

17. The Royal Huntsmen – the Biblical King David portrayed as an image of kingship on the side panel of a sculpted shrine from St Andrews, Fife.

18. The 'Drosten Stone', St Vigean's, Angus. The small inscription on the stone may commemorate one of the last Pictish kings, Uurad mac Bargoit.

While the mac Fergus dynasty had unmistakably Gaelic roots, it appears to have sought to accommodate its Pictish subjects and, indeed, to have adopted many Pictish character- istics. One aspect of this may be seen in the naming of the male members of the ruling house, with Castantin's younger son, who apparently succeeded Óengus in 834, being given the Pictish name Drest. This 'Picticizing', however, should not be overstated, for Drest's successor, Óengus's son, had the decidedly Gaelic name Eóganán. Where this hybridized dynasty would have led the kingdom of the Picts and the Scots is, however, a matter of conjecture, for the experiment was terminated abruptly in 839. It is with remark- able understatement that an Irish annal for that year notes that 'a battle was fought by the gentiles [Vikings] against the men of Fortriu, and in it fell Eóganán, Óengus's son, and Bran, Óengus's son, and Áed, Boanta's son; and others fell, almost without number.' In a single battle with Danish raiders, the male membership of the mac Fergus line had been eliminated. Their slaughter, however, did not mark the end of the Pictish state, for although the traditional histories suggest that Eóganán's successor was Cináed mac Alpín, who was to emerge by c.840 as king of the Scots of Dál Riata, the Pictish king lists show that he was probably opposed by a short-reigned succession of rulers, possibly descended from a female line of the mac Fergus kings, all of whom appear to have met violent ends within the space of six years. The first of the line, Uurad mac Bargoit, who may be commemorated in an inscription at St Vigean's in Angus, died in 842, the year in which Cináed began his conquest. Uurad's sons, Bridei (d. 842), Kineth (d. 843) and Drest (d. 848), followed him in succession, possibly ruling a rump territory restricted to eastern Perthshire and Angus. It seems that Cináed's kingship may not have been secure until the elimination of the last of these rivals and that the year 848 rather than the traditional earlier dates marks the confirmation of his power, for in 849 the relics of Columba were brought to the monastery of Dunkeld in a symbolic transfer of Gaelic Dál Riata power from Argyll to the heart of Pictish territory. Although neither Cináed nor the Picts may have recog- nized it, a new entity was coming into being.

RO

THE KINGS OF ALBA c.843 TO 1058

Most lists of kings of Scots start with Cináed mac Alpín (Kenneth mac Alpin or Kenneth I) and claim that he was the first to rule over both Dál Riata and Pictland, uniting the two kingdoms to form Scotland. That claim is now known to be false, but he is still credited with being the first Gaelic ruler to establish a lasting dynasty, which was eventually to monopolize on kingly power in the northern British Isles. Indeed, it is from him that the modern British monarchy traces its descent. Although he was the founding figure of the longest-lived royal family in Britain, very little is known about him. While he is labelled as *Cenél nGabráin*, his exact relationship to the old Dál Riata ruling house is very obscure, and the best that can be said is that he came from a junior branch of the family. He was, however, spectacularly successful. Within three years at most from the elimination of the mac Fergusa rulers by the Danes, Cináed had established control over Dál Riata. By the early 840s, however, the Scots' homeland in Argyll was coming under sustained attack from marauding Norsemen, some of who may already have been settling in the Isles. Chronicle accounts credit Cináed with providing for the defence of Dál Riata by inviting Gofraid mac Fergusa, a man whose name

19. The handbell of St Columba, one of the holy relics of the Dál Riata saint which were moved to Dunkeld in 849.
20. Dunkeld Cathedral, Perth and Kinross. Cináed mac Alpín re-established the Pictish monastery here as the cult centre of his new dynasty.

21 & 22. 'Sueno's Stone', Forres, Moray. The largest piece of Dark Age sculpture in Europe, the reverse of the cross-slab (left) carries a 'cartoon-strip' depiction of battle and its bloody consequences for the defeated, possibly recording the Scottish conquest of Moray in the ninth century. At the base of the cross front is a scene depicting a royal inauguration.

23. Kirk Michael Cross, Isle of Man. Ancient Scotland, especially Dál Riata, formed part of a wider Irish Sea cultural and religious community along with Man and of course Ireland.

suggests that he was half-Norse, half-Gael, to come over from Airghialla in Ireland to settle in the west. With Argyll secure, Cináed turned towards the east.

In recent years, there has been a tendency towards emphasizing the possibly peaceable nature of Cináed's takeover of the kingship of the Picts, but this is probably wishful thinking. If the Picts had welcomed him with open arms, accepted his Gaelic lordship, embraced the Gaelic aristocracy that arrived in his wake and willingly given up their whole language and culture in favour of that of the newcomers, they would have been unique amongst the Early Historic peoples of Europe in their readiness to consign their very identity to oblivion. This modern view of peaceful integration, which stresses the evidence for a long process of cultural interchange and accommodation between the two peoples, is sharply at odds with the early chronicle traditions that speak in terms of invasion, treachery, betrayal and slaughter. When Cináed came east in 842-843, it was as a conquering invader. It is probably no coincidence that Uurad mac Bargoit died in 842 and that his family perished with monotonous regularity over the next six years. Indeed, the chronicles suggest that Cináed's final victory over the Pictish opposition occurred as late as 847-848. That his grip was by then secure is indicated by his bringing of relics of Columba to a new church that he had built at Dunkeld. Where *Cenél nGabráin* ruled, their patron was to watch over them.

Only the barest outline survives of the ten years of Cináed's reign that followed his victory. It seems to have been a time of almost constant warfare, and although one chronicle claimed that 'there is not under heaven one king so good, as far as the borders of Rome', most speak of his achievements in terms of his prowess as a warlord. Cináed's ambition was clearly to expand his influence to the south, and he is recorded as having launched six invasions of Northumbria. But his reign also brought renewed conflict with Strathclyde and saw his new kingdom subjected to devastating Viking raids that penetrated the heart of his territory and carried the raiders to the new monastery at Dunkeld. Nevertheless, he was recognized as a major power by his neighbours and his status is made clear by the marriages that were arranged for his daughters. One, Maelmuire, may have been the wife of the Irish king, Áed Findliath, another married Óláfr Hvitr, the powerful Norse ruler of Dublin, while a third married Rhun, son of Arthgal king of Strathclyde. Despite these alliances, however, when Cináed died in 858 and was taken for burial to Iona, it was apparent that the permanence of his success was still far from sure.

His successor was his younger brother, Domnall (Donald I), whose four-year reign may actually have marked the consolidation of the Scottish takeover of Pictland. Domnall is described in the sources as a great warrior, and one recent analysis has suggested that it was his achievement to impose *Cenel nGabráin* rule over the mainland north of the Cairngorms, a triumph that may be commemorated in the great carved slab, known today as 'Sueno's Stone', at Forres in Moray. The consolidation of Scottish rule was further emphasized by his introduction of a code of law attributed to the eighth-century Dál Riata king Áed Find. The victor's imposition of his own laws over those of the vanquished is generally recognized as a signal of conquest.

On Domnall's death in 862, the throne passed to his nephew Castantin mac Cináeda (Constantine I), establishing the pattern of alternating succession whereby the kingship passed not from father to son but between brother and brother or from uncle to nephew or cousin to cousin. It was a practical solution to the problem of accommodating the claims of younger brothers and sons, and ensuring that the kingship passed to a mature adult rather than a child. As the line extended, problems and rivalries emerged, but in 862 the system ensured that the Scots had a capable ruler to lead them through troubled times ahead. Castantin faced threats on several fronts from a variety of Scandinavian invaders. In 866, the heartland of the kingdom was again ravaged, this time by the Norse of Dublin led by Óláfr Hvitr. It may have been at this time that a treaty was arranged, sealed by the marriage of Óláfr to Castantin's sister. Certainly, Castantin was implicated in some way in the Norse capture of Dumbarton in 870 and was credited with counselling his brother-in-law to kill the captive King Arthgal in 872. The Norse onslaught against Strathclyde was certainly highly advanta- geous to the Scots, who used this opportunity to extend their power over their former rivals. But Castantin was dabbling in dangerous waters and after Óláfr's death his kingdom was targeted by the new rulers of Dublin. Raids intensified from 875, and in 877 Castantin was killed in battle against them. By rights, the throne could have gone to Domnall mac Alpin's son Giric, but it was taken instead by Castantin's younger brother, Áed.

After 877, the Scots seem to have enjoyed some relief from serious Viking attack. Unfortunately, the lull did not bring peace and reconstruction, for the Scots now indulged in the first outbreak of the savage bloodspilling amongst the ruling line that became characteristic of its history in the tenth century. In 878, Giric and his supporters defeated and slew Áed in battle. Giric, however, may not have ruled alone, for he is described as sharing his throne with his first cousin Eochaid, son of Rhun, king of Strathclyde. It is possible that Strathclyde's help may have been enlisted in wresting the throne from Áed, help that came at the price of a share of royal power. Alternatively, it is possible that this apparent joint rule was in respect of Strathclyde and that Giric, who is given a generally positive report by the chroniclers, had imposed his lordship over the Britons. Giric's violent seizure of power, however, brought retri- bution once his cousins' children were old enough to command sufficient authority to make a challenge for the kingship. In 889, Domnall mac Castantín (Donald II), succeeded in defeating and deposing Giric and Eochaid, neither of whom seem to have had heirs who were to mount any challenge for the kingship of the Scots in future. From 889, the succession was restricted to the descendants of Cináed mac Alpín's sons, Castantin and Áed.

Domnall mac Castantín's reign saw a renewal of Viking pressure, being recorded in the annals as a time of raids and forays. There are hints, too, that he faced challenges from within his kingdom, but he weathered these to hold power for eleven years. In 900, he died at Forres in Moray. Early records are unhelpful as to why he was in Moray, or whether his death was due to natural causes or violence. His successor, however, was his cousin, Castantin mac Áeda (Constantine II), whose line, it has been suggested, had its power base in the north. It is possible that Domnall's challengers were from within his kin and that his death occurred in a campaign into their territory.

The accession of Castantin mac Áeda marked the opening of a new chapter in the history of the northern British Isles. His reign saw the power of the Scottish kings reach an unprecedented height, and that power was projected far to the south, marking the reopening of the Scots' centuries-old desire to win the rich farmlands south of the Forth. Under Castantin, too, profound changes were taking place in the character of the kingdom. While his predecessors from the time of Cináed mac Alpín had held the titles 'king of the Picts', or 'king of Picts and Scots', during Castantin's reign a new style emerged – *rí Albann* – king of Alba: the two peoples were being fused into one with a common (Gaelic) culture, language and tradition.

By the early 900s this hybrid kingdom was once again facing serious threat from Viking armies. In 903, a great Norse raid penetrated the heart of the kingdom in an orgy of looting and destruction, ransacking Dunkeld and over-wintering somewhere in Fortriu. The main Norse force headed south in 904, but a strong body of Vikings remained in Strathearn, plundering and burning until it was finally overwhelmed and annihilated. The force that headed south succeeded in gaining control of the Danish kingdom of York in 910 and now posed a serious threat to Castantin's security. Ragnall, king of York, pushed his power steadily northwards, settling his people in the country between the Tees and the Wear and attacking the rump of the old kingdom of Northumbria centred on Bamburgh. For Castantin, this was one step too far, for he also cherished plans to bring Northumbria into his orbit. When Ealdred of Northumbria fled to his court, Castantin had the opening he needed and brought his army south to the Tyne to challenge Ragnall. In 918, at Corbridge on the Tyne, the two armies fought to a standstill. Both claimed victory, but the reality seems to have been that Castantin had so badly mauled Ragnall's war-band that the York king ceased to be a threat to him. The country north of the Tyne was now effectively under Castantin's lordship.

The peace that followed Corbridge brought closer co-operation between the Scots and the Norse. Ragnall had succeeded in establishing his power in Dublin as well as York and needed a Scottish alliance to keep the main trade routes between Britain and Ireland open. Both he and Castantin, moreover, were greatly alarmed by a new power rising in the south. By 918, Edward the Elder, king of Wessex, the only Anglo-Saxon kingdom to survive the great Viking onslaught of the late ninth century, had consolidated his hold over the Danish colonies in the English Midlands and clearly harboured ambitions towards York. In the coming years, it became apparent that Castantin tried to preserve the power of York as a buffer between his own kingdom and the expanding authority of Wessex. This struggle was to emerge as part of a wider contest for the domination of Britain. In 920, Castantin made a treaty with Edward the Elder which showed that the balance of power north of the Humber lay with the Scots. Edward needed Castantin's acquiescence or aid if Wessex was to succeed in its ambitions to establish its mastery over Northumbria. Edward's successor, Athelstan, faced a similar problem, and in 927 failed to consolidate his hold on York when Castantin gave his tacit support to the new Norse king, Gothfrith. Indeed, Castantin was later to cement his alliance with Gothfrith's family when he married his daughter to Óláfr Gothfrithsson. Castantin, however, was playing a dangerous game, and in 934 Athelstan mounted a major invasion of Scotland by land and sea. His army penetrated as far north as Dunnottar, while his fleet is reported to have ravaged the Caithness coast, possibly striking against the Scots' Norse allies in this area. If his aim was to break the Scoto-Norse alliance and to force Castantin's submission, Athelstan's invasion can be dismissed as a failure, for in 937 Castantin was the dominant figure in a great invasion of England at the head of an alliance of Scots, Vikings and Britons. Possibly penetrating as far south as Northamptonshire, this great confederation sought to place Óláfr Gothfrithsson on the throne of York and to confirm Castantin's domination of Britain north of the Humber. At the unidentified battlefield of *Brunanburh*, however, it suffered a crushing defeat in which one of Castantin's sons was killed. The defeat did not end the warfare, for Castantin and his allies still dominated the north and Óláfr was to seize York following Athelstan's death in 939.

In a poem celebrating the victory at *Brunanburh*, an English poet described Castantin as 'aged... the hoary-haired warrior'. It may have been age that persuaded the king to resign his throne in 943 and become a monk at St Andrews, where he served as abbot of the wealthy and influential community, or perhaps a desire to ensure spiritual salvation after a career of violence. Castantin, however, had worked closely in alliance with the Church since the

24. Dunnottar Castle, Aberdeenshire. The medieval castle is believed to stand on the site of the fortification attacked by Athelstan of Wessex in 934.
25. York. It was in alliance with the Norse kings based in the city that Castantin mac Áeda invaded England in 937.

beginning of his reign, and may well have understood how he could continue to influence political affairs from a position as head of the chief royal monastery. If one late chronicle account can be trusted, it seems the old warrior found it difficult to entirely give up his past life, for it claims that about seven years after his retirement he came out of his monastery to lead one last raid into England. In 952, very much the elder statesman amongst the competing kings of the British Isles, he died and was buried at St Andrews.

Castantin's successor as king was his cousin's son, Máel Coluim mac Domnaill (Malcolm I). Máel Coluim's reign saw a continuation of the consolidation of Scottish control over the country south of the Forth, a domination that was confirmed in 945 through a treaty with the English king, Edmund. His early successes, however, were undermined by growing tensions within the ruling kindred, and in 954 he was killed in Moray, perhaps at the hands of his mac Áeda relatives. The new king was Castantin mac Áeda's son Idulb (Indulf). He seems to have built on Máel Coluim's achievements and annexed part of Lothian to his kingdom. Indulf's name betrays the strong Scandinavian influence that had characterized his father's reign, and his two sons, Culen Hringr and Óláfr, also had Norse-inspired names. It was Scandinavians, however, who ended his life: in 962 he was killed repelling a Viking raid on the Moray coast. The kingship now passed back to Máel Coluim mac Domnaill's line in the person of his elder son, Dub, but Idulb's sons soon challenged him. In 965, Dub defeated one attack headed by Culen Hringr, but in 966, apparently while attempting to tighten his grip over the mac Áeda's heartland in Moray, he was killed. The victorious Culen did not enjoy power for long, however, being killed in 971 by Rhydderch, son of Dyfnwal, king of Strathclyde, in the course of what appears to have been a feud arising from Culen's abduction and rape of Rhydderch's daughter.

The man who profited most from Culen's death was Dub's younger brother, Cináed mac Máel Coluim (Kenneth II), who moved swiftly to take the throne. By 977 he had eliminated his closest rival, Óláfr mac Castantín, and embarked on the most successful reign since that of Castantin mac Áeda. In 971, in an inaugural raid aimed at winning plunder to reward his supporters and to establish his own reputation as a general, Cináed launched the first campaign of his reign into Strathclyde, following this with an invasion of England. His aim was to gain recognition of his lordship over Lothian and, possibly, Cumberland, for in 973 he attended a major 'conference' of British kings at Chester, where the English king, Edgar, appears to have recognized these claims in return for the security of his northern frontier. Foreign military successes undoubtedly bolstered Cináed's authority at home, and there are indications that he planned to capitalize on this power to finally exclude the rival segments of the royal house from the kingship and to restrict the succession to his own line. That also meant removing the rights of Dub's son, also called Cináed. The king's ambitions in this field were the catalyst that united opposition to him. Cináed mac Máel Coluim's rivals for the kingship were able to draw support from disaffected members of the provincial nobility, some of who had suffered at the king's hands. There are hints in the records of a long-running feud between King Cináed and Cunthar, ruler of Angus and the Mearns, a feud that may have seen the king strip Cunthar of estates which he then used to endow a major new monastery at Brechin. In 995, at Fettercairn, Cináed was assassinated on the instructions of Cunthar's daughter Finella, whose son the king had previously killed. Dub's son, Cináed, may have expected to succeed to the throne, but the kingship was instead taken by Culen Hringr's son Castantin (Constantine III). Eighteen months later, the slaughter continued with Castantin's death at the hands of Cináed, son of Dub (Kenneth III). Castantin's death

26. The Round Tower at Brechin, Angus, all that remains of the monastery founded by Cináed II.

marked the extinction of the lineage descended from Áed mac Cináeda, but it did not end the vicious blood-letting amongst the remaining lines. Cináed mac Duib may have attempted to establish some stability by associating his son, Giric, with him in the kingship, but it is clear that he faced repeated challenge throughout his eight-year reign. Finally, in 1005 Cináed mac Máel Coluim's son, Máel Coluim mac Cináeda (Malcolm II), defeated and slew both Cináed mac Duib and Giric in battle at Monzievaird in Strathearn.

In an age of ruthless men, Máel Coluim mac Cináeda (Malcolm II), known later by the nicknames 'the Aggressor' and 'the Destroyer', emerges as the master-practitioner of single-minded ruthlessness. Interpretations of his reign, however, differ amongst historians. Some view him as one of the most successful of Scotland's early medieval kings, a ruler who imposed his authority over most of the Scottish mainland and who extended his kingdom's borders far to the south. Others, however, see him in a less positive light, noting that while he did extend Scottish power southwards, he lost effective control over the northern mainland and relied on alliances with the Norse rulers of Orkney to keep a check on the rivalry of his Moray-based kinsmen. Nevertheless, it is clear from contemporary accounts in chronicles and annals that he was regarded widely at home and abroad as a great king.

Máel Coluim's reign did not commence auspiciously. Like his father, he launched an inaugural raid into northern England, but, unlike Cináed's expedition, the 1006 invasion ended in a bloody rout outside the defences of Durham. It was perhaps lucky for Máel Coluim that there were no serious contenders for the throne at that time, for the defeat must have been a serious blow to his prestige. Soon afterwards, probably in a move designed to bolster his authority, he married one of his daughters to Jarl Sigurd the Mighty of Orkney, who controlled a realm that stretched from Shetland to the Dornoch Firth in the east, and that extended into the Hebrides in the west. It was an astute move which brought security on Scotland's northern frontiers and left Máel Coluim free to concentrate on extending his power southwards. Furthermore, after Sigurd's death in 1014 at the battle of Clontarf in Ireland, Máel Coluim was able to increase his influence in the northern mainland, where he intervened on behalf of his young grandson, Thorfinn Sigurdsson. This steady expansion in Scottish power climaxed in 1018 when Máel Coluim, in alliance with Ywain, king of Strathclyde, crushed a Northumbrian army at Carham on the Tweed. The battle was one of the most significant in Scottish history, for not only did it confirm that Lothian north of the Tweed would thereafter form part of Scotland, but the death of King Ywain, possibly from wounds received at Carham, enabled Máel Coluim to absorb Strathclyde also into his kingdom. It was thus in the reign of Máel Coluim mac Cináeda that the political map of mainland Britain began to take on its recognizable medieval pattern of division into two major monarchies. The expansion of Scottish might was not altogether welcomed by the other major powers in the British Isles. As long ago as 1006, the Irish high-king, Brian Boruma, had signalled his suspicions of Máel Coluim's ambitions by adopting the title 'Emperor of the Gael', a style that was intended to put the Scottish ruler in his place as a subordinate of the most powerful Gaelic king. Scottish expansion into Northumbria had drawn the attention of the Danish king of England, Knútr (Cnut), who sought to impose his mastery over his northern neighbour. In 1031, Knútr led a great army into the north and received the submissions of Máel Coluim, a ruler named Máel Báeda and Echmarcach, king of a sprawling sea-kingdom that stretched at times from Dublin and Man, through Galloway into the southern Hebrides. As with past treaties, that of 1031 lasted only so long as Knútr was able to maintain his focus on the north, but by establishing a loyal strongman in control of Northumbria in the person of Earl Siward, he was able to contain Máel Coluim's ambitions.

Mael Coluim's submission in 1031 should probably be seen against a backdrop of unrest within his kingdom. Much of the unrest evidently revolved around his intention to pass the throne to his grandson, Donnchad mac Crinain (Duncan I), the child of his daughter, Bethoc, and Crinan, apparently the ruler of Atholl, who entered the Church as abbot of Dunkeld. A sign of Máel Coluim's ambitions for his grandson can be seen in his establishment as ruler of Strathclyde, where he would no doubt have been groomed for succession to the Scottish throne. This manipulation of the succession required him to eliminate the descendants of his uncle, King Dub, and resulted in a fresh series of killings. The chief threat evidently lay in Moray, where Cináed mac Duib's family had married in to the local ruling dynasty. A feud within that family may have helped Máel Coluim to root out his enemies, for in 1032 Gillacomgain mac Maelbrigta, mormaer of Moray, who in 1020 had murdered his uncle Findlaech, was in turn slaughtered, evidently by his cousin Macbethad (Macbeth). Gillacomgain's wife was Gruoch, granddaughter of Cináed mac Duib, and it is possible that Máel Coluim had encouraged Macbethad in his revenge attack. Certainly, Máel Coluim pursued a murderous vendetta against Gruoch's family, in 1033 ordering the murder of her nephew, the last in the direct male line of descent from Cináed mac Duib. Final victory, however, was to elude the Aggressor, for Macbethad married Gruoch and became the protector of Lulach, her son by Gillacomgain. Cináed mac Duib's descendants might one day return to again challenge for the throne.

Although he had failed in the end to eliminate all potential rivals, Máel Coluim had done enough to ensure that he was succeeded by Donnchad mac Crinain in 1034. Shakespeare turned Donnchad into good King Duncan, the kind and gentle white-haired ruler whose wisdom had brought Scotland peace and stability, but this image was created to make his murder by his supposedly loyal general, Macbethad, whom he loved as a son and had showered with honours, seem all the more heinous. Indeed, there is nothing in the Shakespearean image that comes close to the reality. Donnchad was considered young when he succeeded to the throne, possibly still in his early twenties. He has not left much of a positive image in contemporary records, but he was evidently aggressive and ambitious. Like his grandfather, he sought to bolster his authority with a plundering raid into Northumbria. Like his grandfather, too, he met with humiliating defeat at Durham in 1039, but unlike Máel Coluim there were challengers waiting in the wings to capitalize on his failure. Opposition to him may have erupted immediately after the failure of his attack on Durham, and, in 1040, in a bid to end the threat from Dub's descendants for once and for all, he led an army into Moray against Macbethad. At Pitgaveny near Elgin, Macbethad met him in battle, defeated and killed him. With Donnchad's sons mere children, there was nothing to prevent Macbethad from taking the throne as husband of Cináed mac Duib's granddaughter, but Macbethad, too, was cheated of the possibility of permanent security when his defeated rival's family were spirited away to safety in foreign exile.

Macbethad has exercised a strange fascination over generations of historians and writers, most of whom have been concerned with rehabilitating the historical figure and dispelling the myth of the Shakespearean monster. Few people today believe that Shakespeare's tragic figure bears any resemblance to the historical king, but the rehabilitation has perhaps swung too far in that he is now often presented as some kind of far-sighted, benevolent ruler who brought his people peace and prosperity. For all the ink that has been wasted on attempting

27. Elgin Cathedral, Moray. Donnchad I's thirteenth-century descendant Alexander II paid for the
foundation of a chaplainry in the cathedral to say masses for the soul of his ancestor, who was
killed at nearby Pitgaveny.

to establish the character of the king and his reign, we are no closer to agreement, and it should be remembered that for the whole of his seventeen-year reign we have the merest handful of records of events, many of which are open to widely differing interpretations. In the first place, it is evident that his long reign was punctuated by successive challenges to his position. One major threat was posed by Donnchad mac Crinain's cousin Thorfinn of Orkney, with whose family the mormaers of Moray had been at war regularly through the later tenth and early eleventh centuries. The first internal threat, however, came from Atholl, where Crinan still held great influence as abbot of Dunkeld. In 1045, he appears to have attempted a rising in support of his younger son, Maldred, or his eldest grandson, Máel Coluim mac Donnchada, who was living in exile in England under the protection of King Edward the Confessor. The rising was crushed and Crinan killed. In the following year, Macbethad faced a more serious threat when Edward the Confessor sanctioned an invasion of Scotland by Earl Siward, in whose household young Máel Coluim mac Donnchada was living. Siward defeated Macbethad in battle and 'appointed another' in his place. It is unlikely that this English puppet was Máel Coluim, who was probably barely into his teens, more likely being his uncle, Maldred. Whatever the case, Siward's candidate probably ruled over little more than Lothian and possibly Strathclyde, for Macbethad was able to gather a fresh army and return from the north to defeat and either expel or kill him.

The failure of the 1046 invasion may have resulted in a strengthening of Macbethad's position. Certainly, the period 1046-54 saw no further challenges and in 1050 Macbethad felt sufficiently secure to leave his kingdom for several weeks to go on pilgrimage to Rome where, according to one chronicler, 'he scattered money like seed-corn to the poor'. This spiritual side to Macbethad's character is sharply at odds with his traditional depiction as a bloody-handed usurper, but fits more closely with contemporary evidence from within Scotland. There, he and Queen Gruoch, whose character seems also far-removed from the scheming monster of Shakespeare's play, were generous patrons of the Church. This generosity may have had political motivation, for Church support would have been a powerful endorsement of Macbethad's right to rule. Certainly, it won him a good reputation amongst the monastic writers who set down the historical record of his reign: 'in his reign there were productive seasons'.

By the early 1050s, Macbethad may have been feeling less secure. His rivals, the sons of Donnchad mac Crinain, were now grown men and in a position to lead challenges in person. This insecurity may have prompted the king to welcome the Norman knights expelled from England in 1052, for these mounted warriors were a formidable weapon in warfare and had already established their reputation in Edward the Confessor's wars against the Welsh. In 1054, their value received its first test when Earl Siward mounted a fresh invasion of Scotland in support of Máel Coluim mac Donnchada, whom Edward the Confessor planned to install on the throne as a client king. Siward triumphed in a bloody battle that saw the elimination of Macbethad's mercenary knights, but victory was achieved at great cost, including the death of his eldest son, and he was unable to capitalize on his success. Indeed, it is unlikely that Máel Coluim's rule extended north of the Forth and it is clear that Macbethad continued to control the heartland of the kingdom. What followed was a bloody war of attrition that saw Máel Coluim gradually extend his authority northwards. In 1057, Máel Coluim crossed the Mounth and brought Macbethad to battle near Lumphanan, where the road into Moray runs north from Deeside. It is possible that Macbethad's army was victorious, for, although the king died in the battle, Máel Coluim's reign was not considered to have begun until he had

28. Dunsinane Hill, Perth and Kinross. The Iron Age hillfort may have been refurbished by Macbeth.

29. The Craw Stane, Rhynie, Aberdeenshire, at the hub of routes into Moray followed by Máel Coluim mac Donnchada in 1058.

killed Lulach mac Gillcomgain in 1058. Lulach, derisively nicknamed 'the Fatuous' or 'the Simpleton', clearly enjoyed strong support within parts of the kingdom and had a strong power base in Moray. It was in defence of this stronghold, at Essie in Strathbogie, only a few miles north of the scene of his stepfather's death, that he was killed.

Although Máel Coluim's victory in 1058 can be seen with hindsight to mark a decisive turning point in the history of Scotland, to contemporary observers it probably was little more than another swing in the pendulum of power between the rival segments of the ruling kindred. Lulach was to prove the last descendant of Cináed mac Duib's to occupy the Scottish throne, but his family and descendants were to continue to mount challenges to Máel Coluim mac Donnchada (Malcolm III) and his successors into the thirteenth century. In Máel Coluim, however, the ambitions of his great-great-grandfather, Cináed mac Máel Coluim, to monopolize control of the succession in the hands of his own narrow segment of the royal house at last came to fruition. With Máel Coluim mac Donnchada, the long saga of alternating succession between lineages ends and a new chapter begins under what historians now call the House of Canmore.

RO

TWO

THE HOUSE OF CANMORE
1058 – 1290

MALCOLM III OR MÁEL COLUIM MAC
DONNCHADA (1058-1093)

Máel Coluim mac Donnchada, who as king of Scots is better known by the anglicized form of his name, Malcolm III, would not have known in 1058 how permanent his victory over his dynastic rivals was to prove. A ruthless and opportunistic warrior, he stamped his authority over Scotland and was to maintain an unshakeable hold on power for thirty-five years. It was possibly this unquestioned might that won him his nickname, Ceann Mór (Canmore), 'Great Head' or 'Great Chief', from which the dynasty he founded, which ruled Scotland for nearly two and a half centuries, receives its name. With ambitions to match his ruthlessness, Malcolm III used his security at home to project his power abroad, deservedly earning himself a reputation as one of Scotland's greatest warrior kings.

Despite the years that he had spent in exile in England, Malcolm won quick acceptance from the powerful Gaelic nobles of his still predominantly Gaelic kingdom. His Gaelic character appears to have been unblunted by long exposure to Anglo-Saxon culture and there was no trace of the anglicizing influence that was to become such a feature of his later years. If anything, the foreign influences that he had absorbed in his years abroad were Scandinavian in character, the product of his long sojourn in the York court of his Anglo-Danish patron, Earl Siward. English ties, however, remained strong and in 1059, perhaps mindful of the debt owed for past support, Malcolm journeyed to the court of Edward the Confessor, possibly to renew the oaths of former Scottish rulers to be 'sworn helper' of the English kings. By 1061, however, Malcolm was prepared to kick over the traces and, despite being the 'sworn brother' of the current Northumbrian earl, Tostig Godwinsson, took advantage of Tostig's absence on pilgrimage at Rome to launch a devastating raid through his territories. Peace was restored and Tostig was later to find refuge at Malcolm's court when driven out of his earldom in 1065, but this first raid signalled the direction that the Scot's true ambitions were to follow throughout his long reign.

Lasting security on Malcolm's northern frontier was won by c.1065 through his marriage to Ingibjorg, widow of Thorfinn the Mighty. While her sons ruled in Orkney there was peace between the Scots and the Norse. Nothing is known of their relationship other than that the marriage produced two children, Donnchad (Duncan) and Domnall (Donald), before Ingibjorg's death in about 1069. Her death opened fresh prospects for the widowed Malcolm, for by 1070 fate had brought to his shores a shipload of Anglo-Saxon exiles fleeing the most recent failed rising against the Norman conquerors of England. In the ship were Edgar Atheling, the Anglo-Saxon claimant to the English throne, his mother and his sisters Margaret and Christina. It was a heaven-sent opportunity for Malcolm, for marriage to one of the sisters offered the prospect of a realization of his ambitions to extend his influence southwards, an ambition baulked that same year when his attempt to capitalize on the weakened state of Northumbria following William the Conqueror's systematic devastation of the north was bloodily repulsed. Furthermore, there was the chance that a son of such a union would some day succeed to the English throne should the West Saxon dynasty be restored. For Edgar, it was a price worth paying for safe refuge and a powerful military ally. Even though both his sisters had – if Margaret's biographer, the Benedictine monk Turgot who served as her chaplain and confessor, is to be believed – intended to become nuns, he persuaded the elder, Margaret, to accept.

An understanding of the implications of this marriage may have been the catalyst that persuaded William the Conqueror that he had to bring Malcolm to heel. In 1072, William invaded Scotland by land and sea but there was no battle. Instead, at Abernethy on the Tay, Malcolm submitted to the Norman king, promising to expel the Anglo-Saxon exiles, performing homage and surrendering his eldest son, Donnchad, as hostage. For seven years he kept his word, then in 1079, drawn by the apparent collapse of Norman royal power in northern England, he launched a devastating raid into Northumbria. In 1080, William sent his eldest son, Robert Curthose, to subdue Malcolm but the campaign ended in a conference at Falkirk that ostensibly renewed the terms of the 1072 treaty. Often presented as a defeat for Malcolm, this settlement marked the high watermark of his power, for, as Robert's hasty building of a castle at what became Newcastle-upon-Tyne revealed, Malcolm had successfully pushed his frontier far to the south. Indeed, he had come close to rebuilding the old Northumbrian realm of Bernicia that stretched from the Forth to the Tees. The dream of consolidating the Scottish hold over this southern realm was to be a chimera pursued by Malcolm and Margaret's descendants until the thirteenth century.

31. The Brough of Birsay, centre of the the domain of Thorfinn the Mighty in Orkney.
Malcolm III won peace with the Norse by marrying Thorfinn's widow, Ingibjorg.
32. The remains of a sauna, Brough of Birsay.

33. Dunfermline Abbey, Fife. The first Benedictine Abbey in Scotland, founded by Malcolm III
and his saintly second wife, Margaret.

Marriage to Margaret marked a decisive shift in the cultural influences on Malcolm. Instead of the Scandinavian element evident down to 1070, Anglo-Saxon culture now predominated. This is clearest in the names given to the first four of Malcolm and Margaret's sons – Edward, Edmund, Æthelred and Edgar – named after the queen's male progenitors from father to great-great-grandfather respectively. There was more to the move than fashion, however, for the children were probably being groomed to take their place in England after the expected revolt that would drive the Norman usurpers into the sea.

Opinion varies as to the extent of Margaret's influence over Malcolm and his policies. The number of Anglo-Saxon exiles in Scotland was small, but concentrated at court their influence was disproportionately great. As queen, Margaret was in a stronger position than any to influence her husband, but Malcolm was not an altogether unwilling subject. The king was not blind to the opportunities offered by his marriage and he may have been keen to ensure that his sons were schooled in his wife's foreign ways to smooth their future acceptance to the English. Indeed, Malcolm evidently considered that the future lay with his sons by Margaret, for he passed over his sons by Ingibjorg to designate Margaret's eldest child, Edward, as his chosen successor. Turgot suggests that the king venerated her every act and supported her efforts to introduce the culture and sophistication of the Old English monarchy to his rough and ready court. Certainly, she brought a veneer of continental urbanity to the Gaelic household, introducing Anglo-Saxon and Frankish clothing and hairstyles, court ceremonial and refined tableware. More contentious, however, are suggestions that she initiated profound change in Scottish religious life. What is clear is that Margaret, brought up in the spiritual hothouse of recently-converted Hungary and having experienced at first hand the tide of religious reform that was transforming the Western Church, found the native Church in Scotland disturbingly backward in its practices and distressingly poorly organized to offer the level of pastoral care that she considered normal. With Malcolm's support – he is reported to have acted as her interpreter – she assembled the leading Scottish clerics in a bid to instigate reform, and it seems that some limited success was achieved. To aid in the reform process, again with Malcolm's support, she wrote to Archbishop Lanfranc of Canterbury to request that he send a colony of Benedictine monks to form the basis of a monastery to be founded beside the royal stronghold at Dunfermline. It was a faltering start, for the priory at Dunfermline had barely put down roots when its monks were expelled in the political upheavals that followed the king's death in 1093. Rather than Margaret, it was her sons who were to carry through her dreams of religious revival.

Despite Margaret's efforts to polish her husband, Malcolm remained an inveterate warlord in the Gaelic tradition. Ever the opportunist, in 1091 he took advantage of William II's absence in Normandy to launch a plundering raid into England. Retreating in the face of the inevitable retaliation, led by William and his brother Robert in person, Malcolm once again made an easy submission, offering his homage and fealty in return for William's promise to restore properties formerly held by the Scottish kings in England. The apparent generosity of the terms despite Malcolm's repeated breaches of faith should not mask the fact that Norman power in the north had grown considerably since the 1070s, and when in 1092 William took control of Carlisle, where he built a castle and started a programme of colonization, that power reached the borders of Malcolm's kingdom. Perhaps confident of his new-gained authority in the north, William baited Malcolm by repeated failure to implement his side of the 1091 agreement. In August 1093, Malcolm travelled to Gloucester in a final bid to secure William's fulfilment of the treaty. Possibly in a deliberate move to provoke Malcolm into again breaking his word, William slighted him. Infuriated, Malcolm returned to Scotland, swiftly raised an army and in early November, accompanied by his son Edward, invaded Northumbria. Bogged down by the rain and mud, Malcolm was outmanoeuvred by the Norman earl and on 13 November was ambushed and killed near Alnwick. The Scots fled, taking with them the seriously wounded Edward, who died of his injuries two days later near Jedburgh, but leaving the king's body behind on the field. On 16 November, gravely ill, her body worn out by the demands of at least eight pregnancies and by the rigours of a life of fasting and self-denial, Margaret received the news she had dreaded shortly before she herself died.

RO

DONALD III or DOMNALL MAC DONNCHADA (1094-1097), DUNCAN II or DONNCHAD MAC MAELCOLUIM (1094) AND EDMUND (1094-1097)

The death of Malcolm III, his designated heir and Queen Margaret in the space of four days in November 1093 unleashed a backlash against the Anglo-Saxon influence that had dominated the Scottish court since the 1070s. The chief beneficiary was Malcolm's younger brother, Domnall mac Donnchada (Donald III), nicknamed *Bàn* – the White or Fair-Haired – known from Shakespearean tradition as Donaldbane. Beyond the tradition that when Malcolm had fled to England in 1040 he had instead gone west to the Norse-Gaelic kingdom of the Isles, nothing is known of his life until his sudden emergence in old age as the figure-head in this violent reaction against foreign influence. As the eldest surviving adult male of the family, Gaelic tradition would have marked him out as Malcolm III's heir, but it had clearly been his brother's intention to exclude him in favour of the sons of his second marriage. This break with tradition may have been the catalyst that united the opposition to Malcolm's family behind Domnall mac Donnchada, but there is next to no record of how his coup was mounted. Later hostile chronicle accounts speak of his invasion of the kingdom, siege and capture of Edinburgh Castle, and expulsion of his brother's surviving children. With his nephews all in exile, Domnall was enthroned as king at Scone, probably early in 1094.

The first challenger to Domnall's position was his eldest nephew, Donnchad, better known under his anglicized name, Duncan, the surviving son of Malcolm III by his first wife, Ingibjorg. Duncan, who in 1072 had been handed over as a hostage to the English king, William the Conqueror, had largely been brought up at the Norman court in England, schooled in English ways and trained as a Norman knight. On the Conqueror's death in 1087, Duncan had been released and knighted by the new king, William II Rufus, but had opted to remain in England. For William, Duncan offered an unparalleled opportunity to establish a pliant vassal on the Scottish throne, thereby ending the twin threat of Scottish support for rebels in England and Scottish challenges on his northern frontier. Having given oaths of homage and fealty to William, and bolstered by marriage to Octreda, daughter of the former Northumbrian earl, Cospatric, whose family were powerful figures in the shifting borderlands between the kingdoms, Duncan marched north with an army of Normans and English. In May 1094 he defeated Domnall and his supporters in battle and was enthroned as King Duncan II. His grasp on power, however, was short-lived. Within a few months, a coup had forced him to dismiss his foreign soldiers while permitting him to retain the throne, but on 12 November 1094 he was murdered at Mondynes near Stonehaven by Maelpedair, ruler of Mearns. Octreda fled to England with their son, William, and before the year's end Domnall had been re-established on the throne.

The defeat and death of Duncan opened the fault lines in the family of Malcolm III. Early in 1095, Edmund, the eldest of Malcolm's surviving sons, opened negotiations with his uncle and secured a share of power. Domnall had at least one daughter – Bethoc – but no sons, and Edmund, as his eldest nephew, may have been recognized as his successor. Edmund's actions evidently alienated the rest of his family, and when Domnall and Edmund gave their support to the rebel Norman earl of Northumberland, William Rufus passed over Æthelred – still alive but for some reason seen as unsuitable – and threw his weight behind Edmund's younger brother Edgar as a rival for the Scottish throne. After a long struggle, in 1097 Domnall and Edmund were defeated in battle and captured. Edmund was at first consigned to chains and imprisoned, but subsequently became a Cluniac monk and died in obscurity in Montacute Abbey in Somerset, safely removed from his former kingdom. History records a more gruesome fate for Domnall, who was blinded at the urging of his youngest nephew, David. His date of death is unknown, but tradition narrates how he was permitted to live until 1107, when he was killed on the instructions of King Alexander I. First buried at Dunkeld, his remains were later translated to Iona, a more fitting resting-place for this last king in the Gaelic tradition.

RO

EDGAR (1097-1107)

In 1095, passing over his elder brother Æthelred, William Rufus, king of England, selected Edgar, fourth son of Malcolm III and Margaret, as his candidate for the Scottish throne. Edgar, who had been living in exile at the English court since late 1093, had accompanied William north on his 1095 campaign against Robert de Mowbray, the rebel earl of Northumberland, and had been invested by him with the kingship of the Scots at this time. Edgar, however, was in no position yet to turn his title into a reality. Around him was gathered a group of exiled Scots opposed to Domnall mac Donnchada, but his key ally was his uncle Edgar Atheling, the Anglo-Saxon claimant to the English throne. It was only in 1097 with the Atheling's aid, at the head of a largely English army, that Edgar returned to Scotland to wrest the throne from his uncle and brother.

After the violent upheavals of the previous years, Edgar's reign appears to have been a time of comparative peace. A potential threat to this stability had been removed in 1098 when he settled a treaty with Magnus Bareleg, king of Norway, which recognized Norwegian sovereignty over the Hebrides, averting conflict with a king who was intruding his authority into western maritime Britain. His apparent willingness to yield sovereignty of an area that had once formed the political and spiritual core of his ancestral kingdom, however, underscores the fact that Edgar, despite his Gaelic blood, was very much a product of the new English orientation of his family. Indeed, he has been likened to an Anglo-Saxon rather than a Scottish king. There is no evidence that he visited the north or west of his kingdom and he had little sympathy for or understanding of Gaelic culture and society. Edgar instead reinforced a southward-focused perspective by new ties with England, in particular by the marriage of his sister Edith (also known as Matilda) to the English king, Henry I. This attitude can also be seen in his religious policies. In 1098, he granted Coldingham to the monks of Durham – he attributed his victory

34. Iona Abbey, Argyll and Bute. Donald III was the last Scottish king reputed to be
buried on the holy island.

35. Durham Cathedral. Typical of his Anglicizing tendencies, King Edgar was a noted
patron of the community of St Cuthbert.

36. Seal of Edgar.

the previous year to St Cuthbert's intervention – and was present when the foundations of a new church were laid there. He also brought monks from Canterbury to recolonize Dunfermline, which he began to rebuild.

In 1107, still only in his early thirties, Edgar died. There is no record of his ever having married and the throne passed to his younger brother Alexander. His body was taken to Dunfermline, where it was buried alongside his parents in front of the high altar of the church.

RO

ALEXANDER I (1107-1124)

Like his brothers before him, Alexander I succeeded to the throne as a vassal of the English crown. His dependence was emphasized by his marriage to Sibylla, one of Henry I's brood of bastards, a woman described in Scottish chronicles as lacking in both modesty and looks. Henry made great use of his illegitimate children as instruments for strengthening his power, frequently arranging for the marriage of his daughters to nobles whom he wished to bind more firmly in their loyalty to him, or to magnates who occupied key positions on his frontiers. Alexander fitted into just this category and the marriage, a simple act of policy, evidently remained loveless and childless.

New tensions within the family had surfaced soon after Alexander's accession. While the throne passed by right to Alexander, Edgar had apparently bequeathed much of what is now southern Scotland to his youngest brother, David. Alexander had no wish to lose control over so great a territory and sought to withhold it from his brother, for whom he evidently had no great love. David, however, was one of Henry I's favourites and, faced with the threat of English military intervention, Alexander was forced to yield. Despite the strain that this placed on their relationship, Alexander remained Henry's vassal and in 1114 led a force of warriors in Henry's campaign in Wales. It was also to England that Alexander turned for aid in resuming the reforms of the Scottish Church which his mother had initiated. Like Edgar he was a devotee of St Cuthbert – he was present at the translation of the saint's remains to a new shrine – and it was from Durham that he brought his candidate, Turgot, to fill the vacant bishopric of St Andrews, the spiritual head of his kingdom. Turgot's successor, Eadmer, came from Canterbury, and it was from the Yorkshire abbey of Nostel that Alexander secured the Augustinian canons to colonize his new foundation at Scone. Yet Alexander was far from being Henry's lapdog and he refused to permit either Turgot or Eadmer to profess obedience to the English archbishops, an act that would have underlined the subordination of the Scottish Church to the English. Correspondence with the papacy on this and other issues shows that Alexander was deeply concerned for the spiritual wellbeing of his kingdom.

Despite his dependence on England, the loss of control over southern Scotland made Alexander very much a man of Scotia. It was in the Gaelic heartland of his ancestral kingdom in Tayside that his power was based – he had held the earldom of Gowrie during Edgar's reign – and beyond churchmen, there is little evidence that he followed his brother's policy of settling Englishmen and Normans on his lands there. How he consolidated his hold over a territory that his predecessors had neglected is unknown, but the titles 'the Fierce' or 'the Strong' given to him by contemporary chronicles, and the

37. Alexander I as depicted on either side of his great seal.
38. The great seal of Scone Abbey, showing the inauguration of a Scottish king. Alexander I
founded a priory of Augustinian canons at the ancient inauguration site.

comment that he 'held his kingdom with a great deal of effort', suggest that it was not an easy process. Nevertheless, the witnesses to his charters show that he could draw on the support of the leading Gaelic nobles and when he died in 1124 much of that support was bequeathed to his bastard son Malcolm.

RO

DAVID I (1124-1153)

By the natural order of things, David I should never have been king of Scots. The youngest son of Malcolm III and Margaret, he was aged about ten when he was driven into exile in England with his brothers and sisters following their parents' deaths in 1093. Although he may have participated in the campaign that placed his brother Edgar on the throne in 1097 – it was traditionally David's scheming that secured the blinding of his uncle, Domnall mac Donnchada – there was no place for him in the new order in Scotland and he remained in England. The marriage of his elder sister Edith to the new English king, Henry I, opened new career prospects for the young Scottish prince. Referred to as 'brother of the Queen' in English accounts and showered with his brother-in-law's patronage, David rose fast in Henry's service. As one of Henry's 'new men', David could expect rapid social advancement, and a steady stream of offices and lands flowed in his direction.

The first sign of significant change came in 1107 when David's brother Edgar died. David was now the probable heir of the new king, Alexander I. He was also a major landholder, for Edgar had bequeathed him rule over Cumbria, a territory that stretched from the northern end of Loch Lomond to the Solway in the south and eastwards into Tweeddale. Alexander was unwilling to hand over such a substantial portion of his kingdom, but threatened by Henry I's military intervention he submitted by c.1113. Surrender, however, left a bitter taste in Alexander's mouth and relations with David were permanently soured.

David was now a great man, and his status was affirmed in 1113 when Henry arranged his marriage to Matilda de Senlis, the widowed countess of Northampton-Huntingdon. Although she was a widow with children, marriage to Matilda was a great honour for David. The daughter of Earl Waltheof of Northumbria and the Conqueror's niece Judith, she was of royal blood, lady in her own right of great estates and claimant to the forfeited earldom of Northumberland. David now became earl of Huntingdon as well as 'prince of the Cumbrian region', entering the topmost circle of the English nobility and securing the resources of one of the greatest magnate estates in England. Their only son, named Henry in honour of David's patron, was born c.1115. It was a mark of David's standing that his child was given precedence over Matilda's sons by her first marriage. The new man had arrived.

Until this point David had taken little interest in religious issues. His suddenly awakening religiosity may simply be a motif embellished by his biographer, Ælred of Rievaulx, to mark the transformation from dissolute youth to responsible adulthood, but it does appear that marriage and power marked a turning-point in David's life. David's mother, Margaret, and his aunt, Christina, abbess of Romsey, had had a powerful influence over his childhood, but it must be remembered that the English court was also awash with the repercussions of the religious reform that was sweeping western Christendom. In 1113, David showed his awareness of these developments when he founded an abbey at Selkirk in the heart of his Scottish lands. This was no mere act of an *arriviste* proclaiming his status through an example of conspicuous but conventional piety, for the monks chosen for the new community were Tironensians, members of a new and particularly austere order based at Tiron near Chartres. Through this act, bringing the first community of any of the reformed orders of monks into the British Isles, David proclaimed his support for the reform movement in general. He further underscored his devotion in 1116 when he attempted to visit St Bernard of Tiron in person, but the abbot died shortly before David arrived at the abbey. David's religious concerns, however, went far deeper and he also began the process of reforming the Church generally within his domain. His first act was to appoint his chaplain, John, as bishop of Glasgow, the spiritual overlord of the territories that made up Cumbria. Like his brother Alexander, despite his dependency on England, David was determined that his new bishop should be free from the domination of the English Church. This determination opened a struggle that lasted for most of the twelfth century.

In 1124, already in what was for the medieval period his middle age, David succeeded to the Scottish throne. For most Scots, David was an unknown quantity and, for some, unwanted. Equally, for David, the Gaelic culture of his new kingdom was alien and barbaric. Indeed, the inauguration ritual, where the king was enthroned and acclaimed by his nobles with no Church involvement, far removed from the ecclesiastical ritual of English coronation, seemed so pagan to the devout David that he had a crisis of conscience over subjecting himself to it and needed to be persuaded to undergo the ceremony by his spiritual advisors. If this was not warning sign enough of where David's cultural preferences lay, the rapidity with which he began to introduce friends and dependents from England signalled a profound change in direction. There is little sign that David had introduced English colonists on to his lands in southern Scotland before 1124, but possibly as early as his inauguration at Scone he began to grant land to knights from the south, men on whom he came to rely for support and advice. One of the first beneficiaries was Robert de Brus, to whom the king granted Annandale. De Brus was followed by a small but influential group of men, often tenants from David's Huntingdon estates, such as Hugh de Morville and Robert Avenel, or associates such as Walter fitz Alan, the ancestor of the Stewarts. It is wrong, however, to think of David as flooding Scotland with colonists, for none of these men received lands north of the River Forth and there, in the heartland of his kingdom, David trusted in the loyalty of the great Gaelic lords, such as the earls of Fife and Strathearn.

The transition of power was always a dangerous time and for David it proved no less so. Early in 1125 a serious rebellion erupted in support of Alexander's bastard son Malcolm. Little is known of this man, who is not to be confused with another of the Canmores' political rivals, Malcolm MacHeth, who was active in the 1160s. It is clear, however, that he enjoyed widespread support within Scotland's Gaelic heartland, underscored by marriage to the sister of Somerled, lord of Argyll. The greatest challenge came in 1130 when, allied with Angus, earl of Moray, a descendant of King Lulach, Malcolm marched against David. At Stracathro, near Brechin in Angus, the rebels were crushed and Earl Angus killed, but Malcolm escaped to harass David for another four years until his capture and imprisonment in Roxburgh Castle. Victory was exploited ruthlessly, with David marching into Moray determined to impose his authority in the north. Angus's estates were seized by the king: the most important he kept for himself, establishing royal castles at places such as Elgin, Forres and Inverness as bases from which to consolidate his hold. To underpin his conquest, he introduced colonists, most notably the Fleming Freskin, but also based his control of the region on alliance with native families, such as his kinsmen the earls of Atholl and Caithness. By the mid-1130s David had established his hold over most of mainland Scotland, extending the authority of the Scottish crown to its greatest reach yet and confirming his position as the second major power in the British Isles.

David's methods in Moray were characteristic of his policies throughout Scotland. The intrusion of colonists was balanced by a developing partnership with his Gaelic nobility and the retention of key estates as the foci for a network of new royal castles. In time, with David's encouragement, these castles attracted commercial settlements to which he granted charters of privileges – the origin of many of Scotland's royal burghs – thereby encouraging settlement of new colonies of traders and craftsmen to stimulate the economic development of his kingdom and establishing in the process outposts of royal power scattered throughout Scotland. The Church, too, was pivotal in this process. David carried through many of his brother's schemes, such as the reform of the bishopric of St Andrews – which he tried to have elevated to independent archiepiscopal status though in the end he had to content himself with only the consecration of his candidate as bishop, free from English overlordship – and in the course of his reign he was able to spread that process of reform to most of the mainland dioceses. The spread of the reformed monastic orders also continued apace. Soon after his succession to the throne he moved the monks from Selkirk to Kelso, in the shadow of his chief seat of power across the Tweed at Roxburgh. New Augustinian communities were established at Inchcolm and Holyrood, and in 1128 he re-founded Dunfermline as the royal abbey *par excellence*. Dunfermline participated in the royal expansion into Moray, receiving grants of estates and revenues from the king that formed the endowment of a new daughter house, Urquhart Priory. Founded in the heart of Earl Angus's former estate, the priory was a striking symbol of the extended reach of David's power.

The dramatic expansion of David's power down to the mid 1130s had been facilitated by his continuing friendship with Henry I. In the 1120s, the relationship was still primarily one of lord and vassal, indeed, in 1127 David was acting more as an English baron than a king in his own right when he was the first secular lord to swear the oath to uphold the rights of Henry I's daughter, Matilda, to succeed to the English throne should Henry produce no male heir. David's support for Henry in that issue, however, may have brought Henry's acquiescence or active support for David in securing the ecclesiastical freedom of Glasgow and St Andrews from the claims of York: the relationship clearly worked to the benefit of both parties.

On Henry I's death in December 1135 David could not prevent the disinheritance of Matilda in favour of the accession of her cousin's husband, Stephen. Within weeks, however, David had launched an invasion in support of his niece's claims, and also to take possession of those parts of northern England that he felt were his and his son's by right – Cumberland, Westmorland and the earldom of Northumberland. Attacking in the depths of winter, David captured Carlisle and Newcastle before settling down to besiege Durham, the fortress that had proved to be the bane of his grandfather, Duncan I. Swiftly assembling an army, Stephen marched to Durham's relief, but rather than give battle the two kings began lengthy negotiations that eventually produced a truce that greatly favoured the Scots. David, mindful of his 1127 oath, refused to perform homage to Stephen, but permitted his son to do so in order to gain control of the territory that Stephen was prepared to concede. Henry became earl of Huntingdon, was confirmed in possession of Carlisle and was granted the lordship of

Doncaster. David surrendered Newcastle, but only on the understanding that Henry's rights to Northumberland be given justice in future. It was a shaky peace and nearly fell apart in 1137, but lasted until January 1138 when David launched his invasion of Northumberland. Although Stephen launched a counter-raid into Lothian in February, the initiative in the war lay with David. Scottish armies penetrated deep into England, one force commanded by David's nephew, William fitz Duncan, son of the short-reigned Duncan II, defeating an English army at Clitheroe in Lancashire. It was a brutal campaign of terror, marked by the widespread plundering and devastation of the countryside, the elimination of all resistance, and the driving off of female captives as slaves by David's Gaelic levies. Although David's biographers seek to excuse him for the atrocities committed, it is clear that the war was fought on David's terms and, although he tried to ensure the protection of Church property and the respecting of the sanctuary rights of those sheltering within churches, he accepted that 'collateral damage' was inevitable. It seemed that nothing could stop the Scottish juggernaut as it swept south towards York, but on 22 August at Cowton Moor near Northallerton his army was heavily defeated by a hastily assembled force under the nominal command of Archbishop Thurstan of York in a conflict known as the Battle of the Standard.

The Standard was a serious check to David's ambitions, but the spreading civil war in England between the supporters of Stephen and Matilda prevented Stephen from following up Thurstan's victory. As David consolidated his hold on the territory he had seized, Stephen was forced to come to terms. In early 1139, Stephen confirmed Earl Henry in possession of the estates granted to him in 1136 but also added Northumbria (excluding the castles of Newcastle and Bamburgh and the lands of the bishopric of Durham between the Tyne and Tees). While David handed over hostages to secure the peace, Earl Henry was further bound into Stephen's service by marriage to Ada de Warenne, sister of some of the king's key supporters. This time the peace seemed to hold, but in February 1141 Stephen was defeated and captured by Matilda's supporters at Lincoln and she prepared for her coronation at London. Suddenly recalling his oath to support Matilda's rights, David broke his truce with Stephen and marched south to join his niece for her coronation. At London, however, David and Matilda endured the humiliation of being driven from the city and only narrowly avoided capture at Winchester a few weeks later. Although David escaped, his experiences convinced him of the need for caution. After 1141, he concentrated on tightening his grip on the north of England, extending his hold over Durham, the north-western fringes of Yorkshire and at least northern Lancashire. Only in 1149 was a new offensive launched, partly as an inaugural raid by his great-nephew, Henry Plantagenet, the future Henry II, whom David had knighted at Carlisle. The aged David did not lead the offensive this time, command being entrusted to men such as William fitz Duncan. While the Scots once again came within an ace of seizing York, the campaign was at best a stalemate, so characteristic of the long civil war in England.

In contrast to war-ravaged southern England, after 1138 David's gains in the north appear as a haven of peace and prosperity. His secure hold on his enlarged kingdom enabled David to push ahead with the schemes for the development of his government, the modernization of the economy, and the reform and reconstruction of the Church, that he had set in motion soon after 1124. David continued to attract new men into his service, clerks and knights who formed the core of an evolving administration. For its structures, he drew on his early experiences in England, creating officers of state and developing a network of local administration on the English pattern.

39. Clitheroe Castle, Lancashire. Below its walls in June 1138, William fitz Duncan
defeated an English army.
40. Carlisle Castle, Cumbria. David I may have been the builder of the great
twelfth-century keep that dominates the castle.
41. A silver penny of David I, minted from Cumbrian silver.

A chancellor, acting as the king's chief legal advisor, also controlled a writing office from which flowed an increasing tide of the parchment records of government: charters making or confirming grants of property and rights; letters to convey royal instructions to local officers; legal judgements in cases before the king's court; and records of royal revenues, rights and dues. The chamberlain controlled the king's finances, while the steward was responsible for the running of the household. The king's military affairs and the security of his household were overseen by the constable. Together with a host of lesser clerks and officials, these men transformed what had been a fairly small and informal royal household into an effective bureaucracy.

While war governed much of David's life down to 1141, he was more than simply a warlord. Influenced by English and Norman traditions, David projected an image of the king as lawgiver. Law codes attributed by tradition to David form the basis of medieval Scots law and the foundations of a system of sheriffdoms for the local administration of law was laid down by the king. But David was no remote figure, dispensing justice to only an exalted few, and the chroniclers make it clear that he saw it as his kingly duty to open the law to his subjects of all ranks. Ælred wrote of the king sitting at the door of his hall to receive petitions from the humblest of folk and even breaking off from his beloved hunting trips to hear the pleas of widows and the poor. To an extent it was a cultivated image, to be seen most clearly in the portrayal of David in the initial letter of his grandson's great charter to Kelso Abbey. There sits David, long-haired and bearded, presented as Solomon alongside the youthful and beardless Malcolm IV. The Biblical imagery, however, did not end with the wise lawgiver.

Amidst the planning for the war with Stephen, David found time to re-affirm his commitment to Church reform. Although he continued to patronize the established orders, such as the Benedictines and Tironensians, and founded one further Augustinian monastery at Cambuskenneth, most of his favour was targeted towards the new and even more austere Cistercian monks. In a society where austerity and simplicity was equated with piety and spirituality, the Cistercians were seen as enjoying a special closeness to God. For David, embarked as he was on a process of reform, and perhaps with his conscience pricked by the blood that he had spilled over the years, the prayers of these monks was welcome balm for his soul. In 1136, during the lull in his war with Stephen, he brought a colony of Cistercians from Rievaulx in Yorkshire to Melrose in Tweeddale. The colony prospered and in 1140, perhaps in atonement for the atrocities committed by their men in the 1138 campaign, David and his son, Earl Henry, founded an offshoot at Newbattle, followed in 1150 by two daughter-houses at Kinloss in Moray and Holmcultram in Cumberland. As his reign progressed, David may have felt ever more needful of Cistercian prayers.

All of this development was not achieved without cost. Over his reign, David devoted large sums to pious works, founding monasteries and building churches. Indeed, his fifteenth-century descendant, James I, looking at his seemingly prodigal alienation of crown resources to endow what seemed to him an ill-deserving Church, described him as 'ane sair sanct for the croune' (a sorry saint for the crown). Not only did he grant away portions of his land and revenue to the Church, however, but also used his resources to provide land to attract a colonizing aristocracy from England. Yet David clearly regarded his investments as money well spent. Indeed, the monks' policy of economic development of their estates, pioneering techniques in agriculture and stock-management, and the improved administrative methods brought by his colonial dependents, helped to kick-start Scotland's economy. Surpluses from monastic estates, especially wool and hides, stimulated the development of Scottish markets and overseas trade, channelled through David's chartered royal burghs. Growth was further stimulated by David's introduction of Scotland's first native coinage, minted with silver from the royal mines at Alston in Cumberland. In many ways it was on the back of this silver coinage that David's economic miracle was floated. Out of the profits of war, David built his new Scottish kingdom.

By 1150, David had drastically reshaped not only his own kingdom but also the balance of power within the British Isles. What historians term his 'Scoto-Northumbrian' realm, with its centre of gravity on a Roxburgh-Carlisle axis, was the dominant force in British politics, seen by southern English writers as a haven of good government in contrast to their war-torn homeland. The southern emphasis within his kingdom, however, should not obscure the fact that David was also a highly effective king of Gaelic Scotland. While there were many Gaels within Scotland who resented his anglicizing policies and personnel, the twenty years of stability that followed the capture of Malcolm in 1134 showed that he was accepted by and could count on the loyalty of most of the Gaelic nobility. Indeed, it has been said that David became more and more a Gaelic king as his reign progressed, successfully uniting the diverse components of his hybrid domain. The fact that David's extended kingdom proved transitory has led some to dismiss his achievement, but in the eyes of most contemporaries his greatness was unquestioned.

Despite his successes, for David the future held only uncertainty. In an attempt to secure his hold over his English gains, in 1149 when he knighted Henry Plantagenet he extracted a promise that the future king would respect the territorial *status quo*. A secure succession to the throne was an added safeguard and, in the person of Earl Henry, king-designate from possibly 1140 and an active colleague in government for his aged father, that seemed certain. In June 1152, however, aged about thirty-seven, Henry died. It was a devastating blow for David, who had never remarried after Queen Matilda's death in 1130 and who had no other adult son to whom the throne could pass. Now in his early seventies, David knew that he had to prepare for the future. In the summer of 1152, while he himself took Earl Henry's second son, the nine-year-old William, to Newcastle to receive the homage of the men of Northumberland, David sent his eldest grandson, Malcolm, on an arduous progress around Scotland in the company of Earl Duncan of Fife, to secure his recognition as king-designate. Still unsure as to whether he had done enough to secure the future of either his kingdom or his line, David died at Carlisle on 24 May 1153.

RO

MALCOLM IV (1153-65)

Malcolm IV was barely twelve years old when his grandfather King David died. The succession of an untried boy opened the possibility of renewed challenges to the ruling line and, in a bid to limit the threat, Malcolm was inaugurated king at Scone within days of his grandfather's burial at Dunfermline. It was not enough, however, and rebellion swiftly erupted. In the west, Somerled and his nephews, the sons of the Malcolm imprisoned in 1134, moved to re-stake the claims of the mac Alexander lineage, and even in the heartland of the kingdom there were disturbances in support of the rival line. It was an inauspicious start.

By 1156 the domestic challenges were over: Somerled had gone in pursuit of a kingdom in the Isles for his son, Dubgall, and Donald mac Malcolm had been captured and imprisoned with his father in Roxburgh. A greater challenge, however, loomed on the horizon. In 1154, Malcolm's cousin Henry Plantagenet ascended the throne of England. Although he had promised in 1149 to respect the borders of the extended Scottish kingdom, in 1157 he laid claim to Cumberland and Northumberland. With England now united behind Henry the balance of power had swung decisively in his favour and Malcolm was in no position to resist. In return for the restoration of Huntingdon, Malcolm surrendered his grandfather's gains and became Henry's vassal. Further humiliation followed. Malcolm, despite his Gaelic name – the last borne by any of Scotland's medieval rulers – had been brought up in the court of his anglicized father and exposed since early childhood to the chivalric ethos that permeated the noble elite of David's kingdom; for the teenage king, knighthood was the ultimate attainment. He had fully expected Henry to knight him but was rebuffed. A fresh opportunity to achieve knighthood came in 1159, however, when Henry summoned him as his vassal to give military service in his campaign against the Count of Toulouse. Probably against the advice of his leading nobles, who well understood the implications of Malcolm's readiness to accept the summons, Malcolm and his younger brother William embarked for France. On 30 June, at Périgueux, Henry at last knighted him. Although the campaign proved a failure, Malcolm had achieved one ambition.

Malcolm returned to Scotland to face the wrath of the Gaelic nobles who had supported him through the early years of his reign. Incensed by what they probably considered to be his wilful disregard of his kingly duties and by an act that might have compromised the independence of the kingdom, they attempted to seize him at Perth but were defeated and forced into submission. Malcolm immediately followed this success with an invasion of Galloway, whose ruler, Fergus, he defeated and forced into retirement as a canon in Holyrood Abbey, and which he then partitioned between Fergus's sons.

This forceful behaviour and love of military action stands in sharp contrast to the traditional image of Malcolm as weak and effeminate. This image has been reinforced by misunderstanding of his later nickname 'the Maiden', which reflected his personal celibacy and not his physical appearance or personality. Indeed, his celibacy was an extension of his devotion to his ideal of Christian knighthood, being modelled on the virginal purity of the ideal knight of Arthurian chivalric tradition, Galahad. It was, however, a cause for concern to those who wished to see the dynasty secured, especially after the first bout of illness that struck him in 1161, and his mother, Ada de Warenne, urged him to marry. Plans for his marriage to Constance of Brittany proved abortive, however, and after four years of recurring, serious illness he died at Jedburgh on 9 December 1165, still a virgin.

RO

WILLIAM I (1165-1214)

The succession to the throne of the twenty-two-year-old William heralded the opening of five decades of profound upheaval and change in the life of the kingdom. The longest reigning of Scotland's medieval monarchs, William presided over a period that saw unparalleled expansion in crown authority but also witnessed repeated challenges to that authority by pretenders from within the wider royal kin as well as the rigorous subjection of Scotland to the overlordship of the kings of England. The successes and failures of his long reign, however, should not detract from the personal achievements of one of Scotland's greatest rulers.

William was born probably in 1143, the second of Earl Henry's three sons by Ada de Warenne. On his father's death in 1152, William was taken by his grandfather to Newcastle and invested as earl of Northumberland. William, however, had little time to enjoy his patrimony, for in 1157 the surrender of the northern counties to the forceful Henry II disinherited the fourteen-year-old earl. Although Henry compensated him with Tynedale, the loss of the earldom embittered William, who spent twenty years trying to regain Northumberland. It became an ambition bordering on obsession and resulted in humiliation for both Scotland and her king.

Like his elder brother, William was a passionate devotee of the new chivalric ideal that was saturating European noble society. Equally determined to win his spurs as a knight, William accompanied Malcolm on the Toulouse expedition of 1159 and was apparently knighted by his brother at Périgueux. On his return to Scotland he would have had the opportunity to indulge his teenage passion for warfare in the breaking of the protest of the rebel earls at Perth and the subsequent Galloway campaign. William's wholehearted embracing of the glamorous world of Frankish chivalry is underscored by references to him as 'William de Warenne', identifying him with his mother's kin, one of the great families of the Anglo-Norman elite, rather than with his father's royal Scottish ancestry. This apparent preference for all things Frankish was re-affirmed when a later chronicler observed that the Scottish kings considered themselves 'as Frenchmen in race, manners, language and culture; they keep only Frenchmen in their household and following and have reduced the Scots to utter servitude'. It was surely an exaggeration, but this casual remark emphasizes how far William had moved from his Gaelic roots.

A fortnight after the death of his brother, on 24 December 1165, William was inaugurated king at Scone. Almost immediately he used his new status in a bid to regain Northumberland. In August 1166 he met with Henry II in France and requested restoration, but was refused. Two years later, he approached Henry's rival Louis VII of France, seeking his diplomatic aid in the matter. It was a crassly provocative act which seriously damaged Anglo-Scottish relations and reduced Henry to such a fury that any mention of William threw him into a fit of rage. Once, he tore off his clothes and ripped the silk cover from the bed on which he was sitting before cramming his mouth with the straw that filled his mattress! It was hardly a promising start to their relationship.

Relations had improved sufficiently by April 1170 for William to attend Henry's court at Windsor and, using this as an opportunity to visit his Huntingdon estates, he remained in England until June for the coronation at Westminster of Henry's eldest son, also called Henry and known as the Young King to distinguish him from his father. On 15 June, William gave homage to the Young King, forming a personal bond that proved his undoing. In 1173, as the 'Angevin Empire' of Henry II slid into civil war between the old king on the one hand and his estranged wife, Queen Eleanor, the Young King and their ally Louis VII on the other, William was approached for aid by the rebels, who offered restoration of Northumberland. Against the advice of his counsellors but following the urging of a hawkish group of young household knights, William chose war.

In June 1174, following two inconclusive campaigns in 1173 and spring 1174, William again invaded England. Ill-prepared for the siege warfare necessary to take the castles that had been built in Northumberland since his grandfather's day, William made little headway. In early July he besieged Alnwick and dispersed most of his army on raiding missions throughout Northumberland. On 13 July, caught unawares, William and the cream of his nobility were captured in a surprise attack. With his legs shackled beneath the belly of his horse, William was escorted south and consigned to prison at Falaise in Normandy. For Scotland, the humiliation had just begun.

To gain his release, William was forced to accept Henry's terms in what is known as the Treaty of Falaise. On 8 December 1174, having publicly acknowledged his subjection to Henry and promising hostages and the surrender of key fortresses in his kingdom, William was released. He confirmed the treaty on 10 August 1175 at York in a great ceremony where William publicly performed homage and fealty to Henry explicitly for his kingdom as well as his estates in England, promised to enforce the subjection of the Scottish Church to English jurisdiction, and 'ordered' his nobles and clergy to make their personal submissions to Henry. Unlike previous submissions, this treaty formally set out Scotland's vassal status, provided terms by which Henry could enforce compliance and established English garrisons in William's chief castles south of the Forth. Furthermore, it made clear that Henry considered the question of Northumberland and Cumberland firmly closed. Henry regularly reminded William of his status, especially by summoning him to court to explain his actions. He also chose to exercise his right as overlord to choose William's bride. By the 1180s and now in his early forties, William was still unmarried and, although he had fathered at least six bastards, his younger brother David was his only legitimate heir. He wanted a bride who would reflect his royal status and in 1185 requested Henry's permission to marry his overlord's granddaughter, Matilda, daughter of Henry the Lion, duke of Saxony. King Henry, however, had no wish to permit so politically significant a marriage to take place and instead offered him Ermengarde de Beaumont, the young daughter of the lesser nobleman Richard, vicomte of Beaumont sur Sarthe in Maine. William agreed reluctantly. Despite Henry's generous payment for the wedding celebrations – held at Woodstock on 5 September 1186 – and return of two of the forfeited castles as a wedding present, it was clear that the Scottish king felt slighted.

With southern expansion effectively shut off to him, William was forced to concentrate on domestic issues. More than one crisis faced him when he returned from Normandy. In Galloway, the sons of Fergus were in rebellion and had appealed to Henry II that he should take them under his lordship. When one brother, Gillebrigde, had the other, Uhtred, murdered, Henry ordered William to bring the fratricide to justice, but Gillebrigde submitted to Henry and spent the next decade defying the powerless William. It was only in 1185 that William's protégé Roland, the son of Uhtred, took control of Galloway and restored it to a Scottish orbit. More serious was the rising in the north by Donald mac William, grandson of Duncan II, who took the opportunity of William's capture to claim the crown that he felt was rightfully his. Drawing widespread support, the rising rumbled on into the 1180s. In 1179, William, displaying the energy and dogged determination that was a hallmark of the central years of his reign, made the first of several expeditions into the north, extending direct royal power for the first time into Ross through the building of new castles on the north side of the Beauly and Cromarty firths. He failed, however, to bring Donald to battle and it was only in 1187 in a conflict near Garbh in Ross that the rebels were crushed, the pretender's severed head being brought to the king at Inverness.

42. William I as a mounted knight.
43. Prudhoe Castle, Northumberland, besieged unsuccessfully by the Scots during
their 1174 invasion of England.
44. Falaise, Calvados, France. William was imprisoned in the twelfth-century keep
after his capture at Alnwick.

45. Arbroath Abbey, Angus, founded by William I and dedicated to St Thomas of Canterbury, to whom he attributed his defeat and capture in 1174.
46. Nineteenth-century facsimile of the seal of Arbroath Abbey, depicting the martyrdom of St Thomas of Canterbury.

This victory marked a new high point for royal power in the Highlands. Forced to look to the proper organization of royal government in the north, William radically overhauled the structures set in place by his brother and grandfather. The network of castles established as early as 1130 was strengthened and extended, as was the system of sheriffdoms based on them. In the 1190s, despite his faltering health, William again campaigned in the north, intent on humbling the perennial troublemaker Harald Maddadsson, earl of Orkney and Caithness. Royal armies reached the north coast at Thurso and Harald submitted, but it was not until after 1200 that he finally admitted the reality of William's power in the farthest reaches of Scotland. The Church, too, became a more effective bastion of royal power, with William appointing a loyal clerk to the key bishopric of Moray. But the most effective bulwark lay in the establishment of loyal knights in the region. The greatest beneficiary was his brother David, to whom he gave the strategic lordship of Garioch, which straddled the routes between Moray and the lowlands to the east, but the service of great Gaelic lords such as the earls of Fife and Strathearn was also rewarded by the granting of lordships in the central Highlands. Through achieving a balance between native and newcomer, William significantly tightened the royal grip on the north.

Amidst the crises that beset him from 1174 to 1187, William still found time for personal acts of devotion. His capture, which was attributed to the saintly intervention of the martyred archbishop of Canterbury, St Thomas à Becket, had affected him profoundly. In honour of the saint, and no doubt to placate this holy defender of England's borders, in late 1178 William founded the great abbey of Arbroath and over the remainder of his reign endowed it with wide lands and revenues from the royal estates. This was the act of a deeply troubled soul.

The years of frustration and hard work after 1174 finally bore fruit in 1189 when Henry II, beset by his rebellious sons, finally proved mortal. The new king, Richard I, desperately in need of cash for his planned crusade, was prepared to negotiate with William. While again deferring a decision on Northumberland, Richard agreed to sell William back his freedom for the princely sum of 10,000 marks. On 5 December 1189, almost fifteen years to the day since his submission at Falaise, the so-called Quitclaim of Canterbury annulled the terms of the 1174 treaty.

William was now at the height of his power and concentrated on consolidating his hold over the kingdom. That he still hankered after Northumberland is clear: he sought to curry favour with Richard I by opposing his younger brother Count John's attempts to seize power in 1193 following the king's capture in Austria; by contributing 2,000 marks to Richard's ransom; and by arranging the marriage of two of his bastard daughters to important Northumbrian lords. It was all for nothing. When Richard agreed to sell the earldom to him in 1194 for 15,000 marks, it was on the condition that the chief castles remain in Richard's possession. It was, for William, an unacceptable condition and, bitterly disappointed, he returned to Scotland. But the matter did not end there. Later in 1194 William hatched a scheme, with Richard's agreement, for the marriage of his eldest legitimate daughter, Margaret, a child of no more than seven years, to Richard's nephew Otto, son of Henry of Saxony. William, who fell seriously ill in summer 1195, still lacked a male heir and, to the horror of his counsellors, attempted to have Otto recognized as his successor. Such was Richard's enthusiasm for the scheme that he agreed that Cumberland, Northumberland and Lothian would form Margaret and Otto's dowry. Just when it seemed that his life's ambition would be attained, however,

William suddenly and for no clear reason backed out of the agreement. Yet he still sought an alternative settlement. In 1199, when John seized the throne of England, William used threats of military intervention in support of John's rival in a bid to extract concessions from the new king, but when it came to the pitch his nerve broke and he disbanded his army. Fruitless negotiations dragged on leaving the festering issue unresolved.

William's increasing desperation over Northumberland was in part a response to his failing health and lack of a male heir. In April 1198, however, after twelve years of marriage, Queen Ermengarde at last gave birth to the son he craved. William was determined to pass to the child, Alexander, all that he considered to be the boy's birthright, and that included Northumberland. As the last years of William's life was to show, however, that was to be no easy task.

For William, the 1190s had been a veritable Indian summer. Freed from the shame of Falaise, it was in this period that the later reputation of the king had been made. To later generations of chroniclers, the bellicose and impetuous prince had been replaced by 'the Lion of justice', a style from which his most common modern title – William the Lion – is derived. To the chronically ill and ageing king, however, such high-blown titles would probably have held a bitter irony, for in the closing years of his life he watched much of the achievement of the 1180s and 1190s seemingly evaporate. It must have seemed a poisoned chalice that he was to pass to his son.

As had been the case throughout his life, the obsession with Northumberland contributed significantly to the dramatic reversal in his fortunes. William's attempts to ingratiate himself with Richard I in 1193 and refusal to immediately acknowledge John in 1199, both acts motivated by his determination to regain his lost patrimony, had soured his relationship with the youngest of Henry II's sons. Despite seven years of negotiations which produced a series of false dawns, by 1206 a solution was no closer and over the next three years the relationship between William and John descended into crisis as rumours reached the English king that William was again negotiating with his French enemies. In April 1209 William, again seriously ill, received the latest in a series of demands from John for a meeting in person. John came north with an army while William brought his forces to Roxburgh, and the two forces glowered at each other across the Tweed. Bowing to John's threats, William agreed to negotiate, but a return of his illness forced the suspension of talks and John returned south leaving his demands on the table. William's considered response infuriated John, who mustered for war, and, after considering armed resistance, the Scots caved in. On 7 August 1209, at Norham, William came to terms.

John's terms were a fresh personal humiliation for William. In return for a minor concession concerning the English castle at Tweedmouth, William was obliged to pay 15,000 marks to secure the peace, renounce his rights to the northern counties (which were to be given to Alexander to hold of the English crown when he came of age) give hostages as surety for payment and hand over his daughters, Margaret and Isabel, whose marriages John was free to arrange, possibly to his young sons, Henry and Richard. John's plan seems to have been that one of his sons would become the heir by marriage of William's heir, Alexander. Scotland's independence was not compromised on this occasion, but her aged king had been browbeaten and bullied into a one-sided treaty that promised much but had no real substance.

On top of this crisis came natural disaster. In September 1210 rainstorms swept Scotland, flattening much of the late harvest, and spate-filled rivers burst their banks. At Perth, William

47. Tomb effigy believed to be that of William I, found in Arbroath Abbey.
48. Balmerino Abbey, Fife, founded by Ermengarde de Beaumont, wife of William I.

and his brother were almost trapped by floodwaters that swept away most of the royal castle but escaped by boat. Then came disturbing news of threatened insurrection in the north which forced William to drag his weary bones to Moray. In January 1211, as William lay bed-ridden at Kintore, Gofraid mac William, son of the Donald killed in 1187, launched his bid for the throne. As the rising rumbled on into summer, the increasingly frail William, his physician Master Martin bumping along in his baggage train, returned to the north and waged a futile three-month campaign. Leaving others to prosecute the war and fearful for the succession of his still underage son, William headed south with his family and sought a meeting with John in February 1212. Perhaps due to her husband's increasing physical inca-pacity, it is Queen Ermengarde who is credited with mediating a renegotiation of the 1209 treaty. The earlier terms were re-affirmed, but with the added provision that John would arrange Alexander's marriage – presumably to his infant daughter, Joanna – and that each king would come to the aid of the other. The treaty settled, the fourteen-year-old Alexander travelled south with John to be knighted at Westminster, presumably in anticipation of leading his first campaign against Gofraid. There was, however, to be no campaign in which Alexander could win his spurs, for by April 1212 the pretender had been betrayed and executed.

Entering his seventieth year, William, described as 'venerable' by one English clerk, was clearly preparing for his death. Queen Ermengarde, probably over twenty years younger than her husband, seems to have assumed some of his duties; she is found, for example, presiding jointly with the bishop of St Andrews over a complex court case. Alexander, too, was becoming more closely associated in affairs of state, being groomed for the office that his father expected soon to bequeath to him. Through 1213, William was setting his worldly affairs in order and was preparing for the afterlife, making new grants to churches and monasteries for his soul's ease and confirming his earlier gifts. But death did not come. In summer 1214, William made one last journey north to Moray to settle a new accord with John, earl of Orkney. It was an exhausting trip and as William made his slow progress south he was once more struck down by illness. On 8 September he reached Stirling, where his health continued slowly to decline. At last, on 4 December 1214, attended by his wife, son and brother, he died.

RO

ALEXANDER II (1214-1249)

On 5 December 1214, the day after his father's death at Stirling and five days before the old king's body was laid to rest before the high altar of his abbey at Arbroath, Alexander II was inaugurated at Scone. Four days of muted festivity followed, then on 9 December the new king met the funeral cortège as it crossed the bridge at Perth, escorted by the widowed Queen Ermengarde, and processed to Arbroath for William's funeral, Earl David presiding as his brother's chief mourner. Why the seemingly indecent haste? Why had the young prince to be made king before his father was even in his grave?

To the modern observer it perhaps appears obvious that Alexander, as the only legiti-mate son of William, would automatically have succeeded to the throne. But in 1214 male primogeniture – the succession of the eldest male offspring of the previous ruler – was still a recent innovation. It was sheer dynastic accident that the succession had passed through a direct line of descent from David I, not policy. In 1214, however, Earl David was the eldest male of the royal kin, and there was also the unresolved question of the Mac Williams, who clearly still enjoyed considerable support amongst segments of the Gaelic nobility. With Gofraid's rising still a recent memory, and Earl David such an unknown quantity to so many Scots, there was real fear of a challenge to Alexander's succession. Speed, therefore, was of the essence.

The challenge was not slow in materializing. Within weeks of Alexander's inauguration the next Mac William claimant, Donald Bàn, had landed on the mainland and was raising rebellion in Ross and Moray. By mid-June 1215, however, the threat was over: Donald was dead and his head delivered to Alexander. The young king was no doubt relieved at the rapidity of Donald mac William's demise, for he had far bigger fish to fry. On the same day that Donald met his maker, hundreds of miles to the south King John was putting his seal to the Articles of the Barons. Among the concessions contained in the Articles, soon to emerge in fuller form in Magna Carta, was John's promise to do right by Alexander in respect of his sisters' marriages, the return of the hostages delivered up in 1209, and all unresolved questions relating to his liberties and rights. It is highly unlikely that Alexander had been ignorant of developments in England, for among the barons pressing their demands on John were his two brothers-in-law, Robert de Ros and Eustace de Vescy, while one of those on whose advice John accepted the demands was Alexander's constable, Alan, lord of Galloway. Although not yet seventeen, Alexander was already showing himself to be a shrewd political operator. After all, he had been associated for two years in the running of the kingdom and had been exposed abruptly to John's duplicity and manipulation in 1212. He was clearly well informed of the deteriorating political situation in England and had no doubt used his time well in developing his inherited ties with John's disaffected northern barons, a group that included many men with personal kinship or tenurial bonds to the young king.

As England drifted into civil war in September 1215, Alexander prepared to capitalize on John's troubles. In October his army crossed the Tweed and he took the homage of the barons of Northumbria, apparently achieving in weeks what his father had failed to gain in fifty years. But John's men held the great fortresses of the region, and by the end of 1215 only Carlisle was in Alexander's possession. Soon, however, he was to reveal himself as John's equal in cynical manipulation and opportunism. In January 1216, as John moved against the northern rebels, the fearful barons turned to Alexander for aid. Revealing a skill in turning a favourable situation to his best advantage, he demanded and received their homage and fealty. John, however, was at his most dangerous when cornered and, swearing to 'make the fox-cub enter his lair' – no doubt a sneering reference to Alexander's red hair and youth – he led his army in an orgy of destruction through south-east Scotland. Nothing was achieved by the slaughter, for Alexander launched a counter-raid into Cumberland and in May, when the French Dauphin Louis landed in Kent to take the English crown at the request of the rebels, John's position in the north collapsed.

Alexander now established firm control of the northern counties. On 8 August 1216, Carlisle again fell into his hands and became the seat of a Scottish administration over Cumberland and Westmorland. Indeed, the strength of his hold over the region and its effective incorporation into his kingdom has been recognized only recently, for, as with earlier Scottish occupations of Carlisle, it proved impermanent. In late summer 1216, however, Alexander seemed to hold all the aces. Leaving Carlisle later in August, he crossed Stainmoor into Teesdale and from there made an epic journey to meet with Louis at Dover. Behind him, with the ferocity of a wounded tiger, John struck across Alexander's lines of communication and once more threatened the rebel position in the north. To protect his gains, Alexander hurried northwards and had reached Scotland by the time John died at Newark on 19 October. This event marked a decisive turning point in the war and, although Alexander held on to his gains until December 1217, England rapidly reunited around the boy-king Henry III. Determined to pass John's territorial legacy intact to his son, the English regents dropped all reference to Alexander's griev-ances from the re-issued Magna Carta: for them this was non-negotiable until Henry came of age. Furthermore, Alexander now found himself excommunicated by the legate sent by the pope to safeguard Henry's heritage, and Scotland was placed under spiritual interdict. Bowing to the inevitable, in mid-December 1217 Alexander travelled to Northampton and gave homage to Henry for his English lands.

Displaying all his father's dogged determination, Alexander was intent that the effort and expenditure of the past years should not have been in vain. After two and a half years, negotiations dragged to a conclusion in June 1220. The settlement came nowhere near to meeting the broken promises of the 1209 and 1212 treaties. While Alexander was given the hand of one of Henry's sisters, Margaret and Isabel were only to be found 'suitable' but non-royal husbands in England before October 1221. Nowhere in the agreement was mention made of the northern counties. Unlike his father, however, Alexander knew when it was time to back down and bide his time. He was young and the question of Northumbria could wait.

Like his father after 1174, Alexander now focused his attention on consolidating his power at home. Unlike William, however, he was no-one's vassal and was determined to remove any suggestion that his kingship was inferior in status to any in Europe, England in particular. The main stigma in this respect was the fact that Scotland's kings were inaugurated in a secular ceremony, not anointed and crowned in the ecclesiastical ritual common to England and France. In 1221, in the first move towards rectifying what he saw as a handicap, Alexander attempted to have the papal legate to Scotland anoint and crown him. The issue was referred to the pope who, under English pressure, rejected the move. On this point, however, Alexander was not simply going to let the matter drop and in 1233 made a second, equally unsuccessful bid. Further attempts may have followed, but it must have been clear to Alexander that the English, whose influence with the pope was almost always going to outweigh that of the Scots, would never willingly yield on the issue, despite the friendship between their kings. That friendship had been confirmed in June 1221 when Alexander married Henry's sister Joanna, a match that had first been proposed nineteen years earlier. It was, however, a sign of Scotland's improved standing, for while William had been forced to content himself with the daughter of a *vicomte*, his son had married a royal princess.

The next decade or so saw Alexander throw himself into the task of consolidating the authority that his father had struggled to impose over the remoter quarters of his kingdom. Long-running disputes, such as the rival claims to the earldom of Mar, were settled with firmness and justice, but it was in his dealings with potentially more explosive situations that he showed his true mettle. In early 1221, before his marriage, he led an army into the north-west Highlands and in summer 1221 and 1222 mounted naval campaigns in the west, targeted against the troublesome MacRuairidh kindred, descendants of Somerled, the twelfth-century ruler of Argyll, who had provided the Mac Williams with military aid. In autumn 1222, as Alexander prepared to go on pilgrimage to Canterbury, news came that the men of Caithness had murdered their bishop, Adam, the king's agent in the far north. Abandoning his plans, Alexander marched north and wreaked a savage justice on the perpetrators of this sacrilege in an unequivocal demonstration that the king's peace should run undisturbed and the royal will be unchallenged throughout his kingdom. Fresh disturbances in the north in 1228 were met and crushed with equal severity. The contrast with William's reign could not have been stronger.

While Alexander's ambitions in northern England may temporarily have been held in check, he expanded his authority in other directions. Plans to move westwards, into the area of nominal Norwegian sovereignty in the Isles, were driven by the awareness that it was from this quarter that much of the Mac Williams' mercenary aid had come. Alexander also wished to check the influence of the Uí Neill of west Ulster, also backers of the Mac Williams, who had been reasserting Irish power in the Hebrides. To this end, he encouraged the dreams of Alan of Galloway of building a kingdom in the Isles for his bastard son, cynically using his constable's ambitions to bring the crisis in the west to a head. A general war with Norway in 1231 was narrowly averted after one destructive Norse campaign in the Firth of Clyde area and Alan's schemes were halted abruptly, but not before the king had achieved his goal. In 1230, in a further rising, the Mac Williams were finally defeated and eliminated. In a pitiless display of royal justice, Alexander ordered the brutal 'execution' of the last Mac William, an infant girl whose brain was dashed out against the market cross shaft at Forfar. In 1235 it was the turn of Galloway. Determined to end the ambiguity of its relationship with the Scottish crown, Alexander imposed a partition of the lordship between the daughters of Alan, whose husbands were married to dependable Anglo-Scottish barons, crushing bloodily a rising in favour of their bastard brother. By 1236, Alexander was more surely master of the Scottish mainland than any of his predecessors.

It was from a position of some power that Alexander turned once again to the question of Anglo-Scottish relations. From 1234 he was again pressing for fulfilment of the 1209 treaty and, ignoring papal instructions to submit to Henry III, insisted on a final settlement. Rumours of war ran high in both kingdoms, perhaps encouraged by Alexander who knew exactly how the mind of his brother-in-law worked. Finally, on 25 September 1237 in a conference at York a treaty was settled that drew a line under the question of the northern counties and Alexander's long-standing personal grievances. In return for renouncing his claims to the counties and the 15,000 marks paid by his father to John, and abandoning the marriage arrangements for his sisters, Alexander received £200-worth of land in Cumberland and Northumberland with privileged jurisdiction over them. All copies of the 1209, 1212 and 1221 treaties were to be returned to the respective parties for destruction. At first sight, it appears that Alexander had caved in and yielded most of his claims in return for a relatively small return, but in the end it seems that Henry had recognized the dangers in permitting the uncertainty to drag on and Alexander had been bought off. It was not, however, a blueprint for peace and, after the death of Queen Joanna in 1238, Anglo-Scottish relations were tense, even coming to the verge of war in 1244.

Joanna's death presented Alexander with both a problem and an opportunity. With the death of Earl David in 1219 and his son, Earl John, in 1237, Alexander had no clear male heir. Joanna is a somewhat grey character, completely overshadowed by the dominating figure of the dowager queen, Ermengarde, who lived until 1234. Her inability to provide Alexander with any child, male or female, may be the reason why she failed to gain the place in her husband's counsels that Ermengarde held in William's. It also appears that, unlike his father's evident faithfulness to Ermengarde, Alexander had extramarital relationships after his marriage to Joanna, perhaps an indication of the state of his relationship with her. It is possible that the pilgrimage to Canterbury that she began after the York meeting had been intended to secure saintly aid in the question of her fertility. At London, she was taken seriously ill and died there on 4 March 1238. A final sign of Alexander's indifference towards his wife might be marked by his failure to bring her remains north for burial. Instead she was buried in the Cistercian nunnery of Tarrant Kaines in Dorset, a community with which her husband had no previous relationship. While the problem of an heir seems to have been resolved temporarily by the tacit recognition of his nephew Robert de Brus, lord of Annandale, as heir presumptive, Alexander quickly set about finding a wife. This task also provided him with the opportunity to underscore his independence of England, a point reinforced in May 1239 when he married Marie de Coucy, the daughter of a powerful French baron. At last, on 4 September 1241, she gave birth to their only child, a son. He was not named William in honour of his grandfather, nor even David in memory of the founder of the royal line, but Alexander, and perhaps in this we come closest to glimpsing the hidden personality of his father.

King Alexander emerges as a highly complex character. His ambition was matched by an energy, ability and ruthlessness that was closer to that of his great-grandfather than his father. Unlike his father, too, he possessed a pragmatic realism that perhaps saved him from the humiliation of a second Falaise for Scotland. In his religion, he was the greatest patron and founder of monasteries since David I. He supported conventional monasticism, co-founding a Cistercian abbey with his mother at Balmerino in Fife, and showering Melrose with favour, while his special foundation was Pluscarden in Moray, a colony of the new and especially austere Valliscaulian order of monks. Pluscarden was founded c.1231, perhaps as a thanks-offering for his final elimination of the Mac Williams and as a means of salving his conscience for the brutality with which that end was achieved. He was also, however, a supporter of the new orders of friars, especially the Dominicans, whom he invited to Scotland in 1230 and provided with their first convent at Edinburgh. In doing so he was signalling an awareness of and support for the new and still controversial spiritual develop-ments within the Church, something that suggests that his religious patronage went beyond the conventional or traditional pious behaviour of the ruling elites. But, while he clearly supported the processes of internal reform within the regular clergy, he routinely exploited his influence over the Church to provide additional support for his authority. For example, monks from Melrose, his favoured monastery, were appointed bishops in the politically sensitive dioceses of Caithness, Ross and Whithorn, and in Galloway the native heads of the local Cistercian houses were deposed in favour of Melrose monks after Alexander suppressed the 1235 rebellion there. For Alexander, religious patronage and personal piety may have been investments to be cashed in for political considerations.

Royal control over the Church was just one manifestation of Alexander II's firm grip on the political life of his kingdom. The political elite, too, was tightly controlled

49. Alexander II enthroned in majesty, from his great seal.
50. Pluscarden Priory, Moray, founded by Alexander following the final defeat of the Mac Williams.

through a mixture of coercion and patronage. Crown-magnate tensions were not unknown, as in 1242 in a brief crisis which followed the death in suspicious circumstances of the heir to the earldom of Atholl, when a majority of the nobility forced the king to take firm action against the family suspected of his murder, who were currently riding high in his favour. Otherwise, magnate ambitions were harnessed to the needs of the crown, and this can be seen most clearly in the military operations that punctuated his reign. Support for Alexander's military objectives brought tangible rewards in the form of land and office, illustrated most spectacularly by the rise of Farquhar MacTaggart from obscurity to the earldom of Ross. This co-operation between crown and nobility, clear testimony of Alexander's rapport with his lords, served to underpin the consolidation of royal authority in the northern and western mainland, regions where control had been intermittent during his father's reign.

By the 1240s, Alexander's authority within Scotland had reached its zenith. On the mainland, only the MacDougall lordship of Lorn had an ambiguous relationship with the crown, and beyond it beckoned the Hebrides. For Alexander, the Isles represented both unfinished business and a continuing challenge, for so long as they remained outwith Scottish sovereignty they posed a potential threat to the security of the kingdom. In 1244, Alexander offered to buy the Isles from Norway, an offer rejected out of hand by the Norwegian king, Håkon IV, who similarly dismissed subsequent offers. Suspicions that the MacDougalls, who were vassals of both kings, were also involved in negotiations with Henry III, prompted Alexander to end the ambiguity for once and for all. In the summer of 1249 a major royal naval expedition cruised the waters of the Inner Hebrides. In early July, it anchored off the island of Kerrera in Oban Bay, poised to strike against the heart of MacDougall power. On 8 July, at the height of his power, Alexander II died suddenly in his tent on Kerrera, struck down, it was rumoured, by the power of St Columba, protector of the Isles.

RO

ALEXANDER III (1249-1286)

Few kings anywhere, let alone Scotland, have enjoyed for so long a positive reputation such as that of Alexander III. Remembered in tradition as the king of Scotland's 'Golden Age', he has in the past been presented as the ideal monarch who brought the realm to the peak of its medieval prestige, power and prosperity, presiding over a united kingdom in which an incipient sense of nationhood was taking root. Only recently has that view come to be challenged, with the king presented instead as a 'lucky mediocrity' whose reputation was created after his death as part of a propaganda offensive mounted by the Bruce and Stewart kings to establish their legitimacy. For writers medieval and modern, however, what has always been most important about Alexander III is the myth rather than the man. Like all icons, it is probably the aspirations invested in and the dreams symbolized by the king that have ensured his immortality rather than his personal achievements or character. But there must surely have been some substance upon which to build the myth?

Alexander III's reign did not begin auspiciously. Only five days after his father's death and before the old king's burial at Melrose, the eight-year-old Alexander was brought to

Scone for his inauguration. There was immediate controversy over procedures, for Alan Durward, justiciar of Scotia and husband of the new king's bastard sister Margaret, urged that Alexander should be knighted before he was inaugurated. Following recent English precedent, the man who knighted the king would most probably become his regent, and it is likely that Durward was aspiring to do so. Walter Comyn, earl of Menteith, head of the powerful Comyn family and Durward's chief political rival, argued strongly and successfully against the knighting. The ceremony proceeded in its traditional form of enthronement, acclamation and declaration of the king's lineage by a Gaelic *seannachaidh*, although the Scots were soon lobbying at Rome again in an attempt to secure the rights of coronation and unction. Menteith had won on this occasion, but Durward continued to hold the political leadership of the administration and his supporters filled the key offices of state. There were some shows of unity, however: in June 1250 the young king, Queen Marie and the leading clergy and nobles assembled at Dunfermline for the translation of the remains of Malcolm III's wife, Queen Margaret, to a more splendid shrine to mark her canonization by the pope. Durward, however, was manoeuvring to increase his authority, and he appears to have succeeded in combining the justiciarships of Scotia and Lothian, the two key judicial and administrative offices, into a single justiciarate in his possession.

Durward's star seemed to be in the ascendant. In summer 1251 plans for a continuation of good Anglo-Scottish relations through the marriage of Alexander to Margaret, daughter of Henry III, were finalized. On Christmas Day 1251, at York, Henry knighted his future son-in-law, and on the following day the young couple were married. Alexander then gave homage for his English lands and, probably well schooled by his advisors, rejected an English attempt to extract his homage for Scotland too. What followed, however, pulled the carpet from under Durward's feet. Alexander, or more likely Henry acting in his name, demanded the resignation of all the Scottish royal officials present. It soon became clear that Durward's opponents, by presenting him as a threat to Alexander and Margaret, had succeeded in calling on Henry to aid them in prising power from their rival. Durward, indeed, may have played into their hands by attempting to secure the legitimizing of his wife at Rome, for this would have made her and his daughters Alexander's nearest heirs. Rumours were certainly circulating that he had planned to murder the young king and take the throne for himself.

In place of Durward stepped Menteith and a government composed largely of the Comyn family and their associates. The young Queen Margaret, who comes across from her letters as spoiled and wilful, resented their control over her, and wrote at length to her father to complain. He, however, was preoccupied with problems in Aquitaine, and when he wrote to the Scots it was to seek military aid. Few responded to his request but one who did was Alan Durward, who in 1254 travelled to Burgos in Castile with Margaret's brother, the future Edward I. Soon, Durward was riding high in Henry III's favour and turning the king's mind against those who had toppled him from power. Menteith and his allies, however, had also alienated much of their support in Scotland. In July 1255, two English emissaries managed to speak privately with Alexander and Margaret and reported back to Henry with an unhappy tale of mismanagement and mistreatment. Moving quickly north, Henry made contact with leading Scottish opponents of the Comyns identified by Alexander and Margaret, amongst them Durward. In August 1255, Durward and the earl of Dunbar staged a coup, seizing

Edinburgh Castle and with it control of the king. Protracted negotiations involving Henry III, Alexander III and the two noble factions followed, but in September, when the Comyns rejected all proposals, Alexander and Henry established a government of their choosing with a term of office to expire on Alexander's twenty-first birthday in 1262. It lasted barely two years.

The 1255 settlement fell, like its predecessor, to a coup. Throughout 1257, attempts at conciliation between the government and the Comyn faction had been underway but no headway was made. In a night time raid in late October, Menteith and his allies kidnapped the king at Kinross and the government disintegrated in confusion. Growing political crisis in England prevented Henry from making more than a token intervention before January 1258, but by that date it appears that the Comyns had already lost control of an increasingly self-confident Alexander, who summoned a parliament to meet at Stirling in mid-April. A settlement was hard to find, but by September 1258 the opposing factions had been hammered into a lop-sided union in which the Comyns were the dominant force. The years of crisis were now over, and for the remainder of the period until Alexander took personal control of his government in 1260, unity was restored to Scotland.

While Alexander's assumption of personal rule brought an end to the eleven years of political division in Scotland, the portents did not seem to augur well. The year 1260 was one of famine and foul weather. Food shortages saw the price of flour rocket, while a wet autumn brought another spoiled harvest and the promise of dearth to come. While Nature may have frowned, the world of politics, however, seemed to smile on Alexander. His ending of the arrangements for his minority government had brought no response from his father-in-law, who was pre-occupied with a mounting crisis at home. It was perhaps in full knowledge of Henry III's weakness that Alexander and the heavily pregnant Margaret travelled to England. Alexander demanded payment of Margaret's dowry, now nearly ten years in arrears, and it was rumoured that he had even gone so far as to suggest that, since Henry had not honoured his obligations under the 1237 York agreement, the issue of his claim to Northumberland should be reopened. It has been said that the 1260 visit brought a renewal of the friendly relations that had existed between the kingdoms before 1249, but more exactly it brought a return to the balance in the relationship that Alexander II had achieved. Having secured Henry's renewed promises concerning the dowry, Alexander returned to Scotland leaving Margaret behind in England for the birth of his first child (a daughter, Margaret, born in February 1261) – much to the concern of his councillors – but only once he had secured guarantees of their safe return. Arrangements, too, were made for the setting up of a minority council should he die before Margaret and the child returned to Scotland. At least some of the lessons of 1249-58 had been learned.

Alexander returned to his kingdom seemingly intent on finishing the uncompleted business of his father's reign. The question of the Isles had fallen somewhat into abeyance during the minority, Ewen MacDougall of Lorn having come into the Scottish king's peace and been restored to his lands in 1255. But despite growing Scottish influence in the west, this was still notionally Norwegian territory and a source of potential danger to Scottish security. In 1261, Alexander tried a return to his father's original policy of seeking a diplomatic solution and sent an embassy to Bergen to negotiate with King Håkon IV. Having spent his reign in asserting rigorous royal power throughout his domain, Håkon was in no mood to permit any diminution in his authority and refused to bargain. The Scottish embassy was even detained over winter in Norway when it tried to leave without the king's formal permission. The diplomatic route having failed, Alexander turned to warfare.

In 1262, Alexander started to apply pressure to the Islesmen. Instead of submitting, however, they sent frantic messages to Håkon, who in 1263 gathered a fleet with the aim of reasserting Norwegian authority in the west. On 11 July 1263 the fleet sailed west, very late in the year for a campaign in the uncertain waters of the Hebrides. Throughout the summer, Alexander had been making preparations for the coming storm, ordering the repair and strengthening of royal castles on both the east and west coasts – for no-one knew where the Norwegians might strike – and instructing local military levies to be held in a state of readiness. On 10 August, Håkon left Orkney for the Hebrides, already aware that his support amongst the Islesmen was draining away. In early September, after plundering their way south and round Kintyre, the Norwegians entered the Firth of Clyde.

Alexander had made his headquarters at Ayr and from there he spun out the negoti-ations that Håkon now sought. The Norwegians might, militarily, have had the upper hand, but time was on the Scots' side, for Alexander knew that Håkon would have to withdraw soon to a secure winter base. In an attempt to force the Scots into a more pliant mood, Håkon sent part of his fleet up Loch Long, where it was hauled across the porterage at Tarbet and launched on Loch Lomond to spread terror throughout Lennox and Menteith. The Scots, however, bided their time. Towards the end of September, Håkon moved the main body of his fleet across the firth to an anchorage between the island of Little Cumbrae and the mainland at Largs, perhaps in preparation for a landing on the Cunningham coast. On 30 September, the first of the equinoctial gales struck and the following morning found three Norwegian galleys and a merchantman beached on the shore at Largs. Throughout the day, small groups of locals and Norwegians skir-mished around the ships, then on 2 October, Håkon himself landed with a select force to salvage what he could from the wrecks. The scene was now set for what has been described variously as the defining moment in the making of the medieval Scottish state, a battle of epic proportions, or an insignificant brawl on an Ayrshire beach.

Stripping away the myth from the facts, the 'battle' of Largs emerges as an inconclu-sive skirmish between two small forces. Håkon had wisely returned to his ships when the Scots appeared, leaving experienced commanders to stage a planned withdrawal in the face of what was at first assumed to be the main Scottish army led by Alexander himself. An Alexander did indeed command the approaching force, but it was not the king but Alexander Stewart, the most powerful Scottish noble in the west, whose lands in Bute and Cowal had been ravaged by the Norwegians. A running skirmish ebbed and flowed over the shingle banks around the mouth of the Gogo Water, but the Scots were unable to force a more general battle and the Norwegians returned to their ships. Håkon, whose fleet was now running short of supplies, was forced to face reality and on 5 October began to withdraw northwards, reaching Orkney on 29 October. He chose to over-winter there, taking over the bishop's palace in Kirkwall. In November, the king's health began to deteriorate and on 16 December he died.

Håkon's death removed what was still a formidable opponent for Alexander.

51. Drawing of one of the Lewis Chessmen found in 1831 on a beach in Lewis, in the Outer Hebrides. Made of walrus ivory, they are thought to be of Anglo-Scandinavian origin and to date from the twelfth century. They have been valued at over £500,000 each and only individual pieces from several sets have been found. It is assumed that more will surface in the future as the sets were probably buried complete for safe-keeping.

Certainly, the western expedition of 1263 had been a failure by anyone's standards, but Håkon had shown the vulnerability of the Scottish mainland to sea-borne raiders and had returned to Orkney with most of his fleet and army intact. His son, King Magnus, however, had many problems stored up from his father's reign to contend with at home, and was in no position to prosecute the war. From a position of strength, the Norwegians now found themselves on the defensive. Alexander chose now to flex his muscles. An embassy in spring 1264 was sent packing, but messengers in the autumn were told that negotiations could start the following summer: Alexander was not going to be diverted from his prey. In summer 1264 he gathered a fleet in Galloway to invade Man, whose king, Magnus Olafsson, only averted invasion by travelling to Scotland to submit personally to Alexander. When the Manx king died the following year, Alexander annexed his kingdom to the Scottish crown. Part of the Scottish fleet from Galloway turned instead into the Isles, where it received the submission of many of the chieftains who had sided with Håkon the previous year, while a land campaign punished those in Caithness and Ross who had submitted to the Norwegians. By the time the Norwegian envoys arrived in 1265, Alexander had imposed his lordship over most of the Isles; a negotiated settlement was little more than a formalizing of established fact.

The terms of the Treaty of Perth of 1266, by which lordship over the Isles was transferred from Norway to Scotland, show that Alexander was prepared to make concessions to ensure that his possession was secure. In return for a single payment of 4,000 marks, to be paid in four annual instalments, and an annual tribute of 100 marks in perpetuity, Man and the Isles became part of the kingdom of the Scots. The former island kingdom was intended to become the appanage of the Scottish heir apparent, Alexander, who had been born in January 1264, but it was to be controlled until his adulthood by a series of crown bailies. The significance of Alexander's achievement in gaining the Isles has often been overlooked, for the chief prize, Man, was to remain in Scottish hands for only thirty years. By annexing the former kingdom of the Isles to his own kingdom, Alexander had extended his power dramatically, pushing his influence south into the Irish Sea and west into the Gaelic world of north-western Ireland and the Hebrides. It represented a significant shift in the balance of power between Scotland and England in the region, which Henry III, a prisoner in the hands of his own nobles, had been incapable of preventing. Until James III added control of Orkney and Shetland to the Scottish crown in the 1460s, it took Scotland to its greatest medieval extent. The apparent ease of the Scottish takeover, however, was deceptive, for in 1275 Alexander was forced to send an army from Galloway against Gofraid Magnusson, illegitimate son of the last Manx king, who had seized control of the island and proclaimed himself king. Scottish control was reimposed in a tide of blood and steel, but it is clear that although they had been bludgeoned into submission, the Manx were still not reconciled to their new masters.

The Treaty of Perth ended a war and transferred what had become effectively only a nominal overlordship from the Norwegians to the Scots. It did not bring an immediate return to friendly relations between the two kingdoms. Norway, though, was a declining power in the later thirteenth century and, with the succession of the young teenage Eric II Magnusson in 1280, it seemed likely to remain weak until its new king was old enough to make his mark. For the Norwegians in the 1280s, good relations with their North Sea neighbours were an imperative and treaties were sought with both

52. Another of the beautiful Hebridean chesspieces from the beach at Lewis.
53. Monument to the battle of Largs, the last significant conflict in the Scottish-Norwegian struggle for mastery of the Hebrides.

England and Scotland. In September 1281, the Scoto-Norwegian treaty was sealed with the marriage in Bergen of the thirteen-year-old Eric to Alexander's only daughter, the twenty-year-old Margaret. Although the marriage alliance cost the Scots heavily – Alexander promised 14,000 marks and resumption of the 'annual' due for the Isles – it ended the tension that had lingered between the kingdoms since the 1260s. Much hope was placed in the match, but in April 1283 Alexander received the news that his daughter had died shortly after giving birth to his granddaughter, to whom the name Margaret had also been given. It was just the latest in a string of blows to rain down on the king.

The first of these blows had fallen in February 1275 when Queen Margaret died at Cupar in Fife. We have no clear image of Alexander's relationship with his wife, but later tradition speaks of it in terms of warmth, closeness and affection, painting the king as a devoted husband and father. Certainly, Alexander, who was still a young man in 1275, showed no inclination to remarry, and it was only in 1285, with the succession in question, that he bowed to political pressure on that front. Five years after the queen's death the second blow fell and Alexander returned to Dunfermline for the funeral of his younger son, the seven-year-old David. Then came Margaret's death in Norway, the blow softened by news of the birth of his first grandchild. All Alexander's hopes now lay with his surviving son, Alexander, a healthy and newly-married young man of nineteen. Young Alexander had been married in November 1282 to Margaret, daughter of Guy de Dampierre, count of Flanders, thereby strengthening Scotland's ties with one of its most important continental trading partners. Like the Norwegian marriage of his sister, it was a match of great significance and marked Scotland's re-emergence onto the European stage. Like Margaret's, however, it was ill starred. In January 1284, the king was in Dunfermline again, burying the last of his children. Politics now overrode sentiment, for Alexander's only living legitimate heir was his nine-month-old granddaughter in Norway. It was imperative that the king should re-marry.

In February 1285, having taken counsel from his advisors, Alexander sent a high-powered delegation to France to seek a bride for him. They returned with the offer of Yolande, sister of Jean, count of Dreux, and in October 1285 she arrived in Scotland. The marriage was held with great splendour at Jedburgh, but later chroniclers, wise after the event, described how the lavish feast was marred by the sudden appearance of a ghostly apparition amongst the revellers. Few could have foretold its message. On 19 March 1286, Alexander was in Edinburgh holding a council with his nobles that seems to have stretched into a long, wine-lubricated 'business lunch'. Late in the afternoon, he decided to return to Yolande, who may have been pregnant, and who was currently residing at the royal manor of Kinghorn in Fife. Against the advice of the ferryman, he crossed the Forth in deepening darkness and in the teeth of a gathering storm. At Inverkeithing, the bailie tried to persuaded him to stay in his house overnight, but the king was determined to complete the eight miles remaining of his journey and rode off into the night, soon to become separated from his companions. It was the last time he was seen alive. The following morning, Alexander's body was found lying on the foreshore at Pettycur, less than one mile from his destination. Modern tradition would have it that he rode to his death over the cliffs in the darkness, but the contemporary records are less dramatic. Galloping along the track that followed the beach at the foot of the cliffs, his horse had stumbled in the sand and thrown him, breaking his neck in the fall. Scotland held its breath, all eyes on Yolande, who claimed to be with child. If she gave birth to a son, then, although there would be the inevitable long and probably troubled minority, there would at least be security and certainty for the future. Even a daughter would be preferable to a granddaughter in distant Norway. By late summer Yolande had either miscarried or had lied about her pregnancy. There was to be no male heir for the Canmore line.

As a model king, Alexander III is, at first glance, a rather odd choice. Succeeding to the throne as a boy of eight, for the first decade of his reign he was little more than a cipher in the hands of competing noble factions. Asserting his own personal authority, however, he brought the divisions to an end and united the nobility once more behind the monarchy. In a brief demonstration of royal ruthlessness, he concluded the long process of extending Scottish control over the Isles, and showed that he was willing and capable of using overwhelming force to cow dissent amongst his new subjects. War and the rewards of victory served to further unite the nobility behind him, with former rivals from his minority years serving alongside each other in the campaigns of 1262-65 in the north and west. Pragmatism, however, made Alexander realize that he was likely to stand a better chance of securing his grip on the Isles through a negotiated settlement and the Treaty of Perth offered the Norwegians a face-saving exercise that brought some profit from the military failure of 1263. He well understood that Norway, even in decline, was a potent power in the northern world, and the marriage treaty of 1281 marked the normalization of Scoto-Norwegian relations after years of strain. This much is positive and self-evident, but what of the later traditions of his reign as a time of peace, abundant harvests and prosperity?

It is a historical fact that the late thirteenth century in Europe generally was a time of expanding markets, rising population and stability. The picture was not entirely rosy, the beginning of Alexander's personal rule, for example, coinciding with a succession of poor harvests and resultant famine and price inflation. Nevertheless, it is clear that the Scottish economy was expanding rapidly during Alexander's reign, with Berwick emerging as one of the most important ports in the northern sector of the North Sea and the major conduit through which Scottish produce, especially wool, woolfells and hides, flowed in to the expanding European market. The expansion of Scotland's trade brought a net inflow of silver to the kingdom, bringing a time of boom that is most clearly marked in the building programmes undertaken by the major monastic landlords and great nobles, who flaunted their wealth in public display. At monasteries and cathedrals from Dundrennan in Galloway to Dornoch in Sutherland, and castles such as Bothwell, Caerlaverock or Kildrummy, new building marks the prosperity that Alexander's peace fostered. But was this prosperity Alexander's personal achievement, or was he just the lucky beneficiary of the good times for all throughout western Europe?

There is no simple answer to that question. Certainly, Scotland cannot but have benefited from the growing prosperity of Europe and, with her established trading links, was well placed to cash in on the demand for her raw and semi-finished produce. But trade does not flourish in uncertain times and the stability of Scotland after 1265 was clearly a major boost. Alexander may have been lucky in that his war was short and geographically remote from the economic heart of his kingdom, and that both the political situation in England during the 1260s and his good family relationship with the Plantagenets in the 1270s and 1280s ensured lasting stability on his only land frontier.

That is not to say that the relationship was not, at times, strained, but Alexander was always secure enough at home to be able to face down the pretensions of his neighbour. In 1275, for example, when he came to Westminster for the coronation of his brother-in-law, Edward I, it was only with written safeguards that his visit was not a sign of subservience. Similarly, when he gave his homage for his English lands it was made explicit that his submission was for those and those alone, not for Scotland. His conduct of diplomacy and politics, then, seems to be that of a capable man, not the lucky mediocrity of recent tradition. But his achievement in these areas is unremarkable, certainly in comparison to either David I or Alexander II. So why did he become such an icon of the kingly ideal for later generations of Scots?

Two main factors appear to have been behind Alexander's later reputation. The first lay in the needs of the Bruce and early Stewart kings to establish their legitimacy as Scotland's rightful rulers in the face of challenge from the Balliol family and the English crown. Their propaganda saw Alexander III's reign presented as a time when the land flowed with milk and honey, when Scotland was safe, secure and powerful, blessed by God. Their purpose was to paint what came after as a time of darkness and despair, when the country turned from the path of righteousness and chose as its king a man who was not its rightful ruler. God turned his back on Scotland, and blighted the realm with war, defeat and dishonour until the Scots recognized their error and turned instead to their rightful king, Robert Bruce. He was portrayed as the man who inherited Alexander III's legacy and restored the land to the freedom and prosperity that it had enjoyed under its last legitimate king. So, Alexander's reputation was enhanced to make what fell between his reign and that of Good King Robert seem blacker still. The second strand, too, had more to do with a later period than with Alexander's own lifetime, for he was taken up as a model of good kingship in the later fourteenth and earlier fifteenth century by chroniclers who were seeking to stress the benefits of powerful royal government. For them, who lived in a time when some nobles were considered 'over mighty', Alexander, who endured a faction-ridden minority where rival bands of nobles contended for power, but who asserted his own authority over them and harnessed their ambitions to his own ends, was the perfect ruler. Furthermore, not only had he checked noble ambitions, he had projected Scotland's power abroad, defeating the Norwegians and rebuffing English pretensions. Under his firm rule, Scotland had emerged as a recognizable nation. To these later chroniclers, the prosperity of his reign was the reward for strong monarchical rule and was an objective towards which his successors should strive. For them, too, the Golden Age idea became a powerful image of what had been lost through the weakness of Scotland's contemporary rulers.

So, does Alexander III deserve his golden reputation? There is no quick or easy solution to that question, but the answer should probably be a qualified 'No'. He was a successful ruler who governed a stable and peaceful realm, where the nobility worked in alliance with the crown. He did wage one short and highly successful war, and conducted a successful diplomacy with his European neighbours, especially with England. He also presided over a period of almost unparalleled expansion in the Scottish economy. While some of these positive factors can be attributed to good fortune, especially the buoyant economy, others were unquestionably a matter of the king's personal abilities. But they do not make him a paragon of kingly virtues, on whom God showered his blessings. Indeed, contemporaries recorded the years of famine and failing harvests in his reign, and spoke of the deaths of his children as God's justice for the king's immoral and unprincipled ways. One chronicler described the king as a lecherous libertine, who whiled away his evening hours in drinking wine – he left unpaid a hefty bill for Bordeaux for which his successors were to be pursued – and in clandestine visits to nunneries where his objective was not religious devotion. While surely the medieval equivalent of tabloid 'news', these presumably scurrilous tales serve to remind us that, beneath the golden gloss, Alexander III was only human.

RO

MARGARET (1286-90)

There is surely no more poignant passage in Scottish history than the tragically short reign of this child queen. Margaret's mother, also Margaret, only daughter of Alexander III and his first queen, Margaret of England, had married King Eric II Magnusson of Norway (1280-99), in Bergen cathedral in September 1281. This match had set the seal on Norway's developing good relations with her North Sea neighbours, Scotland and England, and sought to draw a line under the breakdown in Scoto-Norwegian relations that had occurred in the 1260s. The match soon proved fruitful and Princess Margaret was born in early April 1283, probably in Tönsberg on the coast south of Oslo. All too typically, Margaret's mother, aged around sixteen, died during or shortly after child-birth. This left her daughter's future firmly in the hands of the leading magnates of the day like Bishop Navre of Bergen rather than under the authority of her weak father, Eric, who only turned fifteen in 1283. Margaret was undoubtedly destined to play an important part through marriage in Norwegian foreign policy: the beginnings of her education in Bergen surely reflected this future role. But the untimely deaths of Alexander III's surviving son and heir in January 1284 and then of the Scottish king himself in March 1286 propelled Margaret into the first rank of desirable heiresses.

In parliament in March 1284 Alexander III had required his subjects to recognise the 'illustrious girl Margaret... as our lady and right heir of our said lord king of Scotland.' When the king perished this promise was honoured: for the first time, six Guardians (two earls, two bishops, two barons) were chosen to govern Scotland in the name of the 'community of the realm', not least because this was the lawful way to avoid full-blown civil war between the rival Scottish claimants to the throne, the houses of Balliol and Bruce, who resented – or sought to exploit – the succession of a mere foreign girl. For their part, the Norwegians were keen to secure Margaret's succession to recover control of the Western Isles and various unpaid monies. But it is clear that it was her great-uncle, Edward I of England, who really began to push the key matter of who would be Margaret's husband and thus King of Scots. In doing so Edward may have acted on Alexander III's hint of 1284 that his grand-daughter might wed the English king's son and heir, Edward, (born April 1284) leading to a peaceful union of the English and Scottish crowns.

It was Edward as statesman who oversaw the treaty of Salisbury (November 1289) whereby Margaret was to be brought to the British Isles as yet un-betrothed and only when Scotland was 'at peace'. The various interested parties were competing doggedly for control of Margaret's person and kingdom, with the Bruces, Comyns and Balliol perhaps even hoping to wed their own heirs to the princess. Edward I and Eric II, however, were set on their match, with the English king even going so far in May 1289 as to secure papal approval for his son's marriage before the terms were finalised with the Scots. It was the treaty of Birgham of July 1290 between Edward, Eric and the Guardians which concluded that Prince Edward would wed Margaret and hold Scotland as a kingdom completely 'separate and divided' from England.

With the deal done, Edward I dispatched lavishly supplied ships to fetch the young bride to England. Yet in late August 1290 Margaret left Bergen – amidst much ceremony – in a Norwegian vessel bound for Orkney under the care of Bishop Navre. Here, on what would remain Norwegian soil until the 1460s, she was to be entrusted to an embassy of Scottish knights sent by William Fraser, bishop of St Andrews, as her escort to her inauguration at Scone: a silver bowl kept at Weymss castle in Fife is said to be a relic of this mission. But by late September-early August the first rumours reached Scotland that Margaret had died of illness upon reaching the northern isle. She never saw Scotland and was returned for burial, after her distraught father had identified her body, in the cathedral church of Christ in Bergen (now destroyed).

In 1301 Eric II executed a false 'pretender' Margaret, giving rise to a minor martyr's cult. Later generations of Scots – beginning with the chronicler Andrew Wyntoun (c.1355-1422) – would lament the death of this innocent 'Maiden of Norway'. Scots and Norwegian ballads survive romanticising the frail seven-year-old queen and her doomed journey: for example, the extremely popular (and possibly contemporary) northern folksong about 'Sir Patrick Spens', a seaman said to have been sent 'To Noroway, to Noroway' to bring princess Margaret to Scotland by King Alexander III himself. But in reality, in 1290 the Scots dwelt little on the little girl's fate as they became embroiled in conflict over the vacant throne.

MP

THREE

THE HOUSE DIVIDED
Bruce vs Balliol
1290 – 1371

JOHN I BALLIOL (1292-96)

No other Scottish monarch has suffered the same dreadful degradation of character inflicted upon John, the first Balliol king of Scots. Most of this feeble reputation would be created after his downfall by his enemies. Yet a lot of his real problems as king lay in the fact that until he was well into middle age, John Balliol was not a royal but just another Anglo-Scottish magnate.

Born in 1249, probably on his family's estates in England, John was the third son of John Balliol of Barnard castle in County Durham, the founder of Balliol College, Oxford, who died in 1269. John Balliol senior had wed Dervorgilla (d. 28 January 1290), daughter of Alan, lord of Galloway, and his wife Margaret, eldest daughter of Earl David of Huntingdon, the younger brother of William I of Scotland. The deaths of John

Balliol junior's elder brothers by 1278 meant that despite early training as a cleric he inherited a vast patrimony, including over thirty knights' fiefs in England. His mother's passing would bring him most of the ancient lordship of Galloway in south-west Scotland, centred on Buittle castle and Sweetheart Abbey. This impressive wealth and pedigree brought John powerful connections: by 1283 his marriage to Isabel, daughter of English lord John de Warenne, earl of Surrey, produced a son, Edward; a second, Henry, soon followed. John's sister, Eleanor, married John Comyn of Badenoch (d. 1303), the leading Scottish noble of Alexander III's government along with his kinsman Alexander Comyn, earl of Buchan.

Yet it was not until the unexpected death of Alexander III in 1286 that John's full fortune came in sight. His descent through the eldest daughter of Earl David gave him the best legal claim to the Scottish kingship after Margaret of Norway. It is likely that under the influence of the Comyns, Balliol declared his position early, bringing him into violent conflict in 1286-7 with the Bruce lords of Annandale and earls of Carrick, local rivals of the Galloway lords and Comyns as well as descendants of the second daughter of Earl David. As next in line to the throne after the Maid, John was probably denied office as a Guardian (1286-90). But Comyn support and his legitimate claim ensured that when Margaret died in autumn 1290, the majority of key Scots, like William, bishop of St Andrews, were prepared to recommend Balliol as the rightful king to the statesman to whom the divided Scots now turned to arbitrate their disputed succession, Edward I of England.

Balliol certainly now assumed the bearing of king, yet remained aware that he would have to impress the feudal lord of his lands in England if he wanted to secure the Scottish throne. Thus in November 1290, John – as 'heir to the kingdom of Scotland' – granted lands in Cumberland held by Alexander III to Bishop Anthony Beck of Durham, the 'fixer' Edward I had sent to Scotland. Here already were signs of what one modern historian has described as John's uncertain 'firmness and pliancy'.

Edward I exploited his relationship with the divided Scots expertly. Balliol and his Comyn supporters were the last to submit at Norham in northern England in May 1291 to Edward's devious request that all claimants for the kingship (of which there were sixteen excluding the English king himself) recognize him as overlord of Scotland: the Bruces did so first. But the English king nonetheless gained control of the key castles and offices of the kingdom before the tortuous 'Great Cause' of 1291-2 – the eighteen-month legal hearing held to decide, really, between the claims of Balliol and Robert Bruce of Annandale. By the time this closed with Edward's declaration in favour of Balliol, Scottish royal authority was fatally compromised.

On St Andrews day (30 November) 1292, John was inaugurated as king of Scots upon the Stone of Destiny at Scone. Yet this was a ceremony overseen by Edwardian officials rather than the traditional Scottish earls and churchmen. Worse, within a matter of two months, John – again summoned to northern England – crumbled under the demand that he renew his homage to Edward as Scotland's overlord and release him from any promises he may have made about Scottish autonomy.

There are signs, though, that in his short domestic kingship, John was not a complete broken reed. Annual parliaments were held, justice apparently attended to and Alexander III's work of expanding royal authority continued, with three new sheriffs appointed for the west coast. The recalcitrant Bruces were also largely held in check. However, King John's highly limited itinerary throughout Scotland suggests that government remained in the

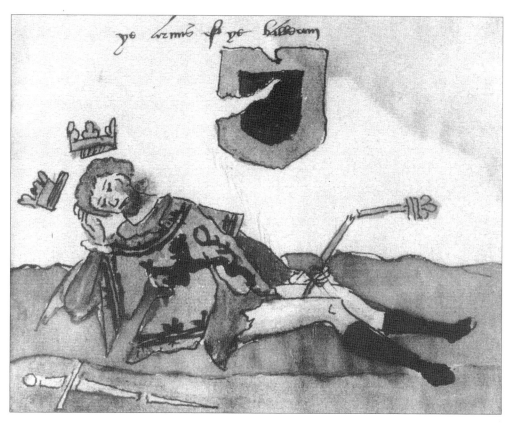

55. The great seal of the Guardians.
56. John Balliol, from a Scottish armorial illuminated between 1581 and 1584. The king is surrounded by the broken symbols of his rule.

57. Seal of John.
58 & 59. Coins of John.

hands of the remainder of the former Guardian administration of 1286-91. While John was closely involved, he failed to impress any personal stamp on his regime and was probably led by the Comyns and their allies.

It was this regime which undoubtedly prepared John carefully for further confrontations with Edward I over appeals from Scottish courts which the law-wielding English king insisted he answer for at Westminster. Here there were glimpses of resistance in John's initial refusal to travel south or to answer without consulting his subjects. But in the face of threats of forfeiture of castles and land John folded.

In the end it took a far more universal threat to the interests of the Scottish nobility for John to stand up finally to Edward. In summer 1294 the English king summoned John and a number of his earls to perform military service for him in his war against France. Unused to such service (and having already sought guarantees against it in the marriage talks of 1289-90), the Scots instead sought a way out of their dilemma through alliance with Philip IV of France. Contemporary English chroniclers insisted that John was so weak a king that at this juncture a Council of Twelve of his subjects removed him from power. But in fact John's familial lands in Balieul in Picardy surely made him crucial to the talks, and helped secure (admittedly vague) promises of French help in the event of open Anglo-Scottish war.

But if John and the Comyns calculated this two-front threat would break England's hold they had underestimated Edward's anger. Perhaps even worse, when Edward led an English army north in spring 1296, sacking the chief Scottish port of Berwick, John failed to lead the Scottish host he had summoned into battle in person. Instead, after his own father-in-law, the earl of Surrey, had routed a Scots cavalry force at Dunbar (27 April), John fled to the north-east only to surrender to Edward at Montrose. He was then taken a short distance west to Stracathro churchyard and ritually stripped of his royal vestments as a traitorous vassal and forced to denounce his French alliance (7 July). Three days later, in Brechin, John was forced to renounce his kingship. This was the punishment that within his own lifetime would see John branded by Scots and English writers as 'Toom Tabard' – empty surcoat.

The disgraced king was then removed to London along with his son, the Stone of Destiny and Scotland's government records. All but John would see Scotland again. It is perhaps hard to believe that inspiring Scots like William Wallace and Andrew Murray – who defeated an English army at Stirling in September 1297 – fought for John's return out of personal loyalty: rather they surely fought for his kingship as the symbol of Scotland's independence. Yet after 1298, the majority of the Scottish political community continued to fight England in John's name and Scottish diplomatic efforts did almost secure his return. In July 1299 Franco-Scottish pressure saw him released by Edward I from the Tower of London into papal custody at Avignon; in October 1301 he was further discharged into French custody and allowed to reside on his Picardy estates. But the defeat of the French at Courtrai in 1302 shattered any hope of a Balliol return backed by a Franco-Scottish army.

John was obliged to live out his twilight years in Hélicourt-en-Vimeau in Picardy, probably dying sometime around April 1313, in his sixty-fourth year. By then Robert Bruce had stolen the Scottish throne and accelerated the blackening of John's name. In 1309 at Robert I's first parliament in St Andrews, the Scottish clergy denounced Balliol as a willing puppet of Edward I. Thereafter, the Bruce regime forbade all mention of the Balliol dynasty and

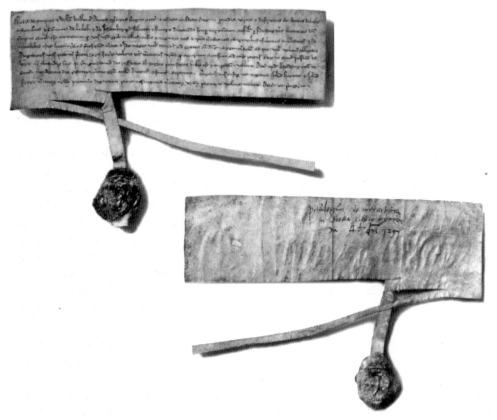

60. Dunbar, East Lothian. The plain between the hills and the coast saw the rout of John's army in April 1296.

61. Letter from William Wallace and Andrew Murray to the important Hanseatic trading communities of Lübeck and Hamburg, assuring them that Scottish ports are open once more following the defeat of the English at Stirling Bridge.

claimed direct lawful succession from Alexander III. These were the points emphasized by late fourteenth and fifteenth century Scottish writers; subsequent historians have been able to do little to rescue John from disgrace.

MP

ROBERT I BRUCE (1306-29)

Almost within his own lifetime, Robert Bruce came to represent the ideal model of strong, patriotic Scottish kingship. Yet the twenty-three years during which Robert I occupied the throne and the glorious reputation he has enjoyed since death reflect an image he himself strove to build, one that masks the very uncertain beginnings of his adult political life.

Robert was the eighth heir to hold that Christian name in the kindred of the Bruces of Annandale, Anglo-Norman in-comers under David I (1124-53). He was born on 24 March 1274, in Turnberry castle on the Ayrshire coast of the earldom of Carrick. His father, Robert (VII) Bruce, had taken this ancient Gaelic title after his dramatic marriage in 1272 to Marjorie, heiress of Neil, earl of Carrick. As a child, Robert saw much of the coastal Irish Sea world of his mother's heritage. As was traditional, he was fostered out for a time to a Gaelic family in the western isles or Ulster and he enters the written record about 1286 when he can be found witnessing a land grant alongside his father on the island of Islay.

Yet Robert was also equally at home in Edward I's England. His family held extensive lands in the northern and middle shires and Robert's father served as keeper of Carlisle castle; the Bruces kept a house in London and Robert and his siblings received some of their schooling in the chivalric and courtly arts in the English royal household. In spanning both realms, Robert was heavily influenced by his grandfather, Robert (VI) Bruce, lord of Annandale (born c.1220), a crusading companion of the English royals. The belief of this wily 'Old Competitor' in his claim to the Scottish throne ahead of John Balliol must have instilled in Robert and his brothers Edward, Neil, Thomas and Alexander (a Cambridge graduate by 1303) an empowering sense of familial destiny. Above all, his upbringing gave Robert the varied skills and contacts that would serve him so well as king.

As he entered adolescence, Robert must have been party to the machinations of his grandfather's royal designs, including the assault on Balliol and Comyn interests in south-west Scotland in 1286-7 and a general campaign to win the support of important Scots and Edward I for the Bruce claim. Thus Robert must have been duty-bound to give homage to Edward I around 1290-92 and to seek the possible division of the Scottish kingdom among the claimants. He was also surely present at Berwick on 7 November 1292 when the eldest Bruce conceded his loss of the Great Cause and resigned Annandale to his son, Robert (VIII)'s father, who in turn looked to resign Carrick to the younger heir.

By 1293, this gave Robert (VIII), at eighteen, a major stake in John I's kingdom, an interest he oversaw – perhaps under the guidance of his grandfather until he died in 1295 – in defiance of his Balliol-Comyn enemies. Robert refused to do homage to the new king, took Isabel, the daughter of his ally Donald, earl of Mar, for a wife, and in

AND EFTER KING ROBERT
YE BRVCE MARIIT YE
DVKE OF HVLLESTERIS DOCHTER

62. A page from a seventeenth-century armorial marking Robert the Bruce's second marriage.

1292-3 perhaps travelled to Norway for the marriage of his sister, also Isabel, to the widowed Eric II. When Anglo-Scottish war erupted in 1296 after John I's alliance with France, Robert surely obeyed his father in siding with Edward I in the hope of receiving the kingship of Scotland as a vassal of the victorious English crown.x

But once Edward had crushed the Scots and stripped Balliol of power, it became clear to Robert that the English king was determined to deny the Bruces their birthright in any shape or form: Scotland would be run as an occupied Plantagenet province. It was this personal and political frustration that provoked Robert to consort with his west of Scotland allies, Bishop Robert Wishart of Glasgow and James the Steward. They launched an abortive attempt to turn the momentum of the risings (in Balliol's name) of Wallace and Murray in summer 1297 into a revival of the Scottish kingship that could be hijacked for the Bruce claim. Patriotism may have been the rallying cry of this sortie, with Robert alleged to have declared his intention to 'join my own people and the nation in which I was born', but political reality soon kicked in: badly outnumbered and distrusted by Wallace and his associates, Bruce and his party capitulated to English forces at Irvine in Ayrshire in July 1297.

Chastened but with his lands intact, Robert now seems to have quietly served Edward I, perhaps even taking part in the English king's defeat of Wallace's Scots at Falkirk in July 1298. Yet almost immediately, probably by reviving his claim for the vassal kingship, he provoked Edward into pursuing him into Carrick, where Robert hid after razing his own castle of Turnberry to the ground. By the close of 1298 Robert seemed to have had no option but to join the patriotic cause of fighting for Balliol, and he became joint Guardian alongside John Comyn of Badenoch. In reality, though, Robert and his supporters may have muscled their way into this administration with a view to pushing the Bruce claim to displace the absent captive, John I.

Tensions erupted quickly between this odd couple. At a council at Peebles in summer 1299 Bruce and Comyn – and their followers – were at each others' throats, violently divided over both the aims of Scottish diplomatic efforts in Paris and Rome and the limited Scottish military campaign. The Comyns made surely well founded accusations of treason against a Bruce party – which now possibly included William Lamberton, the new bishop of St Andrews – pushing for the abandonment of Balliol. Robert for his part was worried by the private agendas behind the Scots' assaults on the English in southwest Scotland on what included Bruce family lands; he must have been shaken by news of the release of Balliol by Edward into papal custody in July 1299.

x Robert was clearly losing ground and the next three years saw him almost completely excluded from Scottish government and besieged by both English and Scots in his Carrick lands. By May 1300 he had been ousted as Guardian in favour of a pro-Balliol Comyn supporter, Enguerrand d'Umfraville. By early 1301 the Scottish patriot administration was preparing for a Balliol return with a French army, a hope confirmed by John's transfer to the French king's custody in October. Bruce by then was widowed (Isabel of Mar died sometime before 1297), without any sons and outcast: he had no option but to protect his family interests and – perhaps through his father's role as keeper of Carlisle – to re-submit to Edward I. This he achieved in January-February 1302, not only retaining his lands but also winning a valuable second marriage to Elizabeth de Burgh, daughter of Richard, earl of Ulster, an ally of the English crown in its Scottish campaigns. Robert also secured a general promise that Edward – who had struggled for the past three years to find the time and resources to reconquer Scotland – would back Bruce's claim for the kingship in any English or foreign court. By July 1302 the wisdom of Robert's decision seemed obvious as a massive French defeat at Courtrai in Flanders left the English free to over-run the Scots.

Once more Robert seemed outwardly content to take part in an Edwardian occupation of Scotland. He provided troops along with his father-in-law for the 1303-1304 campaigns of Edward I and the Prince of Wales and even helped pursue a defiant Wallace to ground. However, once again his allegiance was wavering. It may be that Robert's stomach turned at the prospect of war with some of his countrymen; he must also have realized that there was now no real prospect of a vassal Bruce kingship on the back of Scottish military collapse. England would simply impose another colonial regime.

Thus, as Edward's campaign progressed, Robert's service became first increasingly reluctant and then actively duplicitous. Emboldened by the death of his father in April 1304 and inheritance of all the Bruce lands in Scotland and England, Robert stalled in providing Edward with siege engines to destroy the symbolic Scottish garrison in Stirling castle. Even as the castle fell in June 1304 – some four months after the rest of the Scots had surrendered – Robert was sounding out allies for a future revival of the kingship. Bishop Lamberton certainly agreed to ditch Balliol and support Robert in this future 'enterprise'; other influential Scots were also surely asked to do so in secret in 1304-05.

Meanwhile, Robert played the obedient subject, acting as sheriff of Ayr and of Lanark and advising at Westminster on plans for a new Scottish administration. But by the second half of 1305 it must have become clear that Robert, distrusted by Edward, would have no place in this government, which would instead be dominated by English officials and the old Comyn-led establishment.

It was perhaps in part to discuss this state of domestic political affairs that Robert arranged to meet his former co-Guardian, John Comyn of Badenoch, at the church of the Greyfriars in Dumfries on 10 February 1306. But as this represented neutral holy ground between Bruce and Comyn lands it was more likely the case that Robert wanted either to see where his antagonist would stand on a Bruce bid for the kingship or to broach accusations that Comyn had betrayed Robert's plans to the English. The meeting soon became more heated than that of 1299 and in a moment of livid frustration rather than long-term calculation, Bruce 'struck [John] with his foot and sword'. Although Comyn and his few companions had to be finished off by Bruce's attendants, Robert had become the first of two kings of Scots who would commit murder. But it is ironic that while James II (1437-60) would slay his magnate opponent as an adult king, Robert's killing of Comyn was the act that actually compelled him to take up the crown.

In March 1306 Robert was almost thirty-two, in the prime of his life. But his assumption of the kingship at this time was unarguably forced upon him by the crisis provoked by Comyn's death. He could expect no pardon from Edward I and now the powerful kindred and supporters of Comyn would hunt him down. In many ways his only safety lay in adopting the royal banner of authority and making the Scottish cause his own.

To do this he had few key allies. But after gathering a small retinue of southwestern men and securing his castles in this region, Robert rode to Glasgow where Bishop

63. Seal of Robert I (the Bruce).
64 & 65. Coins of Robert I (the Bruce).

66. The plaque commemorating the murder of John Comyn at the site of the
Franciscan convent in Dumfries.
67. The ruins of Turnberry Castle, Ayrshire, birthplace and stronghold of Robert Bruce.

Wishart absolved him of Comyn's sacrilegious murder and produced the trappings necessary for a royal inauguration. Word must then have been circulated to those whom Robert had sounded out in the past two years and on 25 March he was inaugurated as king of Scots at Scone by Bishop Lamberton of St Andrews, presumably using a make-shift crown.

It was not a confident or impressive ceremony. Numbering only two earls, three or four bishops and abbots, Robert's new wife, his daughter Marjorie, his sisters and brothers and a few south-western lords, this factional band was so desperate for some stamp of credibility that a second ceremony was held on 27 March when Isabel, countess of Buchan, arrived to act out the traditional role of her absent nephew, the earl of Fife, in making any new king of Scots. Bruce may have been determined to make a go of it but everybody else in Scotland must have expected the self-made Robert I to be almost instantly destroyed by either Edward or the Scots.

This was so very nearly Robert's fate by the year's end. After his inauguration he had almost nowhere to go. An English cavalry force routed his meagre army of a few hundred men at Methven near Perth on 19 June. Thereafter Bruce's band were hunted fugitives with many captured and killed, including his brother Neil. Fleeing on horse towards the west coast Robert was bested again at Dalry (11 July) by Scots led by John Macdougall of Argyll. Now seeking only escape, Robert sent his women-folk north to Tain in Ross-shire and Kildrummy castle in Mar while he and his surviving brothers disappeared into the western approaches to Scotland which Robert had known as a child. As he wintered and regrouped, probably off Ulster or in the western isles, Robert must have heard not only of the forfeiture of all his lands but of Edward's vengeful imprisonment of all the Bruce women (with Robert's sister and the countess of Buchan locked notoriously in iron cages).

Few medieval royal exiles failed to make some attempt to recover their kingdoms and Robert I was to be no exception, not least because he literally had nothing else to lose, a sore point driven home when his brothers Thomas and Alexander were betrayed and executed in early 1307. But after Robert returned to Scotland he would make first slow and then increasingly rapid progress against his Scottish and English enemies. To do so he undeniably enjoyed a lot of luck and at times suffered gravely. Yet it should not be doubted that Robert brought enormous personal bravery and skill to his task: a lesser man might have easily failed. In particular, historians have praised his ability to learn from his early mistakes and adopt devastating new tactics, to win over men's loyalty with sound patronage and, above all, to inspire and overawe by leading from the front in war.

Robert landed wisely in his homelands of Carrick in February 1307 and used his natural followers to harass the English occupation forces in southwest Scotland with guerrilla warfare, denying them a decisive pitched battle, remaining on the move and making best use of the rugged terrain. Before Edward I could lead an army north, Robert had come off best in two skirmishes of note at Glen Trool (April) and Loudoun Hill (May). But it was with the eagerly anticipated death of Edward at Burgh-by-Sands near Carlisle on 7 July that Robert got his big break.

For as stark a contrast as Edward I had been in ability to John Balliol, so Bruce was to Edward II (1307-27). The new English king made only a token show of force in summer 1307 before withdrawing to England to create many domestic problems for himself. Robert was thus left free to leave his sole surviving brother, Edward Bruce, to tackle south-west Scotland while he made the gruelling march north to smash the pro-Balliol/Comyn Scots – in English pay but now deprived of aid from London. Robert led his men through Argyll and up the Great Glen taking Inverlochy, Urquhart and lesser castles and forcing his Scottish enemies to submit or flee one by one. He never occupied these strongholds, adopting early the tactic of razing them to the ground. He was clearly intent on breaking the Comyn power-base in the northeast. To do so he inflicted a brutal 'herschip' or destructive burning on the lands of the earldom of Buchan. Then in May 1308 he bested the Comyn Buchan earl at Inverurie. The invaluable port of Aberdeen fell to Bruce by August.

Although reportedly exhausted and confined for a time to a litter – perhaps with the first signs of the wasting disease that later (mostly English) writers would characterize as leprosy – Robert recovered to lead a march back to the west coast. There he brilliantly defeated the Macdougalls by late 1308. His eighteen months of success seem now to have convinced many that he was a winner worth backing. Local Scots were inspired to overthrow the English garrisons of Forfar and Cupar, while many lords now sought to enter Robert I's peace. The king typically forgave such Scots, so pressing was his continued need for support.

All this gave Robert 1309 as a year for consolidation. March saw him call his first parliament at St Andrews where he oversaw the issue by his growing number of noble and church supporters – though really still a minority of the community – of declarations of loyalty to his kingship, denouncing John Balliol. At this time Robert's kingship was also recognized by Philip V of France (with Norway following suit by 1312). However, Robert still had a massive job to do in clearing his English and Scottish enemies from the many garrisons in Scotland south of Perth and Dundee. In this he applied a similarly hands-on approach. One chronicler describes how in 1313 Robert himself led his men to wade across the moat around Perth and was first up the scaling ladder over the burgh walls. Using such stealth tactics rather than long sieges, Robert's swelling support picked off an incredible string of major fortresses. By spring 1314 only Stirling castle and the border strongholds remained in English possession.

There seemed little Edward II could do about Robert's success. When he had finally led an army north in 1310, Robert had retreated to the north emerging only to harass the English troops' withdrawal after an ineffective campaign. By then Edward and his favourites were extremely unpopular with his magnates and heading for civil war (1312). In contrast, Robert was able to turn to a growing band of able, well motivated and generously rewarded noble supporters, headed by his brother Edward (whom he made earl of Carrick and lord of Galloway about 1312), Thomas Randolph (created earl of Moray) and Sir James Douglas. The king even led these generals in person to carry devastating and highly organized raids into northern England after 1311. These extracted crops, livestock and large sums of money and otherwise scorched the earth in a bid to force the troubled Edward II to make peace and recognize Bruce as sovereign of an independent Scotland. Robert must also have been boosted about autumn 1313 with news of the death of John Balliol: such was his confidence that in October that year he declared a twelve-month deadline in which his remaining Scottish opponents – now lumped in as traitors with the English – had to submit to his peace.

This ultimatum helped set the stage for Robert's most triumphant encounter with the English, the battle of Bannockburn of 23-24 June 1314, fought to prevent Edward's relief of Stirling castle with an army of some 16,000 men. Robert's bold personal leadership in this fight was to be a decisive factor in the surprise Scottish victory (the exact site of which at Stirling still remains a focus of heated debate). The king was cautious at first: awaiting the English approach towards the woods surrounding the castle from the south he was fully prepared to withdraw his 8,000 or so men to fight another day. But when the English vanguard of cavalry proved ill disciplined and easily routed by mobile hedgehogs (or 'schiltroms') of Scottish spearmen, Robert may have sensed the chance of victory. His men were undeniably inspired by his own example, for when charged by a young English knight, Henry de Bohun, who spotted the king standing out from his host on his small grey horse, Robert cleaved his attacker's skull with his battle-axe, an act later immortalized in the epic poem *The Bruce*, written by the Scots cleric John Barbour about 1371-5.

During the night of 23-24 June, Robert was further convinced by Scottish defectors from Edward's unhappy army that the field could be won. Dawn revealed the English to have expended considerable energy in a march to bypass the small streams, ditches and bog between the castle and Forth estuary in search of firm open ground. Robert denied their cavalry and archers this luxury, sending his first two or three divisions from the woods under Edward Bruce, Randolph and Douglas to close with the English over a sorely constrained front. When Robert finally brought in his own division, the English – unable to deploy their full force – broke and fled with many drowning in the mud and shallows. Edward II narrowly escaped capture in full flight while Robert despoiled his lavish royal baggage train.

Robert was quick to capitalize on Bannockburn. Not only was he able to recover his Queen and daughter from captivity in exchange for English prisoners but also, at a parliament in November at nearby Cambuskenneth Abbey, he forfeited his chief remaining Anglo-Scottish opponents of their Scottish lands. This gave him extensive resources with which to reward his supporters and subjects in order to secure their loyalty. Robert also intensified his attacks on northern England both in a search for cash and to force Edward II to recognize Bruce kingship of a free Scotland.

However, a darker but typically ruthless side of Robert's kingship now emerges, one until recently neglected by Scottish historians. The bleeding of northern England in 1314-15 really did little to pressurize Edward II. Thus Robert turned to an option which offered several strategic advantages in war with England but also promised to satisfy the Bruces' natural ambition for power, resources and revenge: the invasion of Ireland. Some medieval writers later suggested that Robert sent his brother Edward to conquer Ireland in summer 1315 as a means of ridding himself of a troublesome rival. In reality, not only did Robert recognize Edward as his heir apparent in parliament shortly before he embarked but the king committed massive resources to the Irish plan and took part himself in three brutal winter campaigns. It was, however, a campaign too far. Although the Scots quickly over-ran Ulster, they could not capture the English colonial capital at Dublin or persuade the native Irish to unite against English imperialism: instead they became bogged down in Gaelic Irish in-fighting. Yet Robert seemed determined to help his brother – who was made High King of Ireland in 1316 – make a breakthrough, even going so far as to participate in a winter campaign in southern Ireland in 1317 in which the king, Edward and Randolph might all too easily have been killed or starved to death: Robert's health surely suffered. The king must have been re-energized in April 1318 by the Scots' recapture of Berwick, a stronghold and port Robert thereafter determined to maintain as Scottish. But this led him to neglect the Irish campaign and cost him the life of his impatient brother and heir, Edward, who emerged from Ulster with his army in October 1318 only to be destroyed at Dundalk. This signalled the beginning of a crisis for Robert.

Robert had at least three sons (and a daughter) out of wedlock, but after Dundalk his only legitimate male heir was his two-year-old grandson, Robert Stewart, son of his daughter Marjorie and Walter the Steward. In parliament in November 1318 Robert I sought the boy's recognition by the Estates as heir apparent against a background of growing resentment in some quarters about the favouritism of his redistribution of the lands forfeited from his opponents in 1314. Although this parliament enacted many praiseworthy new laws (and confirmed old ones) to help ease Robert's resettlement of lands and offices, it also outlawed 'murmuring' against the king. A major plot was in the air involving out-of-favour Scottish lords hoping for a coup in favour of the son of King John, Edward Balliol, who had been in Picardy since 1315 but crossed to Edward II's court after Dundalk. The conspirators' preparations were fuelled by England's gleeful exploitation of the Pope's excommunication and summons of 'Robert de Brus' as a sacrilegious murderer. This was an external threat which Robert and his churchmen responded to by penning the famous 'Declaration of Arbroath' of April 1320, sent to the Pope in the name of the Scottish baronage to trumpet support for 'our most valiant prince, king and lord, the lord Robert' as independent Scotland's champion against England.

Fortunately for Robert, while the Declaration achieved little in its day, the murderous 'Soules conspiracy' of William Soules, Enguerrand d'Umfraville and other former Balliol men was betrayed. Those involved were either imprisoned, exiled or brutally 'hangit and heidit' after a trial in the so-called Black Parliament of August 1320. But this scare must have confirmed the pressing need for Robert – now forty-six – to solve several key areas of policy. Not the least of these was the need for a peace settlement with England and provision for a Bruce heir.

The first of these goals he attempted to secure for war-weary Scotland in 1321-3, even negotiating a peace not with Edward II but with his lieutenants in northern England. Yet faced with the English king's refusal to give up Scotland, Robert had to settle for a long, uneasy truce in 1323. At least this gave him valuable time to stabilize his internal affairs and here he had some success. While he continued to grant out large amounts of lands, money and offices to ensure he had loyal supporters in all corners of Scotland, he was also blessed on 5 March 1324, at the age of fifty, with a son, David (who may have been the younger of twins, the elder, John, dying in infancy and being buried at Restenneth Priory) to add to his two daughters by Elizabeth de Burgh.

Robert now had a direct male heir but he must have been painfully aware that David was only too likely to succeed as king while a child. The years of struggle had undeniably taken their toll on Bruce. His decision, probably after the death of Queen Elizabeth in Moray in 1327, to build a manor house retreat – complete with pantry, garden and aviary for hawks rather than stone defences – at Cardross near Dumbarton may reflect a desire for personal peace in his few remaining years as the disease which afflicted him took hold. Nevertheless, Robert did not withdraw from politics and worked hard to ensure a relatively stable inheritance for his son.

68. Seal of Robert the Bruce, earl of Carrick. Appended in 1301 to a charter in favour of the Abbey of Melrose.

69. The arms of the King of Scotland. The drawing represents a lion within a bordure, pierced by ten fleurs-de-lis.

70. Arms on the tomb of Sir James Douglas in St Bride's church, Douglas, South Lanarkshire. Sir James was killed in Spain on the way to take the heart of Robert I to the Holy Land.

A new mutual defence alliance agreed with France in 1326 was part of this, but a full peace between England and an independent Scotland was still Robert's ultimate goal. Thus in 1327 when Edward II's queen, Isabella, overthrew and killed her husband, Robert seized the opportunity to exploit England's internal chaos. Leading his host across the border once more, Robert saw his divisions humiliate the army of the teenage Edward III and by the close of the year force Isabella's regime to accept the dictated peace terms of the treaty of Edinburgh-Northampton, signed in June 1328. Robert was required to pay £20,000 for his demands, but the treaty was well worth it, bringing recognition of Scottish sovereignty, English support in lifting Robert's excommunication, and a royal marriage for David Bruce to Edward III's sister, Joan.

This appeared to cap conclusively Robert's massive achievements since the dark days of 1306. However, Robert himself may have had doubts about this settlement and the years ahead. He must have known that he had not dealt with the issue of those 'Disinherited' Scottish and English lords forfeited of Scottish lands who now waited in England for Edward Balliol to lead them to revenge. It was also likely that as an adult Edward III would naturally seek to undo the humiliation of 1327-8. Concerned about this future, Robert seems to have spent the last few months of his life combining practical preparation of his kingdom with the readying of his own soul and image for life after death.

As king, Robert had consistently combined religion with his political ends, commemorating the feast days of Scotland's national saints, Andrew and Margaret, just as he marked the anniversaries of the battles of Stirling and Bannockburn. In 1318 he had also overseen the consecration of Lamberton's completed cathedral at St Andrews much as in the same inspiring manner he had ordered the relics of St Columba to be carried into battle by the Scots in 1314.

Yet at the same time, Robert was aware of the importance of local devotions. He continued to mark the Bruces' old debt to an Irish saint, Malachy, and in 1329 he spent some weeks travelling from Cardross through Clydeside and south-west Scotland to the shrine of St Ninian at Whithorn, Galloway. In 1327 it had been reported that while Robert was on a visit to Ulster he was so sick he could move only his tongue to speak; in 1328 he was allegedly too ill to attend the parliament that ratified peace with England. He was clearly dying and his 1329 pilgrimage was surely a parting act of faith. But it also allowed Robert to travel through the most sensitive region of Scotland, where much Balliol and Comyn support still lingered, and to improve the defences of the western approaches by making more land grants in return for military services.

On his death bed, Robert is said to have urged his son never to fight a pitched battle, a clear stress of his limited but winning guerrilla tactics against England. Before he breathed his last at Cardross on 7 June 1329, Robert also arranged that after death, while his body was to be buried at Dunfermline Abbey beside his second wife (a very conscious association with the Canmores' spiritual home), his internal organs were to be otherwise disposed of. Most of his organs were to be interred at St Serf's Chapel near Dumbarton, but Robert asked Sir James Douglas to carry his heart on crusade to the Holy Land in fulfilment of the king's deep personal ambition and to make a bold statement of his power to Europe. Douglas was killed in Spain fighting the Saracens in 1330 but Robert's heart was returned and interred at Melrose Abbey on the border as per his will, again surely to act as a deterrent to future English armies and to rival the heart of John Balliol's father buried at Sweetheart Abbey in Galloway.

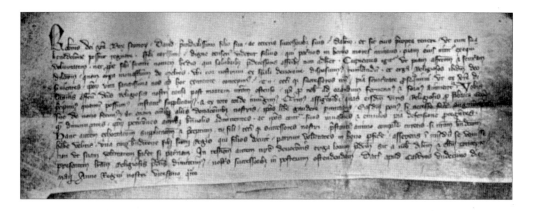

71. The letter written by Robert I on his deathbed instructing that his heart should be buried at Melrose and commending the monks thereof to his son.

72. Melrose Abbey. A casket said to contain the remains of Robert I's heart was excavated here in 1921 and again in 1996.

Robert had triumphed against colossal odds to establish a Bruce dynasty and recover Scotland's independence. But his place as Scotland's greatest king was assured emphatically by the inflation of his life and legacy after 1329. Taking their cue from Robert's own propaganda, the later medieval Scottish chroniclers took him as their model of good, strong kingship supported by loyal subjects. Fifteenth-century writers were convinced by Archdeacon John Barbour's portrayal of the hero king in *The Bruce*, a chivalric work paid for by Robert's grandson, Robert Stewart (Robert II 1371-90), which became the favourite of generations of Scots reared on war with England. Scottish kings and magnates were drawn to association with Robert, 'the symbol of the integrity of the realm', James III, for example, using Bruce's sword as a talisman for support.

Inevitably, Scottish popular imagination and historians became obsessed with Bannockburn as Robert and Scotland's greatest hour. After the Scottish poet Blind Harry wrote *The Wallace*, around 1474-8, Bruce's reputation was perhaps dulled in favour of that of Scotland's other favourite son. But eighteenth- and nineteenth-century writers re-fired Robert's image, especially after the excavation of 'Bruce's skull' from the royal tombs at Dunfermline in 1819 and the rediscovery of the Declaration of Arbroath by Sir Walter Scott (1771-1832), who also popularized the story of Robert being inspired by a plucky spider struggling to weave a web in a cave to 'try and try again'. Robert thus became a respectable symbol for nineteenth-century Scots of both unionist and nationalist political persuasion, a king who had either kept England and Scotland apart until they were ready for fruitful union or had protected Scottish freedom. The modern image of Bruce is thus still dominated by the many Victorian statues of a tall, strong, moustached or bearded figure in armour, Scotland's fatherly protector, an image cemented by the Bannockburn Heritage Centre statue of the 1950s. However, there was considerable fresh interest in 1996 in both the excavation of Robert's heart in its silver casket from Melrose Abbey and in pathologists' recreation from the Dunfermline skull of his face. Scarred by battle and severe illness, this latter has offered us an alternative view of the king, something historians have also sought out of late.

As a result, it is increasingly apparent that in reality the hero king had a difficult reign and contributed to considerable change affecting Scotland and its monarchy. He remains a hugely impressive warlord and politician but he was not surely as powerful or free-willed a king as, say, Alexanders II or III. The cost of the years of Guardianship (1286-92), John I's troubled reign (1292-6) and then Robert earl of Carrick's violent seizure of the throne and destruction of his opponents was a recasting of kingship. There was a greater expectation among Robert's subjects that they should not only be protected in war, served of royal justice and rewarded through patronage by their king, but should also be increasingly consulted in affairs of state. Robert – just another magnate until his thirties – was the first king of Scots who had to call almost annual Councils or Parliaments to seek his subjects' approval of the Succession, laws and foreign policy. But most significantly of all, because of Robert's unavoidable granting out of so much land and his delegation of local authority to win support he was also, between 1326 and 1329, the first Scottish king so impoverished as to ask for annual taxation from his subjects to meet his living costs. In addition, he had been obliged to elevate several families to positions of regional dominance which in later years these nobles would seek to expand and protect in opposition to the crown.

This new relationship would create tensions for subsequent Scottish monarchs now unable to 'live of their own' resources. In the same way, Robert left a legacy of unfinished business with England for his son and subjects as well as a potent Scottish formula and identity for facing these challenges.

MP

DAVID II (1329-71) AND EDWARD BALLIOL (1332-56)

David Bruce had an incredibly hard act to follow when he succeeded as king at five years old. Born on 5 March 1324, probably in St Andrews, David was given the family title of earl of Carrick. He spent the years after his mother's death in 1327 in nursery residences with his sisters on the bishop of St Andrews' manor at Inchmurdoch in Fife, at Cardross and in Carrick's Turnberry castle, where his household stewards were some of Robert I's loyal knights, including Sir Malcolm Fleming of Lenzie, keeper of Dumbarton castle, who may have been David's 'foster-father' in the Gaelic tradition. David may also have made early 'state' appearances, for example at the parliament of August 1326 when an Act of Succession confirmed him as Robert's heir. Then on 12 June 1328 he was married to Edward III's sister Joan (aged seven) in a lavish but, with both kings absent, strained ceremony at Berwick as part of the peace with England.

This mixture of optimism and unease for David's future continued after 1329. While he received his early schooling, government and law and order lay in the firm hands of Thomas Randolph, earl of Moray, Guardian as per Robert I's and parliament's wishes. Yet some Scots must have had grave doubts about the infant monarch. Remarkably, although David was to be the first king of Scots to be crowned and anointed with holy oil thanks to a papal grant secured by his father, his coronation with special child-sized crown and sceptre did not occur at Scone until 24 November 1331. By then there must have been an inevitable expectation of the armed return of the 'Disinherited' lords under Edward Balliol, who was in England by early 1331.

Balliol was now forty-eight and had been denied his political birthright since youth. In 1289 he may have been offered as a match for Margaret of Norway; in 1295 he was set to marry a niece of Philip IV of France. But in 1296 Edward was removed to London with his father. After spells in the Tower and the households of Edward I's sons he was paroled from his role as hostage for his late father's conduct and in 1315 allowed to take up his family lands in Picardy. However, Edward craved an opportunity to reclaim his Scottish inheritance, albeit as an English vassal. In 1318-20 he was in England in anticipation of the 'Soules' plot to kill Robert I. In late 1330-1 he may have hurriedly annulled his marriage to an Italian noblewoman to return to England with the Disinherited.

Balliol landed in Fife in August 1332 with about two thousand men and only unofficial backing from Edward III. Nonetheless his arrival caught the Bruce Scots reeling and arguing amongst themselves after the death (perhaps by poison) of Randolph in July 1332. Many Scots came out in Balliol's favour and after routing the army of the new Guardian, Donald of Mar, at Dupplin near Perth on 12 August, Edward was able to have himself crowned king of Scots at Scone on 24 September using John I's old regalia. Yet his revenge would never reach a higher point. With David safe, probably in Dumbarton castle, his loyal magnates ejected Balliol from Scotland in December 1332

73. Dumbarton Castle, the near-impregnable fortress where David and his child-bride, Joan, took refuge before being spirited to France.

74. Hestan Island in the Solway Firth , Dumfries and Galloway, which served Edward Balliol as a refuge in his turn as the Bruce party fought back.

(when Edward's only brother, Henry, was slain). Balliol did return and this time with an English army led by Edward III: the Scots were again heavily defeated at Halidon Hill near Berwick which was now lost (22 July 1333). But Balliol soon found that the cost of being England's puppet was stifling. In 1333-34 he would have to renew his homage to Edward III and grant him all the valuable southern shires of Scotland which the English now occupied. Despite rumours of a peace plan whereby David would surrender and divorce Joan who would then wed Balliol as king of Scots, Edward III had little interest in helping the pretender assert his kingship beyond this southern zone. Instead, after 1337, England's war aims turned to France. For the next decade Balliol would become an increasingly forlorn figure based primarily in his old family lands of Galloway but pushed further and further south as the Bruce Scots fought back. By the 1340s, Balliol really only held his island fortress of Hestan in the Solway Firth as one of Edward III's several border captains.

Meanwhile, for David things had nonetheless been deemed so bad by May 1334 that he became the second Bruce king of Scots to be sent into exile, taking passage by ship from Dumbarton. Philip VI of France gave the ten-year-old David, his queen and sisters and a number of other Scottish noble children refuge in Château Gaillard in Normandy. Here David was tutored by the abbot of Kelso and trained in arms by Robert Keith, the Marischal. As he grew to adulthood he must have been impressed by the massed armies of chivalry at war after England's invasion – in 1339 David would fly his own banner in Philip's army at Buironfesse in Flanders. It was in France too that David developed his interest in crusading, when Philip planned an expedition to the Holy Land. But the Scottish nobles and churchmen with him must also have driven into the adolescent king the great history of Robert I and kept David informed of developments at home.

This meant that David was determined to return to lead the fight but also that he became increasingly aware that certain Scottish nobles, fighting in his name, had increased their own lands and influence in the absence of a strong adult king. In particular, Robert Stewart, David's half-nephew (though eight years older) and heir presumptive, acted as Guardian between 1338 and 1341, recovering much of central and south-western Scotland from Balliol and English occupation but at the same time clashing with David's close advisors, headed by John Randolph, earl of Moray, over control of royal resources and policy. The Steward was in power when William Douglas – another self-made man of the 1330s and famous since as 'the knight of Liddesdale' – recaptured Edinburgh castle in April 1341, a strong signal that it was time for David to return while the enemy retained castles only at Stirling and the border.

Yet David's return was not triumphant. His party landed quietly at Inverbervie on the Kincardineshire coast about 2 June 1341 and the seventeen-year-old king's tentative tour of his kingdom in the following weeks underlined his awareness that some of his magnates had considerably more power than he did in key regions: clashes were evidently expected as David tried to reassert royal authority. The next five years, indeed, were characterized by mounting tension as David tried to build up his power, support and image and challenged ambitious nobles like Robert Stewart, Douglas and William, earl of Ross – whose families had first been rewarded by Robert I – for control of valuable earldoms and lordships, royal revenue and the vital judicial offices and castles of Scotland. On several occasions the young king's will was defied openly, leading in

1342, for example, to the loss of the earldom of Atholl to the Steward and to Douglas's murder of a royal favourite, the military hero Alexander Ramsay of Dalhousie.

But David learned his king-craft well and quickly began to build up a large following of lesser knights and civil servants impressed by his energy as one interested in jousting and leading war-raids against England. By 1344 the king had gained the upper hand over his rivals. About 1346, he may even have been able to propose parliament's recognition of his new full nephew, John Sutherland (born c.1346, son of William, earl of Sutherland), as his heir presumptive ahead of Robert and his four Stewart sons; yet this also hinted that David doubted his own ability to produce a son by Queen Joan.

This situation formed the background to Scotland's invasion of northern England of October 1346 in response to French pleas for aid while Edward III was campaigning in Europe. David clearly intended the leisurely progress of his 12,000 or so troops towards Durham as a statement of his power. However, the Scots were surprised on 17 October at Neville's Cross by 8,000 English militia led by the Archbishop of York. As the Scots engaged the enemy on narrow, broken ground the resentment of those nobles excluded from favour by David since 1341 surfaced. Robert the Steward and Patrick Dunbar, earl of March (with the earl of Ross already having deserted), abandoned the host as the first two Scottish divisions were overwhelmed. David was captured by an ambitious English esquire, John de Coupland, and twice wounded in the head by arrows: almost all the king's key supporters and officers were captured or killed. By January 1347, David was recovering from his wounds in the Tower of London.

Edward Balliol – now sixty-three – had led eighty men into battle for the English at Neville's Cross. But any hopes he had that Edward III would now support his kingship claim were to be dashed: if 'David de Brus' was to be of any value to England he would, ironically, have to be recognized as king of an independent Scotland. Yet over the next eleven long years it proved problematic to persuade enough of the Scots – led for most of that period by Robert the Steward as 'King's Lieutenant' – that the terms proposed for their king's release should be accepted. On two occasions – 1351-2 and 1354 – David came close to negotiating his release only to see the Steward and others raise crippling objections. In the first instance this was understandable, for David is now known to have proposed that as part of his release he would recognize a younger son of Edward III (probably John of Gaunt, David and Joan's nephew) as heir presumptive to Scotland's kingship ahead of Robert Steward; he would also allow the restoration of Scottish lands to some of the Disinherited. David even went so far as to come to a Scottish parliament on parole in February 1352 to sell this idea, provoking Edward Balliol to insist that Edward III should guarantee the Balliol claim. But not for the last time David met with trenchant opposition in a Scottish parliament and the idea was rejected. The Steward may even have threatened to depose David.

Much the same fate befell the release talks of 1354. The Steward persuaded the Scots to reject plans to ransom David for 90,000 merks (about £56,000) and twenty noble hostages and instead to join the French in attacking northern England in 1355. In the end, it was not until a French army (including Scots) was destroyed at Poitiers in September 1356 and John II of France captured that the Scots – deprived of their ally – were forced to finalize David's release in return for 100,000 merks to be paid over ten years, hostages and a long truce. This confirmed that the feeble Edward Balliol (who had even briefly considered defecting to the French) was only too right to resign his

75. The arms of some of Scotland's powerful nobles: Dunbar, earl of March; Randolph, earl of
Moray; Douglas, earl of Douglas; and Douglas, earl of Angus.
76. A gold noble of David II.
77. Seal of Edward Balliol.

claim to Edward III in disgust at Roxburgh in early 1356. He was compensated with a large pension that sustained his quiet final years in Yorkshire until his death in January 1364, aged eighty, but his historical reputation as a failed English pawn was sealed.

David – now thirty-three – returned to Scotland in October 1357 with many scores to settle. He must also have brought back his experience of a different style of rule. In England he had developed what one chronicler called 'a rycht gret specialtie' of friendship with Edward III and, after being invited to tournaments of that king's new knights' Order of the Garter, had grown to appreciate a style of monarchy in which the nobility respected the political initiative of the king. David knew by bitter experience to be cautious and at first he recognized the established magnate powers in Scotland. But for the remaining thirteen years of his mature rule David would combine his assertion of royal authority over his great subjects both with a growing interest in chivalry, the crusades, piety and the royal court and with bold attempts to renegotiate his ransom terms with England.

From 1358 this programme saw David once more building up his own loyal supporters at the expense of the control of key territories, offices and castles by the Stewarts, the earls of March and Ross and William, the new earl of Douglas. Generally, David managed by 1363 to gain control of the key earldom of Fife and disputed lordships in Perthshire, of the chief law offices of justiciar north and south of Forth, and of Dumbarton, Stirling and Edinburgh castles. At the same time, the king used his growing mandate to seek Edward III's cancellation of his ransom in return for recognition of a younger English prince as Scotland's heir presumptive instead of the Steward. This was a gamble David still thought worthwhile, despite his estrangement from Queen Joan, who returned to a life of courtly piety in London from 1359 and died there around September 1362. In her place David took mistresses: first Katherine Mortimer, probably a relative of a minor Forfarshire knight in David's favour and the wife of another knight whom David made earl of Fife in 1358. Katherine was killed on the orders of the out-of-favour Thomas Stewart, earl of Angus, in 1360, for which the king imprisoned and probably starved Angus to death after laying the girl to rest at Newbattle Abbey near Edinburgh. By 1361-2, David had a second mistress, Margaret Logie (née Drummond), a member of a useful Perthshire kindred. Neither of these liaisons would produce Bruce children but they had clear local political value.

Altogether, these were highly controversial royal policies. In spring 1363 David's progress in these areas – with Margaret Logie about to become David's second queen – provoked a grave crisis, the rebellion of Robert Stewart and his sons and the earls of March and Douglas against what they decried as David's lack of 'fair lordship' and his misuse of taxation for the ransom, of which David only paid two full 10,000 merk instalments by 1360. These rebels intended 'bending [David] to their will or banishing him.' However, a military expedition led by David, and money and land grants to royal supporters, ensured that this revolt was swiftly crushed and the earls forced to ritually submit before their king and his new queen. David used this emphatic victory to renegotiate a fresh succession deal in London in late 1363. Yet when he returned to parliament at Scone in March 1364 to sell the idea the still badly limited power of this king without a direct male heir was made starkly apparent: once again, the opposition of the Steward and others saw David's plans rejected.

The king was allowed to continue discussing such a treaty with England over the next four years. His close relations with England were matched by a great traffic in Scottish pilgrims, university students and merchants heading south. But it was clear that David had sorely misjudged the now defining spirit of anti-Englishness of many of his noble subjects as well as the entrenched power of the Stewarts and other families favoured by Robert I. Nor was David helped in this predicament by his new wife (or so the king thought). Margaret proved adept at advancing the fortunes of her own family but she and David failed to produce children. By 1368 they were estranged and the king had to seek an annulment of the marriage before his opponents exploited his dynastic vulnerability. He turned instead to Agnes Dunbar, sister of his allies George and John, the new earl of March and lord of Fife, as his prospective third wife and a likely mother of royal sons. This marriage to Agnes would bring the added support of her kinsmen and other royal favourites like Archibald Douglas, the new lord of Galloway, James Douglas of Dalkeith, Robert Erskine – David's chief political 'fixer' – and Walter Leslie, a crusading legend whom David had intruded into the earldom of Ross.

This new royal party appeared to allow David to enter into a period of dominance. In the years 1368-70, shrewd administration and tax and customs increases granted by annual parliaments skilfully controlled through committees (which from 1357 included representatives from the royal burghs) allowed David to increase his revenue to some £15,000, a record high. He negotiated smaller ransom payments to England and maintained sound relations with Edward III through such shared interests as pilgrimage to the tomb of St Thomas à Beckett at Canterbury. David also managed seemingly to cow his great magnate antagonists in the north (Ross and John MacDonald, lord of the Isles), in central Scotland (Robert Stewart and sons) and in the borders (the earl of Douglas). David's court, too, based at Edinburgh castle, where the king planned to build a new tower house, projected an image of fatherly authority. Many influential clerics and laymen were attracted to royal service by David's expressed desire to go on crusade, his patronage of works and men of chivalry and his devotion to religious sites: for example his building of a church at St Monans, Fife, to give thanks either for his cure from severe headaches caused by his old wounds or for salvation from shipwreck (as well as to give the crown a foothold in this disputed earldom).

However, there were serious cracks in David's ascendancy. He still had no son of his own and was not likely to marry Agnes Dunbar while Margaret, who had appealed to the Pope, blocked their annulment (Margaret, indeed, had financial support from the English, and even encouraged the Pope to contemplate an interdict on Scotland, a threat which only passed when Margaret died in 1374 and was buried in Avignon). Meanwhile, in parliament between 1368 and 1371 David faced criticism of his failure to control Highland violence. Overall, it was unlikely that David could continue to satisfy the ambitions of his own supporters while containing those of his opponents without the stability a Bruce heir would guarantee. In short, if David had not died from illness (probably related to his old wounds) just short of forty-seven in Edinburgh castle on 22 February 1371, his reign might all too easily have erupted into a major civil war which the king could not be sure to win surrounded as he was by Stewart, Douglas, Dunbar and other noble scions. Yet as Robert Stewart – now Robert II – had his predecessor buried quickly, not at Dunfermline as planned by David but in nearby Holyrood Abbey (in a marble tomb destroyed in the seventeenth century), he must have breathed an immense sigh of relief.

David had clearly been his father's son, an extremely capable politician, but one sorely hampered by unique political circumstances. Yet until recently modern historians have failed to appreciate his qualities. Victorian and early twentieth-century writers especially damned David for his capture and adultery, his apparently vindictive treatment of nobles and those 'unpatriotic' deals with England. As a dismal 'degeneration from the magnanimity of his father' they preferred to forget him.

Yet medieval Scots knew their man. Even those chronicles written after the accession of David's opponents, the Stewarts, praised above all David's 'raddure', his fearful personal authority which was an effective tool in keeping over-mighty magnates in check and maintaining law and order. In many ways, David was a model of strong kingship that would not be seen again until the adult rule of James I (1406-37).

MP

FOUR

THE HOUSE OF STEWART
1371 – 1625

ROBERT II STEWART (1371-90)

Robert the Steward was fifty-five when he unexpectedly became king. Like John Balliol, his rule was plagued from the start by the fact that many powerful Scottish nobles continued to view Robert as their equal or less. Yet even without this problem, Robert would have offered very different prospects as king after the east-coast, anglophile, authoritarian and chivalric David II.

Robert was probably born in early 1316, about a year after the marriage in April 1315 of his father, Walter, the 6th High Steward of Scotland, to the eldest daughter of Robert I, Marjorie Bruce (who died after a fall from her horse probably in 1317). But Robert grew up as a west-coast magnate on the Stewart family lands in Renfrew, Clydeside and the Gaelic-speaking isle of Rothesay, and was perhaps fostered out as a child to an Isles or Argyll family. His household and private faith would remain centred on this region throughout much of his life.

There is no doubt, however, that Robert was, even in adolescence, an extremely ambitious and capable politician. If all went well for the Bruce dynasty, Robert would remain simply the next head of his family to take up the now purely honorary title of High Steward of Scotland, a royal household role that his Breton ancestors (the FitzAlans) had been given by David I (1124-53). But as we've seen, Robert I's line was by no means secure. Thus Robert Stewart's importance in the kingdom had been inflated from the first.

Between Edward Bruce's death in 1318 and the birth of a royal son in 1324, the infant Robert Stewart was recognized as heir to the throne; the 1326 parliamentary Act of Succession recognized him as second behind prince David. With this role came extensive new estates in Knapdale (Argyll), the Lothians and Roxburghshire. Robert may also have been promised the possible inheritance of the earldom of Fife. That made the new Steward (after the death of his father on 9 April 1327) the most important regional magnate of Scotland alongside the key Bruce allies, the Randolphs and the Douglases. So when Edward Balliol and England threatened through war to deprive Robert Steward of his inheritance he would play a crucial part in the recovery of Bruce Scotland. On 19 July 1333 – aged just sixteen – he led a division of his landed followers against Edward III in the army of Guardian Archibald Douglas at the defeat of Halidon Hill. Then in 1334 Robert only narrowly escaped by boat to Dumbarton Castle as his western lands were overrun by his Anglo-Balliol enemies. But while David was taken into exile in France, Robert stayed to fight and, teaming up with the Campbells of Lochawe, waged a campaign to recover castles and land around the Clyde and in southwest Scotland.

At this stage, a fifteenth-century Scottish chronicler describes Robert as winning the loyalty of many Scots: 'a young man of attractive appearance above the sons of men, broad and tall in physique, kind to everyone, and modest, generous, cheerful and honest.' But this influence, and Robert's undoubted attempts to increase his landed interests during the war, brought him into conflict with David's chief councillors while he was King's Lieutenant in 1334-5 and again – although Robert seems to have submitted to Edward III briefly in between – in 1338-41. By the time David returned in June 1341 the lines were drawn for a tense struggle between crown and heir presumptive for control of territories and policy. As part of this rivalry, David and his supporters would influence contemporary Scottish writers to ignore and defame Robert's achievements as Lieutenant before 1341 (and again between 1347 and 1357).

This personal contest dominated David's adult reign and the best years of Robert's life. On the whole, David managed to continually intimidate and frustrate Robert's landed ambitions, even imprisoning him briefly with at least one of his sons in 1368. Yet without a Bruce son David could never completely break Robert. The Steward – nearly always at the royal court throughout the reign – repeatedly proved himself able to sabotage or limit the king's power, abandoning him in battle in 1346 (the only time Robert would ever cross the border into England), delaying David's release from captivity (1347-57), joining a rebellion against the crown in 1363 and, on several occasions, mustering opposition in parliament to obstruct David's plans to admit an English royal to the Scottish succession. In doing so, Robert's strength lay in the control he and his growing family exerted over much of western, central and north-eastern Scotland by 1360-70. For while David was barren, Robert had four sons and several daughters by his first wife, Elizabeth Mure (d. c.1349-55), daughter of Adam of Rowallan in Ayrshire, although Robert had to seek legitimation for this brood in 1347 and perhaps go through a formal marriage; he then had several more children by his second wife, Euphemia, widow of John Randolph, earl of Moray, and sister of William, earl of Ross, whom he wed in 1355. Robert also had several illegitimate children by various mistresses.

79. Tomb effigy believed to be that of Marjory Bruce, daughter of Robert I and mother of Robert II, in Paisley Abbey, Renfrewshire.

80. Dundonald Castle, Ayrshire, the seat of Stewart power.

It was naturally to this 'family firm' or network that Robert turned in 1371. While David II had sought to overawe his great regional magnates with his own authority and household government, Robert was prepared to compromise with the great families in power in the various quarters of Scotland, and to delegate power to them there while seeking either a useful marriage to one of his daughters or advancement of the lordship of one of his cunning adult sons. This approach enabled Robert to buy his way out of an immediate crisis in spring 1371 – a challenge before his Scone coronation from William, earl of Douglas. By 1382 it had also seen the Stewarts sideline many of David II's old supporters and gain control of eight of the fifteen Scottish earldoms and of many more valuable lordships, as well as most of the key royal castles and offices north of the Forth-Clyde line. This included the earldoms of Fife and Menteith, snapped up by Robert's second surviving son, Robert; Buchan, Ross and Badenoch, all grasped in the north-east by the fourth son, Alexander; and Caithness, which fell to Robert's fifth son (his first by his second wife), David, who also inherited the earldom of Strathearn thanks to the strong-minded influence of his mother, Queen Euphemia. All these lands were added to those held by Robert II before 1371, namely the western Stewart lands and the Perthshire earldom of Atholl. In addition, John MacDonald, lord of the Isles, John Dunbar, earl of Moray and James, the future 2nd earl of Douglas, were Robert's sons-in-law. Robert managed to quash doubts about the royal Stewart line through further parliamentary Acts of Succession in 1371 and 1373 which entailed the kingship in turn on each of Robert's sons and their male heirs only: the memory of the problem-filled female succession disputes of 1286-92 clearly still haunted the community and there was an equally pressing need to vanquish doubts about the legitimacy of Robert II's first family. At the same time, Robert pushed the Stewarts' image as the true heirs of Robert Bruce and – along with the Black Douglas family in the south –Scotland's champions against England. This patriotic strengthening of the new royal house was enshrined in John Barbour's *The Bruce*, one of several such court works paid for by Robert II by 1375.

For the best part of a decade this loose, decentralized style of kingship seemed to work well enough. During the 1370s, Robert II was mostly to be found in and around the burgh of Perth and his nearby lordship of Methven or making devotional visits to his ancestral lands in the west: predictably, he was in no way as energetic a king as either of the younger Bruces. However, because much of Robert II's power throughout the realm lay in the hands of 'the sons he maid rych and mychty' as well as other regional magnates, all of whom he normally left to their own devices, it was very difficult for Robert to be seen to lead from the centre when a crisis arose. This was especially true when open rivalry erupted between the Stewart princes.

By 1382 Alexander Stewart, the king's justiciar and lieutenant in the north, had obviously became part of the problem of, rather than the crown's solution to, mounting Highland lawlessness, having built a territorial empire using 'caterans' – Gaelic mercenary companies. While this was decried by fearful parliaments in the English-speaking lowlands, the king was unable to punish his fourth son's violent acquisition of land in the northeast and Ross. Fatally, Robert's impotence provided his eldest son and heir, John, earl of Carrick, impatient for power, with a pretext to remove the king from government.

In a council at Holyrood in November 1384 a bloodless palace coup was effected. It was recorded that

> because our lord the king, for certain causes, is not able to attend himself personally to the execution of justice and the law of the kingdom, he has

willed... that his first-born son and heir... is to administer the common law everywhere throughout the kingdom.

This was to be the first of several occasions over the next three decades when powerful magnate interests – the real authority throughout Scotland – would manoeuvre to control the proceedings of council or parliament in a transfer of Scottish government out of royal hands.

Carrick's assumption of his lieutenancy brought control of gifts of royal lands, offices and pensions and, crucially, the direction of foreign policy to a magnate coalition headed by James, 2nd earl of Douglas, and the Lindsays. This meant an instant escalation of the bubbling conflict with England. The southern border had been an uneasy front on which Robert II – though he had continued the truce and payment of David II's ransom until the death of Edward III in 1377 – had been prepared to allow southern Scots to raid and seize disputed border lands, putting an end to the Scottish pilgrim, church and trade traffic to England of David's reign. After 1378, during a period of papal 'schism', Robert promised Scotland's support to the pro-French Pope in Avignon while England backed the rival Pope in Rome. Continuing this course, in 1383 Robert agreed to a renewed alliance with France which included promises of men and money for a joint campaign against England's troubled Richard II: this allowed Carrick and the Douglases to step up their aggression. Ultimately, however, King Robert was not prepared to initiate all-out war, and he sought Scotland's inclusion in Anglo-French peace talks in 1384.

His removal from power later that year cleared the way for war. By June 1385, a company of some 1,200 French troops led by John de Vienne were billeted in Scotland. The great contemporary chronicler Jean Froissart would later describe this expedition. Influenced by Scots loyal to Carrick and Douglas, he would also paint the revealing picture of a feeble Robert II which forever coloured the first Stewart king's historical reputation. For just as he had done when a smaller French expedition came to Scotland in 1355, Froissart's Robert did not come to greet the French knights in 1385. Instead he remained in 'le sauvage Ecosse', surely a reference to either Perthshire or his ancestral lands in the Gaelic west. Worse, he had 'red-bleared eyes, of the colour of sandal-wood, which clearly showed that he was no valiant man, but one who would rather remain at home than march to the field'.

Thus it was Carrick, Douglas, the king's third son, Robert Stewart, earl of Fife, James Lindsay, earl of Crawford, and the Dunbar earl of March who joined the French on a prof-itless campaign in 1385. The Scots and French quickly quarrelled and the English retaliated, burning much of Lothian including Edinburgh. The Scots were forced to accept truces until 1388. For Robert II in the west this meant little, but it gave a critical voice to rivals of Carrick's administration. At the same time, like his father, Carrick was unable to cope with lawlessness in the north and Alexander Stewart's power there increased.

Nonetheless, it required a dramatic shift in the balance of magnate power in Scotland to allow for another coup in royal government. This came in August 1388 when the Douglas earl was killed in the course of what was actually a famous victory over English forces at Otterburn in Northumberland. The Douglas inheritance fell into dispute and Carrick became quickly isolated. In a council at Edinburgh on 1 December that year he was obliged to resign the lieutenancy to his brother Robert, earl of Fife, who pointed to Carrick's inability to see justice done in the north and defend the realm from English attack. Yet in reality Fife swept into power on the back of several political deals. In 1384 both Fife and Archibald Douglas, lord of Galloway, had exempted their lands from Carrick's lieutenancy powers; now in 1388, Fife promised to support Archibald as the next Douglas earl. Fife also vowed to deal harshly with Alexander Stewart in the north, a stance favourable with many lowlanders in council. In addition, Fife could continue to bleed the financial resources of the crown: he had controlled these since the murder in 1382 of Sir John Lyon, Robert II's son-in-law and chamberlain, an office which Fife thereafter assumed for himself.

For the last two years of his life, then, Robert II was once again at the beck and call of one of his powerful magnate sons, expected to appear at councils and private meetings when necessary to confirm grants to Fife's and Archibald's followers or to approve their redirection of policy. This saw him involved in a Stewart civil war, acting at the fringes of Fife's campaign to oust Alexander as lieutenant and justiciar north of Forth and to deprive him of his influence in Moray and Ross.

These clashes were a direct legacy of the buildup of his family's power that had character-ized Robert II's tactic for governing Scotland in the 1370s. Now they formed the backdrop to the end of the old king's life. For after a royal circuit around the north-east in January 1390 – to show crown approval for Fife's actions – Robert retired to die, aged seventy-four, at his private tower castle of Dundonald in Ayrshire on 19 April. Yet he was buried in late April not in the nearby Stewart family foundation of Paisley Abbey, or at the Canmore-Bruce resting grounds of Dunfermline, but in the abbey of Scone, the inauguration site of the kings, close to the Stewart lands of Strathearn and Methven and presumably beside his queen, who had died in the winter of 1387-88.

It would probably have been of little comfort for Robert to know that the Stewarts would long reign in Scotland. It was during these Stewart kingships that much of the historical damage to his reputation was done. Late fourteenth-century writers were split between those before 1371 who favoured David II and sought to blacken Robert Steward's career and those writing after 1371 who fell in with either Carrick or Fife and had to justify their removal of a weak King Robert II. His name never recovered from his failure in old age: in 1521 historian John Mair could write that 'I cannot hold this aged king... to have been a skilful warrior or wise in counsel.' Modern historians have only very recently shown that with regard to Robert Stewart's career and policies before 1382 this was unfair. But in the end, Robert II was overtaken by time and the ambition of his own dynasty.

MP

ROBERT III (1390-1406)

According to the fifteenth-century Scottish chronicler Walter Bower, when asked by his Queen what epitaph should adorn his tomb, Robert III, by then in his sixties, is said to have declared with characteristic gentle humility his preference to be buried instead 'in a midden', or at best with the legend: 'Here lies the worst of kings and most wretched of men in the whole kingdom.' By 1406 – if not much earlier – this would have been a completely understandable, bitter reflection on a career that had begun with the promise of so much.

The second Stewart monarch was actually born, probably around 1336-37, as John Stewart, eldest son of Robert Stewart (Robert II) and his first wife, Elizabeth Mure. Much of his early life must have been spent on the Stewart lands in west Scotland. It was from there as 'Lord of Kyle' in Ayrshire that John Stewart first emerged on the political stage about 1350-55 – during his father's lieutenancy and David II's captivity – as the leader of a Scottish force recovering part of the old Bruce family lands of Annandale from English occupation.

Plate 1: Bamburgh, the citadel of the Angles of Bernicia, which was stormed by Urien of Rheged in the 590s.

Plate 2: 'The Picts were here', Pictish Class I sculptures cut into the rock at the entrance to the hillfort on Trusty's Hill, Dumfries and Galloway.

Plate 3: 'Pictish Warrior', a
sixteenth-century watercolour
by John Smith.

Plate 4: Gaelic Sunset. Tradition reports that Domnall Bán found refuge with the Norse-Gaelic rulers of the Hebrides after the killing of his father in 1040.

Plate 5: David I as king and warrior. Images from the king's great seal.

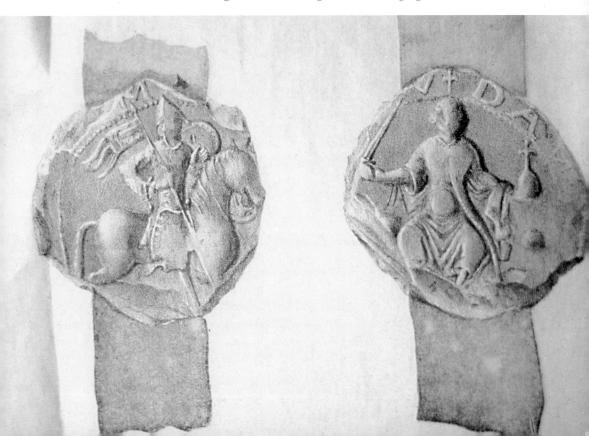

Plate 6: The initial letter M of Malcolm IV's great charter to Kelso Abbey, with portraits of David I (left) and Malcolm himself.

Plate 7: Statue of Robert I at Stirling Castle, the Victorian ideal of the hero king.

Plate 8: David II as a child in France, from Froissart, *Chroniques*.

Plate 9, opposite: The arms of the Scottish king and leading nobles, from the Armorial de Gelre, c.1369, the oldest surviving roll of Scottish arms. The largest coat is that of the king. The others are: earl of Ross; earl of Carrick; earl of Fife; earl of Strathearn; earl of Douglas; earl of March; earl of Mar; king of Man; earl of Moray; earl of Lennox; lord of Annandale.

die co
nīc bā
scortāt

gˢ de
rog

gˢde
carric

gˢ
de
biue

gˢ a
straerc

gˢ
a
douglas

gˢ
de
maerche

gˢ
de mar

kin
caman

gˢ
de morref

gˢ
a
teue
lenos

anaderdeel

Jacob von gots genaden küng von Schottland

Plate 10: Jörg von Ehingen portrait of James II. This is the only authentic representation we have of James II.

Plate 11: Melrose Abbey. Robert I's heart was interred here following its return from Sir James Douglas's disastrous journey to Spain.

Plate 12: Finlaggan Castle, Islay, symbolic heart of the lordship of the Isles.

karolus von gottes genaden kiing von franckrich

Plate 13: Jörg von Ehingen portrait of Charles VII, king of France, ally of James II.
Plate 14, opposite: The capture of David II at the Battle of Neville's Cross, from Froissart, *Chroniques*.

Plate 15, opposite: Aeneas Sylvius Piccolomini meeting James I, a fanciful image of the king and his court from a fresco in the Piccolomini Library, Siena Cathedral.

Plate 16, above: Edinburgh Castle, the centre of James III's government and his prison in 1482.

Plate 17: The truncated towers of James IV's ceremonial gatehouse at Stirling Castle.

Plate 18: Mary, Queen of Scots, as a young girl.

Plate 19: Portrait of Charles I wearing a white satin coat, with the Marquess of Hamilton in attendance. Sir Anthony Van Dyck (1599-1641), Flemish School.

Heraldry, clockwise from top left:

Plate 20: The rose and thistle badge of James VI of Scotland and I of England.
Plate 21: James VI and I's coat of arms.
Plate 22: The coat of arms of Charles I.
Plate 23: The arms of Charles I's wife, Henrietta Maria.

More regal heraldry, clockwise from top left:

Plate 24: The coat of arms of Charles II.
Plate 25: The arms of James VII of Scotland and II of England.
Plate 26: The arms of William II of Scotland and III of England.
Plate 27: The arms of Queen Anne, who became the first Queen of the United
Kingdom in 1707.

Plate 28: Rullion Green, Lothian, where a memorial stone marks the site of General Tam Dalziel's victory over the Covenanters during the Pentland Rising of 1666.

Plate 29: Glencoe, in the Highlands, scene of the massacre of the MacDonalds by government soldiers in 1692.

81. The Cavers or Percy Standard. This is said to have been the standard of James,
earl of Douglas and Mar, which was carried by his son, Archibald Douglas of Cavers, at the
Battle of Otterburn in 1388.
82. Seal of Robert II.
83. Elgin Cathedral, Moray, sacked by the king's brother Alexander Stewart, in 1390.

Tempted with cash, John may also have joined the small French expeditionary force that fought in Scotland briefly in 1355. He must have been greatly relieved to be able to do so at a time when he had been named as a possible hostage to guarantee David II's release. After David was ransomed in 1357 it is likely that between 1359 and 1363 John Stewart did have to endure spells in English captivity in this capacity: this experience – and the concentration of his lands in southern Scotland – surely helped intensify the aggression towards England which John would act on in later years.

It also meant that John joined his father's failed rebellion against David II in spring 1363 and subsequently submitted publicly to the king. By then, however, most Scots must have realized that if David failed to produce heirs but outlived the older Robert Steward, then John Stewart of Kyle would become king. As such, David II seems to have turned to him as a means of reconciliation with, and influence over, the Stewarts. In 1366-67 the king arranged for John – at the surprisingly late age of about thirty – to wed Annabella Drummond, niece of David's second queen, Margaret. This unofficial recognition as heir-in-waiting to the throne brought John the earldom of Atholl from his father in May 1367 and a grant of the old Bruce earldom of Carrick (adjacent to Kyle) from the king in June 1368. However, David's hasty annulment of his fruitless marriage to Margaret in 1368 threatened to destroy John's future. Stewart opposition to David's plans to wed Agnes Dunbar may have seen John briefly gaoled along with his father and brother Alexander in that year, and generally subjected to royal interference in his lands. John must have been just as relieved as his father to see David die in 1371.

As we have seen, the accession of the Stewart dynasty revived John's fortunes dramatically. Doubts about the legitimacy of his parents' marriage and his place in the royal succession were quashed by parliamentary acts of 'entail' in 1371 – when John alone was named as heir – and 1373, when the potential succession was plotted ahead through the male heirs of John and his three brothers and two half-brothers. John also emerged in the 1370s as the leading prince of the blood south of the Forth-Clyde line, in charge of border commissions (regular so-called 'March days') to maintain the peace with England, keeper of Edinburgh castle and with strong marriage connections to the various strands of the Douglases, the dominant family of the borders. But John's natural political ambition created tensions with his brothers and father. This last was a breach surely betrayed by John's baptism of his first son and daughter as 'David' (born 1378) and 'Margaret', after the Stewarts' former royal antagonists, David II and his second wife.

John's cunning and successful manoeuvre into power as 'King's Lieutenant' in the place of his 'infirm' father at a council in November 1384 released his frustrated aggression towards England. This was a policy which was popular with John's main ally, James, 2nd earl of Douglas, and many other Scottish nobles, as well as being highly profitable: John himself would receive some £5,500 for supporting the French military expedition to Scotland in 1385 (though this was still less than the Douglas earl's £7,000). But the embarrassing Scottish maltreatment of their guests, Douglas's death at Otterburn in 1388 and the southerner John's failure to tackle the problem of Highland lawlessness perpetrated by his younger brother Alexander fatally undermined his regime. Moreover, when the challenge from his brother Robert, earl of Fife, came at a council in December 1388, John was not merely politically incapacitated: he had also recently been rendered lame – at the age of fifty or so – by a kick from the horse of one of his past allies, Sir James Douglas of Dalkeith. Fife's assumption of the lieutenancy with the support of Archibald 'the Grim', the new third earl of Douglas (whose inheritance John had opposed), seemed to indicate that the fate of the heir to the throne would mirror that of his father, his time to be spent on the sidelines of power in the Gaelic Stewart lands in the west.

However, recent research has shown John Stewart to be a rather more resilient political player than his father. True, when Robert II died in April 1390 there was an uncomfortable four-month gap until 14 August before John was crowned at Scone. This was a period during which Fife was able to have his lieutenancy confirmed in the wake of Alexander Stewart's wolf-like destruction of Elgin cathedral in the summer. But John's accession to the kingship – and his name-change to 'Robert III' for the sake of family continuity and to avoid association with John Balliol and John II of France – seemed to offer hope of a revival of his fortunes based in part on the legitimate personal authority of the monarchy.

Fife and the other great magnates of the day continued to enjoy a large degree of control over the offices and resources of royal government and to act for the community and crown in the localities. But Robert III expended considerable energy in promoting – with much success – the political profile of his eldest son, the youth who would be king, David Stewart, now earl of Carrick. As a result, in 1393, Fife's lieutenancy was discontinued (although he remained chamberlain) and the king was increasingly able to associate David as Fife's partner in government while maintaining a large measure of personal control over the teenage prince.

Faced with a shortage of royal lands, the king's attempts to use pensions to buy the loyalty of nobles to the crown and prince were inevitably undermined by the drastic devaluation of Scottish money at this time. But by the mid-1390s Robert III, through his son, was once again at centre stage in royal Scotland. The king seems to have resumed control of Anglo-Scottish policy, maintaining a wary peace with Richard II alongside a dormant Franco-Scottish alliance. He was also able to build up the power of the Red Douglas earls of Angus in southeastern Scotland as an alternative to Fife's allies, the Black Douglases. Robert III turned his attention as well to reasserting order in the north. The years 1393-99 saw a number of royal campaigns – jointly headed by Fife, the Lindsay earl of Crawford and, latterly, David of Carrick – directed against Alexander Stewart and his sons as well as other clans in the north and west. As a Gaelic lord and earl of Atholl as well as king of Scots, Robert III had a close interest in pacifying the region. Thus, 28 September 1396 found him at Perth personally overseeing a staged clan combat-to-the-death between the kindreds of Kay and Chattan.

This unusual royal policy does not seem to have worked. Nor, really, would the king's calculated elevation on 28 April 1398 of Carrick as 'duke of Rothesay' (after the Stewarts' ancestral home on Bute) and Fife as 'duke of Albany' (after *Alba*, the traditional Gaelic designation of the Scottish kingdom north of Forth). These were honorary titles designed at once to satisfy egos and to signal a royal partnership in overcoming Donald MacDonald, lord of the Isles and pretender to the earldom of Ross, in a campaign planned for summer 1398. But these promotions came in the wake of strong criticism of the king's government in Council and of the royal failure to police the north, complaints which would seem to be borne out by the contemporary chronicler of Moray's assertion that:

> in those days there was no law in Scotland, but he who was stronger oppressed him who was weaker and the whole realm was a den of thieves; murders, herschips and fireraising and all other misdeeds remained unpunished; and justice, as if outlawed, lay in exile outwith the bounds of the realm.

Crucially, the invalid king's weakness in the north gave certain magnates vital ammunition to add to other local complaints, for example, the crown's failure to recover Dumbarton castle from the possession of a certain Walter Buchanan despite a prolonged siege in 1398, or

84. The tomb of Alexander Stewart, the 'Wolf of Badenoch', brother of Robert III, in Dunkeld
Cathedral. Alexander's exploits in the north played a large part in the downfall of both his father,
Robert II, and his elder brother Robert III.

85. The North Inch, Perth, scene of the judicial combat between Clan Chattan and Clan
Kay. This was one of Robert III's more unorthodox methods of dealing with the fractious
north of his kingdom.

Robert III's alienation of the Douglases by favouring the earl of Angus. However, in the end it was the ambition of David, duke of Rothesay, which proved decisive.

As Rothesay reached adulthood he sought to throw off his father's controlling influence. In part, this was a perfectly natural aspiration for a young, vigorous royal, one who had cut an impressive figure in a tournament organized by Queen Annabella in Edinburgh in 1398 to showcase the prince's talents. But Rothesay's hopes also sprang from friction with his father, in particular over the king's messy annulment of Rothesay's proposed marriage to the daughter of George Dunbar, earl of March, in 1395-96. This match would have given Rothesay valuable border allies in determining Scottish policy towards England. More generally, Rothesay was anxious to assume a more independent role in control of his future royal government. It followed that in January 1399 Rothesay was prepared to collude with his uncle Albany and Archibald, earl of Douglas, to reuse the excuse of the king's infirmity and the failure of royal officers to impose order in the north as a pretext for the transfer of power. The twenty-one year old Rothesay was named Lieutenant for three years in a council held at Perth. However, he was not a free agent. He was to report to and accept the advice of a council of twenty-one chosen nobles, a body dominated by Albany and Douglas and their followers. Thus, once again, Robert III found himself marginalized to his family lands in the west, at the beck and call of his younger blood relatives to legitimate their control of royal policy and patronage. On this occasion, though, the coup had been partly engineered by the man he had sought to build up as his associate in power, his son, Rothesay.

In the light of this betrayal, Robert III must have looked on with mixed feelings over the next three years as Rothesay's considerable energy and ambition almost inevitably brought him into conflict with the entrenched interests of Albany and Douglas. The king had played a large part in the alienation of the March earl but Rothesay made matters far worse by taking up with the daughter of the earl of Douglas, provoking March to seek help from Henry IV of England. Rothesay's retaliatory forfeiture of March in 1400 brought Henry north with an army to Edinburgh with vague claims to the Stewarts' throne (surely harking back to the deals David II had tried to cut with Henry's father, John of Gaunt, in the 1360s). The English soon went away but Rothesay's independent action had also alienated Albany.

Albany was further angered by Rothesay's seizure of customs revenue in 1400-1401 and his interference in the vacant bishopric of St Andrews in Fife, where the Lieutenant also targeted some of the officials of Albany's earldom. It is clear that Albany later circulated cunning propaganda denouncing Rothesay as a power-mad degenerate, loose-living, pleasure-seeking and above the law, who had to be removed from office (these were tales which Sir Walter Scott adapted for his novel *The Fair Maid of Perth* in 1828). But Albany may also have been able to use such exaggerated proof of Rothesay's independent action to persuade Robert III to agree to his son and heir's arrest in late 1401, shortly after the death of Queen Annabella at Scone and her burial at Dunfermline. Rothesay's lieutenancy under the council's control was due to expire officially in early 1402 and Albany clearly feared this would herald a general assault on his interests by the future king. To defend his empire Albany decided to act. Here, Robert III's policy of using pensions to ensure loyalty to the prince proved dangerously uncertain. For Albany was able to use Rothesay's own household retainers to arrest the duke at St Andrews then have him transferred to Albany's own Falkland castle and starved to death in the dungeon around 25-27 March 1402.

In destroying Robert III's heir, Albany had the crucial support of the new 4th earl of Douglas. The aged king had no choice but to countenance their actions, acquiescing to a fixed council declaration in spring 1402 that Rothesay had died 'by divine providence and not otherwise' and that all murmuring against Albany and Douglas was to cease. Albany was appointed King's Lieutenant for two years and Douglas got his war with England. Admittedly, this quickly met disaster at Humbleton Hill on 14 September 1402, where Douglas was captured along with Albany's own son and heir, Murdac. But the magnates continued to control most royal policies and resources, even, for example, depriving the king of the earldom of Atholl, which Albany gave to his half-brother Walter Stewart.

However, Rothesay's death and Douglas's capture gave Robert III a window of opportunity. The king was now able to venture out from the Stewart lands to promote the political profile of his remaining son and heir, James, now earl of Carrick. The creation of a 'regality' in Carrick – a special jurisdiction which excluded Albany's power as Lieutenant and Douglas's as justiciar south of Forth – was clearly designed to build James up as a focus of support for a crown revival. This seems to have had some effect, as Robert III became increasingly influential in negotiations with England after 1402. Yet this would prove a fragile resurgence in the face of noble blocs that had already acted to destroy one future king. When the royalists Henry Sinclair, earl of Orkney, and Sir David Fleming of Cumbernauld tried to use Prince James as a figurehead in a mounted campaign to challenge Albany and Douglas power in Lothian in early 1406 things went badly wrong. Fleming was killed by a force led by Sir James Douglas of Balvenie, while Orkney and James were forced first to take shelter on the Bass rock in the Forth estuary (normally used as a prison) and then to take passage on a German ship bound for France.

A fearful Robert III clearly approved of this transfer of his last heir to the protection of Charles VI of France. But James never got there: his ship was captured by English pirates on 22 March 1406 and the prince taken as a captive to Henry IV. Robert III died a broken man within a matter of days in Rothesay castle on Bute, aged about seventy. He was buried in the Stewart vault in Paisley Abbey, fortunately spared the epitaph he himself insisted summarized his shortcomings as a king. But it is this view of Robert III's weak personal rule which historians have largely sustained, lumping him in with his father as a failed pair, both of whom were able to provide amply for the succession but lacked the dynamism and natural authority any forceful effective ruler should have. As a whole their reigns are characterized by what the chronicler Abbot Bower described as 'a great deal of dissension, strife and brawling among the magnates and the leading men, because the king, being bodily infirm, had no grip anywhere.' Only recent, closer examination has revealed Robert III to have been a determined political fighter, if one unable to prevent his own noble relatives from eclipsing the crown.

MP

JAMES I (1406-1437)

The reign of James I could scarcely have begun less auspiciously. His capture by English pirates in the spring of 1406, shortly before the death of his father, Robert III, left the Scots with the problem of establishing a caretaker government to rule for an indefinite period (which was to turn out to be eighteen years). Traditionally, the king's closest male relative assumed the role of governor or lieutenant, and Robert Stewart, 1st duke of Albany and earl of Fife and Menteith, qualified for this role despite his involvement in the death of his

86. The Bass Rock, from Tantallon Castle. James I was confined to this barren outcrop for weeks before taking ship for France.

nephew David, duke of Rothesay, in 1402. Diplomacy with England was conducted on the basis that although the Scots acknowledged James I as their rightful king and demanded his return, they would not obey any instructions ostensibly issued by him while under the influence of the English king for fear of compromising their hard won national sovereignty. Henry IV and Henry V both tried to use their royal captive to their own advantage, but the Scots' far from conciliatory response was to attack English-held garrisons in southern Scotland and renew the 'Auld Alliance' with France in 1407.

The nature of the Albany governorship was necessarily different from that of a king, and the problems posed by opportunist members of the nobility, such as the earl of Douglas who extorted money from the royal customs, had to be resolved without recourse to parliament (which could not be called in the absence of the king). Unable to forfeit lands and titles, Albany could only offer political solutions through his status as head of the Stewart family, such as marriage settlements or tacit recognition of aggrandizement. Problems in the Highlands flared up in 1411 over the earldom of Ross, resulting in a bloody engagement at Harlaw between Donald, lord of the Isles, and Albany's nephew Alexander Stewart, earl of Mar. The struggle for influence in the northeast Highlands remained unresolved and was to prove troublesome for James I when he returned to rule in his own right.

Robert, duke of Albany, was in his eighties when he died at Stirling in September 1420, and his son Murdac succeeded him as governor. Depredations and unruly actions by the family of the new governor, particularly his sons, elicited deep censure from contemporary writers concerning Murdac's inability to control them, further undermining his position. The return of James I to Scotland after eighteen years of captivity in England came as something of a jolt to his subjects, grown used to the *laissez-faire* style of government operated by the Albany Stewarts during their governorship. A king attaining his majority after succeeding as a minor was hardly an unknown phenomenon in Scotland, but for that king to have spent his minority forcibly removed from the influence of his councillors and countrymen rendered him a somewhat unknown quantity in terms of his personality and likely attitude to government. Any uncertainty was soon removed in 1424. The returning king was thirty years old, well educated and experienced in English methods of government, but he was also deeply resentful of the time he had spent in captivity and highly suspicious of those who had administered power in his absence. It was soon evident that James I was determined to avoid governing as *primus inter pares*, deciding rather to establish strong, centralized leadership with the king enjoying unchallenged authority at the head of the hierarchy.

In order to achieve this, certain measures had to be taken, not least of which was the eradication of threats to his position, and James perceived those threats to come from his own family, particularly the Albany Stewarts. Relations with the important border family of Douglas were also strained, and James had to tread warily at first because Archibald, 4th earl of Douglas, and John Stewart, earl of Buchan, were in France with a Scottish army, fighting alongside the French. However, when much of this force, including Douglas and Buchan, were wiped out at the battle of Verneuil in August 1424, James felt secure enough to take action. In March 1425 the king launched his attack on the whole house of Albany, and Duke Murdac, two of his sons and his father-in-law the earl of Lennox were executed following their condemnation in parliament held at Stirling in May. These showcase executions had a purpose other than simply disposing of the king's perceived enemies, which was to instil fear, establish respect for James I and make his subjects understand that unquestioned loyalty was demanded.

87. Linlithgow Palace, Lothian, begun by James I as the symbolic seat of his new monarchy.
88. The royal arms of James I over the Old Entry at Linlithgow Palace.
89. Coin of James I, 1406-1437.

90. Harlaw, Aberdeenshire, scene of the lord of the Isles' challenge to the power of the Albany Stewarts in 1411.

91. Doune Castle, Stirlingshire, stronghold of the Albany Stewarts.

Having fired this warning shot to demonstrate his authority, James I set about establishing the Scottish court on the distinctly European model that had so impressed him during his time at the court of Henry V and on his visits to France. While in England, James had met and married Joan Beaufort, niece of Thomas, duke of Exeter, and Henry, bishop of Winchester. These were powerful men in the English administration, therefore the marriage was a prestigious one as well as being that rare thing in royal alliances, a love match. The royal couple showed every determination to demonstrate their status by spending lavishly on luxuries such as jewellery, fine clothes, tapestries and furnishings, with the palace of Linlithgow being constructed not along defensive lines but as a showcase for this opulent style so that foreign diplomats and visitors would be impressed by the wealth and taste of the Scottish court, and also to underline royal status to native subjects. It was not only the possession of domestic luxuries which provided evidence of princely power, but also royal outlay on the latest artillery pieces, particularly cannon from the Low Countries, the most powerful of which was called the Lion, their purpose being as much to impress rival rulers as intimidate possible aggressors.

The release of James I from English captivity had not been without conditions. A large ransom had been negotiated which was to be paid in instalments, security for which was given by sending hostages from Scottish noble families (usually the eldest son) to be kept in England at their family's expense, to be redeemed as and when the ransom was paid. The massive financial burden of the ransom led James I to impose onerous taxation and levies on a scale unprecedented in Scotland. At first, the Scots appeared to accept that taxation was necessary to pay the ransom and secure the release of the hostages, but parliament would not approve regular taxation and James resorted to other measures such as seizing lands and appropriating revenues, extorting loans from merchants and burgesses and exploiting customs and rents. Hostility to these impositions was heightened by the fact that they were not being used to pay off the ransom or finance national security, but instead to finance an opulent royal lifestyle to which the Scots were not accustomed and with which they must have had little sympathy. Such was the level of distrust between the king and his subjects that a tax levy agreed to by parliament in 1431 was raised only on the understanding that the money was to be kept in a locked box, paid out only in accordance with parliament's specific instructions and not squandered by the king.

James I and Joan Beaufort had six daughters, but the succession was not secured until 16 October 1430 with the birth of twin boys in Holyrood abbey. A contemporary writer described the celebrations, stating that

> bonfires were lighted, flagons of wine were free to all and victuals publicly to all comers, with the sweetest harmony of all kinds of musical instruments all night long proclaiming the praise and glory of God for all his gifts and benefits.
>
> *Liber Pluscardensis*

The elder twin was called Alexander, but died in infancy, leaving his surviving brother, James, as his father's only male heir.

James I strived for strong centralized authority, but the nature of medieval Scotland was such that this was not easily accomplished, as royal authority was strong in the lowlands but less established in the Gaelic-speaking highlands and islands. Alexander Macdonald, lord of the Isles, was in a strong enough position, geographically removed from the centre of government, to ignore royal instructions if he chose, and it was James I's firm intention to bring these areas under his control and put an end to the open flouting of his authority. In 1428, the king went north and arrested Alexander at Inverness. A subsequent rebellion the following year led to Macdonald's forces being scattered after an engagement with the king's army at Lochaber, but James was to learn that success in individual skirmishes did not put a significant dent in the position of the lord of the Isles. In 1431, the earl of Mar, acting as royal lieutenant, was defeated at Inverlochy, and James agreed to restore Alexander to his lordship. A tacit truce was then established for the remainder of James I's reign, but the problem of tension between the Gaelic northwest of Scotland and the central government was far from resolved.

In terms of foreign diplomacy, it was soon clear that James I had no intention of being under English influence, notwithstanding the ransom, and within four years of his return, he had negotiated an alliance with France. By exploiting the Anglo-French conflict, James secured the marriage of his four-year-old daughter Margaret to Louis, dauphin of France, in 1436. This was an extremely prestigious marriage, as it meant that Margaret would become Queen of France (although she died, very unhappily married to Louis, before this could happen). Two of James I's other daughters also secured prestigious European marriages, with Isabella marrying Francis, duke of Brittany, in 1442 and Eleanor marrying Sigismund, archduke of Austria, in 1449, building on the international standing of Scotland in the courts of continental Europe which their father had been so assiduous in promoting.

James I was seen as a cultured and literate man, and he composed the poem 'The Kingis Quair' (The King's Book) concerning his time in England and his love for Joan Beaufort, his future queen. However, the personality of the king as far as his subjects were concerned showed less gentle sensibilities, his arbitrary nature stimulating fear rather than respect and causing alienation and distrust. Some of this distrust might have been offset through sufficient rewards and patronage, but James failed to do this, further increasing the hostility of threatened and dispossessed magnates. The first major blow at the king's authority was struck in 1436 after he decided to mount a campaign to recapture the border castle of Roxburgh, still in English hands. The campaign, on the face of it a potentially popular one, degenerated into chaos, as the king fled from the field (perhaps fearing a plot against him) followed by his army who left the king's precious artillery to be captured.

Failing to appreciate the warning, James attempted to raise more money to finance the renewal of the campaign, and his uncle Walter, earl of Atholl, sponsored an attempt to arrest the king in parliament. Robert Graham of Kinpunt was chosen as speaker for the three estates, as he was articulate and had received some legal training, although his known hostility to the king was no doubt a factor in his selection. The Albany Stewarts had been friends and patrons of Graham's family, and he had himself been arrested in 1424 as a supporter of Walter, earl of Lennox. His enmity towards the king was deep seated and implacable, and although he may have gone beyond his brief in attempting to seize James I in parliament, he is unlikely to have been operating without the backing of more powerful confederates, notably Atholl. Insufficient support was forthcoming from the three estates on that occasion, and Graham's attempt failed, but it must have seemed to the conspirators that the only course of action left to them was the removal of the king by death.

Clearly unaware of the extent of the danger facing him, James I had Graham arrested, then banished, but he does not seem to have suspected a wider conspiracy involving his elderly uncle. A mixture of hatred for past actions and fear of the king's intentions motivated Robert Graham and a group of armed men, comprising servants of the late duke of Albany including

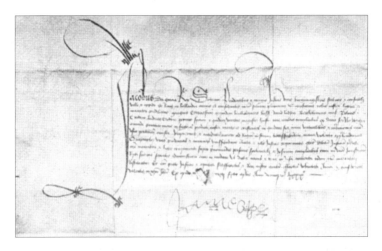

92. Letter of James I. James was a literate man, and composed 'The Kingis Quair'
in honour of his wife.

93. The remains of Roxburgh Castle, Borders. James I's failure to capture the English-held castle
shattered the myth of the all-powerful king and contributed to his downfall.

94. Methven Castle, Perthshire. The seventeenth-century castle stands on the site of the
stronghold of Walter Stewart, earl of Atholl.

95. John Slezer, 'Prospect of the Town of Perth', from *Theatrum Scotiae*. The Blackfriars' convent and royal lodgings, where James I was assassinated, occupied the site of the large structure on the extreme right of the engraving.

96. Blackfriars, Perth, modern plaque recording the assassination here of King James I.

97. Gold matrix of the privy seal of Joan Beaufort, Queen of James I, found while excavating the foundation of a house at West Green, Kinross, in 1829.

Thomas and Christopher Chambers and two Barclay brothers of Tentsmuir, when they entered the king's lodgings in the Dominican convent at Perth on 20 February 1437. Robert Stewart, Atholl's grandson and heir, assisted the entry of the assassins, but scuffles with members of the king's household gave James I brief warning. He fled to hide in a sewer tunnel, the outlet of which had been blocked recently to prevent balls being lost from the king's tennis court. Thus cornered, he was discovered and stabbed to death. Beyond the removal of James I, the conspirators do not seem to have prepared their ground particularly well, although they may have felt that Atholl, as the nearest male relative to the king, would be accepted automatically as regent for the young James II. This would require the elimination of the queen, but although she was wounded during the attack on her husband, the assassins failed to kill her and she managed to escape, losing no time in sending word to Edinburgh to prevent seizure of her son by the conspirators, removing John Spens, a man with connections to Atholl, from custodianship of the six year old duke of Rothesay and replacing him with John Balfour, untainted with such associations.

Regicide was the ultimate crime in medieval feudal society, and notwithstanding the unpopularity of James I, there seems to have been little support for the perpetrators after the event. The queen's survival was to prove the undoing of Atholl's plot. She organized her own faction in the ensuing confusion and pressed for the apprehension and arrest of her husband's assassins and those suspected of being a party to the plot. Queen Joan had some powerful cards to play in the form of the valiant figure she cut as the tragic widow bearing physical wounds from the struggle with her husband's assassins, and the butchered body of the king which was put on display before his burial in the Carthusian Priory, founded by him just outside Perth. The papal nuncio, Bishop Anthony Altani of Urbino, was present in Perth and declared James to have died a martyr. Having heightened the sense of revulsion for the crime, the queen's party turned their attention to the immediate problem of political survival.

Conflicting views of the king were the result of competing propaganda after the murder. To those who wished him dead, James I was a tyrannical ruler who arbitrarily attacked members of the nobility, including his own family, in order to lay claim to their lands and wealth. His financial demands were too frequent and too pressing, and he failed to deliver justice to his people. Against that view was the one that James had provided strong leadership against magnate excesses and depredations and that his removal was a disaster for the Scottish people, leaving them to endure the instability of years of consequent faction fighting. Whatever his shortcomings, James I established the model of Stewart kingship which placed Scotland firmly within a European context and which would be continued and evolved by his successors.

CM

JAMES II (1437-1460)

The reign of James II began with the usual problems to be faced at the outset of a royal minority compounded by the civil unrest and power struggles that followed the assassination of his father. The queen had lost no time in hurrying to her son in Edinburgh in order to ensure his safety while the conspirators were tracked down, put on trial and executed and the extent of the threat was assessed. The assassination of James I had taken place during Lent, which may explain why James II's coronation did not take place until 26 March (the beginning of the administrative year 1437 by medieval calculation), although safety concerns were clearly also an issue since the traditional site of Scottish royal coronations, Scone, was not used because of its proximity to Perth. Instead, the six-year old king was crowned at Holyrood, following which Atholl was tried and executed, although he was spared the grisly torture and dismemberment suffered by the other conspirators. This accomplished, the problem of administering the realm during the minority was addressed.

The problem was rendered more complex than usual by the severely depleted ranks of the higher nobility, brought about by James I's purges and the random accident of failures of lines, and a number of noble houses themselves had minors at the helm. Archibald, 5th earl of Douglas, was the obvious choice for lieutenant-general, as he was the king's nearest adult male relative in keeping with precedent, however, the queen retained her husband's distrust of Douglas and he does not appear to have been awarded the office immediately. The queen's faction included William, 2nd earl of Angus, and James Kennedy, bishop of St Andrews, although Angus died in October 1437, by which time Douglas was established as lieutenant-general. Localized feuding and civil unrest continued relatively unchecked, according to contemporary sources, and any influence which the lieutenant-general might have been able to exercise was short-lived, as he fell victim to the plague which afflicted Scotland in 1439, leaving an heir who was only thirteen years old. In these circumstances, it was possible for opportunist members of the lesser nobility to exercise a level of power and influence that would have been unthinkable in the usual hierarchical system that had evolved from feudalism. Two rival families rose to prominence during the minority, the Crichtons and the Livingstons. William, Lord Crichton, derived his status from consistent administrative service to James I, and had risen to the highest state office of chancellor. In addition to this, Crichton was the keeper of the strategically important Edinburgh castle. Sir Alexander Livingston of Callendar based his influence on his family's systematic acquisition of various offices and strongholds, including Stirling castle.

The imprisonment of the queen in 1439, shortly after it became known that she had remarried (to James Stewart, 'Black Knight' of Lorne), resulted in a brokered agreement known as the 'Appoyntement' the terms of which secured the queen's release but effectively ended her political influence, confining her role to taking care of her children. She went on to have three sons by her second husband, and died in 1445. The sweeping of the queen's faction from the political stage did not stabilize minority politics, as the young king was used as a pawn in the manoeuvrings for power of Crichton and Livingston. Documentary evidence for the 1440s is scanty, lending weight to the view that this was a time of turmoil, but such official documents as survive seem to bear out the colourful stories related by the sixteenth century chroniclers, such as Bishop John Lesley and Robert Lindsay of Pitscottie, including that of the king being smuggled out of Edinburgh castle by the queen and taken to Stirling; then Crichton's counter-stroke of abducting the king while he was out riding from Stirling and taking him back to Edinburgh.

These were bold actions indeed, but when the young sons of the late lieutenant-general were executed at the so-called 'Black Dinner' in Edinburgh castle in November 1440, a more powerful influence was clearly at work. The execution of William, 6th earl of Douglas, and his younger brother David, along with their adherent Malcolm Fleming of Cumbernauld, resulted in their great-uncle James Douglas of Balvenie, also known as James 'the Gross' because he was so fat, falling heir to the Black Douglas estates. He had a record of court attendance and steady ambition behind him, having assumed the title earl of Avondale early in the minority, and it is

98. Holyrood Abbey, scene of the coronation of James II in March 1437.

99. The tomb of James II's lieutenant-general, Archibald, 5th earl of Douglas.

100. Crichton Castle, Midlothian, stronghold of James II's scheming chancellor, William Lord Crichton.

highly unlikely that Crichton or Livingston would have taken it upon themselves to attack the 6th earl of Douglas without the covert backing of the future 7th earl. Certainly, the new earl took it upon himself to placate Fleming's outraged family by offering one of his own daughters in marriage to Fleming's heir, and it is significant that the boys were not forfeited (which would have required parliamentary sanction), thus facilitating Avondale's succession.

Ambition unmasked, James the Gross set about consolidating his family's position, obtaining the earldom of Moray by the somewhat dubious measure of marrying his son, Archibald, to the younger co-heiress, ignoring the claim of the elder sister, married to James Crichton, son of the chancellor, and securing the marriage of his eldest son, William, to Margaret, the 'fair maid of Galloway', sister of the executed 6th earl. The intention behind this somewhat insensitive arrangement was to recover the unentailed Black Douglas properties to which Margaret fell heir, although the marriage did not actually take place until 1443, after the death of the 7th earl. The forcible shift of the line of Black Douglas descent must have caused disquiet and resentment amongst the remaining family and retainers of the 6th earl, but, on the surface at least, the cracks were papered over and the succession of William, 8th earl of Douglas, left the Black Douglases and their allies the Livingstons dominant at court.

That dominance was not to be challenged seriously until after the king's marriage in July 1449. On 1 April, the treaty of Brussels was the culmination of negotiations for James II to marry Mary of Gueldres, daughter of Arnold, duke of Gueldres, and niece of Philip the Good, duke of Burgundy, who was one of the wealthiest rulers in western Europe. This marriage marked one of the most prestigious unions for a Scottish king since the thirteenth century, and followed in the pattern of important European marriages secured for his sisters: Margaret to Louis, dauphin of France, Isabella to Francis, duke of Brittany, Eleanor to Archduke Sigismund of Austria and Mary to Wolfaert van Borselen, lord of Veere. Trade access to the Low Countries, including the financial powerhouse of Bruges, strengthened Scottish links to the wealth of mainland Europe, while Burgundian skill in the development of artillery weapons gave James II the opportunity to indulge his passion, inherited from his father, and build up a formidable battery of armaments for his military campaigns.

However, all of this came at a price. Important though Mary's dowry of £30,000 was in augmenting the royal coffers, it was to be paid by the duke of Burgundy in instalments, and the Scots for their part were to provide the new queen with £5,000 as her *tocher* (marriage portion). Failure to do this would lead to the withholding of further instalments from Burgundy, therefore James had an immediate concern, on assuming the reins of personal power, to look to his royal finances. With their network of offices, including the justiciarship, the captaincy of the castles of Stirling, Doune, Dumbarton, Dunoon and Methven, and the important fiscal office of comptroller, the Livingstons were prime targets for James II's acquisitive schemes. Suspicions of financial irregularities, which seem to have had some foundation, formed the basis for charges against the family, and the Livingstons were forfeited in January 1450, chief beneficiaries being the queen and William, earl of Douglas, who appears to have accepted the downfall of his erstwhile allies with equanimity.

This political muscle-flexing by the king, who was his father's son in the sense that he had no desire to see royal authority challenged or impeded and who had endured the frustration of a long minority, should have sent a message to Douglas. That he did not perceive the fragile nature of the king's favour is evident in his decision to travel to Rome for the papal jubilee in the winter of 1450-51. Shortly after Douglas's departure, Margaret, widow of Archibald, 5th earl of Douglas, and James II's aunt, died. She had been granted her late

James the second
Begon his Raygne
1437, He married
Marie dochter off Arnoll
Duke off Gilder

101. James II and his queen, from a Scottish Armorial illuminated for Robert Lord Seton
towards the end of the sixteenth century.

102. Tomb of James 'the Gross', 7th earl of Douglas, in St Bride's Kirk, Douglas, Lanarkshire.

103. Tomb of Margaret Stewart, countess of Douglas and duchess of Touraine, aunt of James II, in the collegiate church of Lincluden, Dumfries and Galloway.

104. The 'Douglas Window' at Stirling Castle, from which tradition reports that the corpse of the murdered 8th Earl of Douglas was thrown.

husband's earldom of Wigtown by her brother, James I, to be held in life-rent. This earldom had been a bone of contention between the Black Douglases, who had acquired it without royal sanction in 1372, and James I. By granting it in life-rent to his sister, James's intention was that it should return to the crown following her death, and James II seized it promptly in 1451. His motives almost certainly went beyond simple legality. The Black Douglases had achieved a spectacular level of expansion which gave them lands, titles and influence in places as diverse as Galloway, Lanarkshire, Lothian, Moray and the north-east, and James would have wanted to curb their power and set limits on their expansion. However, the seizure of the nominally Douglas territory of Wigtown at a time when the earl was not there to contest or defend the action, awakened memories and fears of the arbitrary ruthlessness of James I among other members of the political community who, although they may have had no great regard for the Douglases, nevertheless felt the potential threat to their own positions. Confrontation was avoided on Douglas's return by his overt demonstration of loyalty and the ceremonial surrendering of his possessions to the king in parliament and their subsequent re-granting. However, it was clear that Douglas now had good cause to be wary of the king, and James II, for his part, would not have relished having to back down over the issue of Wigtown, which he only restored, reluctantly, in October 1451.

Jealousy and distrust of the Black Douglases could be exploited by the king, and he resolved to work towards the undermining of his overtly powerful subject by courting the loyalty and service of men whose allegiance to Douglas as their immediate feudal superior was at best lukewarm. The vulnerable part of the Black Douglas power base was the south-west, traditionally Black Douglas heartland, but where those loyal to the 5th earl's line would have been offended by the nature of the transfer of power following the 'Black Dinner'. Anticipating future royal hostility, William, 8th earl of Douglas, sought allies for his own protection, and formed a bond of alliance with Alexander Lindsay, earl of Crawford, and John Macdonald, earl of Ross and lord of the Isles. The actual bond has not survived, but there is no evidence that it indicated a plot to attack the king. News of its existence proved unacceptable to the king, however, as the men involved had a history of defiance and troublemaking, and James would have been aware of troublesome magnate coalitions in France. With the issue of Wigtown still rankling, Douglas's use of the title 'earl of Wigtown' on a charter issued by him in January 1452, coupled with the discovery of the bond, provoked James II sufficiently for him to summon Douglas to appear before him in order to answer for his actions.

The fact that a safe-conduct was demanded by Douglas before he would agree to attend the king at Stirling on 21 February 1452, indicates how far their relationship had deteriorated. On the second day of discussions, tempers flared and James II stabbed Douglas to death, aided in his attack by several courtiers to the extent that (according to a contemporary chronicler's account) the earl's body had twenty-six wounds. This was a shocking event that would have outraged contemporaries because of the violation of the medieval code of honour involved in reneging on the safe-conduct issued to Douglas. The king, said to have personally stabbed Douglas twice, was not confident in his own security and moved fast to limit the damage and prepare for any backlash. He stepped up the programme of securing support, offering reassurance and providing patronage as a reward for loyalty, significantly concentrating his initial efforts in the south-west. Evidence for his concern is shown by his removal of the pregnant queen from Stirling to the comparative safety of Bishop Kennedy's palace at St Andrews, where the future James III was born in May. Some vindication for this decision came when James, now 9th earl of Douglas, arrived in Stirling at the head of a force of six

105. Threave Castle, Dumfries and Galloway, the last stronghold of the Black Douglases.
106. Ravenscraig Castle, Kirkcaldy, one of the earliest artillery works in Britain, which was
begun by James II.

hundred men to denounce the king for the murder of his brother, burning the town in a gesture of defiance to the king, who had left Stirling only a couple of days before.

The necessity of reading history backwards may make the ultimate downfall of the Black Douglases seem inevitable. James II's position was strengthened by the greater resources at his disposal and the ultimate allegiance owed to him by his subjects, whereas the Black Douglases, already undermined within their own kin-base, could give vent to their righteous indignation but were ultimately faced with the problem that defiance of the king was treason. The attitude of the other members of the political community was crucial. Unpopular though the Douglases may have made themselves in their rapid rise to prominence, the king's methods were alarming and he had to work very hard to placate his other important nobles and churchmen. Parliamentary exoneration, albeit grudging, was given in June 1452, but James disturbed the fragile balance once more in his subsequent summer campaign in the south of Scotland, intended to root out lingering support for the Douglases, where his raids had the effect of alienating some of those who had been supportive or at least neutral. This enabled his counsellors to press the king to come to terms with James, 9th earl of Douglas, in an agreement made at Douglas castle in Lanarkshire on 28 August 1452 and again, by bond of manrent given at Lanark, on 16 January 1453.

Unlike James I, his son seemed better able to learn from experience, and although he had no intention of allowing the rehabilitation of the Black Douglases, he took more care over the nature of his pursuit of the family's ultimate destruction, trying to allay fears of arbitrariness and using patronage to deliver rewards for loyalty. This took time, but the king's final attack on the lands of the Black Douglases began in March 1455, and the capture of their last stronghold at Threave was followed by their forfeiture in the June parliament.

The desire to reap some benefits in return for the support offered to the king was pursued by the three estates with the Act of Annexation in 1455, which sought to ensure that the Douglas lands annexed to the crown and other royal resources would not be squandered in patronage but held to generate income, thus negating the need for taxation or any systematic encroachments on his subjects' resources. Having dealt with the threat of a territorially powerful magnate house, James II's patronage as regarded replenishing the ranks of his higher nobility took the form of creating the earldoms of Rothes, Morton, Erroll, Marischal and Argyll, although only the Campbell earldom of Argyll may be said to be territorial, and that was in recognition of the need for a loyal crown agent to act as a buffer against the predations of the lord of the Isles. In the same way as certain members of the lesser nobility were rewarded with the creation or recognition of the title 'lord of parliament', these titles conferred prestige and underlined the political status of their recipients at little or no cost to the crown in terms of land or fiscal grants.

Having stabilized domestic affairs, James II was able to devote his attention to foreign diplomacy, and negotiations for the marriage of his son, James, duke of Rothesay, were set in motion in 1459, with a view to securing a Danish match. The instability created by the civil war in England was exploited by James II with variable success. His raids on Berwick in 1455 and the Isle of Man in 1456 did not achieve their objective, but his campaign in 1460 to recapture Roxburgh was more effective, although at an enormous cost to the Scots. The use of the king's beloved artillery was a feature of this campaign, including the famous 'Mons Meg', acquired from Burgundy in1458. On 3 August 1460, James II was killed when one of his own guns broke apart as he was watching it being fired, a fragment of metal severing his thigh and causing his death through shock and loss of blood.

A contemporary portrait of James II shows the red birthmark which covered the left-hand side of his face, rendering him physically striking and earning him the sobriquet, 'James of the fiery face'. His posthumous reputation comes largely from later writers who sought to interpret his struggle with the Black Douglases in the light of their own views on over-mighty magnates and the breakdown of 'natural order'. He embodied certain Stewart characteristics such as ruthlessness and acquisitiveness, but he tempered these with an ability to learn from his mistakes and to appreciate the necessity of courting support rather than forcing it through fear. A broadly positive view of his character may stem from straight comparisons with his father's ruthlessness and his son's disastrous shortcomings, but he fulfilled many of the criteria of 'good lordship' expected of a medieval king and was killed, aged only twenty-nine, on a campaign popularly backed by his subjects, with the succession secured.

CM

JAMES III (1460-1488)

Following the death of her husband, the queen ordered the continuance of the siege of Roxburgh castle, and it fell to the Scots just two days before the new king's coronation at Kelso on 10 August, within a week of his father's death. Mary of Gueldres was to prove a strong influence in the early years of the minority of her son, stealing the march on James Kennedy, bishop of St Andrews, who was abroad at the time of Roxburgh, by placing her own people in positions of influence. Her political leadership was a considered continuation of her husband's policy in terms of her dealings with England, securing the diplomatic cession of Berwick to Scotland in March 1461 as return for offering shelter to the fugitive Lancastrian king, Henry VI, and his queen, Margaret of Anjou, although political expediency and her natural inclinations following the victory of the Yorkists caused Mary to switch her support to Edward IV.

Criticisms of her which appear in both contemporary and later chronicle sources seem to have their foundation more in the misogyny of the writers and the bitterness of political rivals such as Kennedy himself and disappointed Lancastrians. Her chosen counsellors, such as James Lindsay, provost of Lincluden and keeper of the privy seal, continued in office after the queen's death, and there is no evidence for turmoil and dissent in the early years of the minority. Expenditure by Mary of Gueldres included considerable building work undertaken at Falkland palace and at her castle of Ravenscraig, at Dysart in Fife, designed with great artillery battlements looking over the Forth to the south, in keeping with her late husband's passion for guns. More pious considerations lay behind her expensive foundation and endowment of Holy Trinity Church in Edinburgh, for which the later altarpiece depicting James III and his queen, Margaret of Denmark, was painted by the Flemish artist, Hugo Van Der Goes.

Challenges by the Kennedy family to the queen mother's political ascendancy led to compromise, and in an attempt to capitalize on the political confusion created by the 'Wars of the Roses', a Scottish force led by the uneasy alliance of James Kennedy, bishop of St Andrews, Queen Mary and the eleven year old James III laid siege to Norham castle, stronghold of the bishops of Durham, in the summer of 1463, although they failed to take it. Kennedy was almost certainly the instigator of this unsuccessful strategy, as his influence in government was increasing, probably at a time when the queen's health was deteriorating, since she died in December 1463.

107. Personal seal of Mary of Gueldres from a nineteenth-century facsimile. The queen mother controlled the government of her young son James III until her death in 1463.

108. The medieval town walls of Berwick. Mary of Gueldres succeeded in recovering the town for Scotland as the price of safety for Henry VI of England.

Bishop Kennedy's assumption of the guardianship of the king was followed by the collapse of his pro-French/Lancastrian policies as the Yorkists emerged triumphant from the struggle between the two sides. Turning his attention to internal matters, Kennedy organized a royal progress in the summer of 1464 which took the young king north of the Forth as far as Aberdeen, Inverness and Elgin, affirming loyalty to the new regime. This, and a winter progress at the end of 1464, offered a stark contrast to the king's disinclination for travel in the years of his personal rule! Kennedy's long awaited dominance in Scottish politics was to be short-lived, as he died on 24 May 1465. A truce with England was negotiated, and the Kennedy family's rivals, the Boyds of Kilmarnock, headed by Robert, Lord Boyd, and his brother, Sir Alexander Boyd of Drumcoll, the king's instructor in the use of arms, challenged them over the running of the minority government by seizing control of the fourteen-year-old king while he was out hunting near Linlithgow on 9 July 1466.

Alexander Boyd, having assisted in the coup to seize possession of the king, found himself discarded by his elder brother, whose idea of advancing the Boyds' position involved principally himself and his son Thomas. During the period of his ascendancy, Lord Boyd had his son created earl of Arran and secured his marriage to Mary, the elder sister of James III. Extensive land grants were made to Thomas, and Robert's ambition and acquisitiveness did not end there, securing the marriage of his daughter Elizabeth to Archibald Douglas, earl of Angus, and adding the office of chamberlain to those he already held. Although not in control of royal government, the major offices of state remaining in the hands of men not of the Boyd faction, the actions of the Boyds created sufficient animosity to place them in a precarious position, particularly in view of James III's growing animosity towards them.

Arrangements for the king's marriage proceeded along the same diplomatic lines envisaged by his father, with the Treaty of Copenhagen in 1468 securing a marriage alliance between James III and Margaret of Denmark, daughter of Christian I of Denmark and Norway. The king assumed control of government in his own right after his wedding in the summer of 1469 at the age of seventeen, and he followed the pattern established by his father and grand-father in attacking those who had wielded power during his minority. In this case, that meant the Boyds, who were forfeited and stripped of political influence, although only the hapless Alexander Boyd was executed, Robert and Thomas having taken flight.

After the forfeiture of the Boyds, James III was in the enviable position of having no great potentially hostile magnate power bases to deal with. Peace had been made with England, and diplomacy with Scandinavia had resulted in the pawning to the Scots of the earldom of Orkney and lordship of Shetland by the impecunious Christian I, in place of a dowry for his daughter. By 1472, James had converted this arrangement to the annexation of Orkney and Shetland to the Scottish crown, but ambitions in foreign diplomacy did not end there. The marriage alliances that the Stewarts had been making with some of the major royal and magnate houses of Europe gave James III a dangerously exalted view of the nature of Scottish kingship as exercised by him. He embraced the political theory that the king is emperor in his own realm to the extent that there are examples of his portrait on pieces of silver coinage minted towards the end of his reign in which he wears an imperial crown.

There was certainly a distinctly imperial flavour to his ambitions in Europe between 1471-73, which included proposals to invade Brittany, personally heading an army of 60,000, annex Gueldres and acquire Saintonge from the French; schemes which were greeted with near total lack of enthusiasm from his subjects, realizing the expense and effort which would be

109. James III and his queen, from a Scottish Armorial illuminated for Robert Lord Seton towards the end of the sixteenth century.

110. A silver groat of James III, the first example of Renaissance portraiture on coinage north of the Alps. The king is shown wearing a closed-arched imperial crown.

involved, and the almost certain futility. The policy of peace and alliance with England, pursued assiduously by James III and culminating in the Treaty of 1474, was sufficiently unpopular, particularly with his border subjects to whom cross-border raiding was a way of life, to make it unworkable by the late 1470's.

In terms of fulfilling the traditional role of medieval monarchy, James III failed dismally to make himself accessible to his people, concentrating almost his entire personal rule in Edinburgh rather than travelling round the country on justice ayres, curbing local feuding and being seen to dispense royal justice. Despite repeated requests to fulfil this function, including a plea from parliament in 1479, the king ignored the problem and several areas of the country were racked with serious feuding: Ayrshire, where the Cunninghams fought the Montgomerys, Strathearn, where the Drummonds fought the Murrays and the northeast, where Huntly fought Ross.

The centralizing of the justice system in Edinburgh facilitated the king's practice of raising money through the granting of remissions for serious crimes, provided that the perpetrators were prepared to pay, for which he was criticized severely in parliament for undermining the system of royal justice based on weight of evidence. James III also tried to revive his grandfather's efforts at frequent taxation, strongly resisted by parliament, but unlike James I, lavish spending was not his primary objective; he preferred to hoard the money he had acquired. In 1480, he went a step further and debased the Scottish coinage by issuing a copper currency, the infamous 'black money', the face value of which was highly inflated.

The exploitation of various methods of raising money extended to the king's dealings with the Church, and he became involved in a bitter struggle with the important border family the Humes over the disputed revenues of Coldingham priory. Deep friction was also caused by the elevation of St Andrews into an archbishopric for Patrick Graham, involving the Church and crown in a long and unpleasant dispute. Graham succeeded to the bishopric of St Andrews following the death of his uncle, Bishop Kennedy, in 1465, although his appointment to this, the senior Scottish bishopric, at the age of only thirty, created considerable resentment. James III's determination to bring the Scottish Church under greater royal authority, limiting papal interference in taxation and provisions, alarmed the papacy, and Pope Sixtus IV saw in Graham an ally for the papacy, issuing a bull on 17 August 1472 raising St Andrews to the status of an archbishopric with metropolitan authority over the other twelve Scottish bishops. The prospect of deferring to Graham was not pleasing to the other Scottish bishops, and the potential for Graham to enforce papal policies against Crown interests would have infuriated James III. Concerted domestic opposition left Graham a broken man by 1475, deserted even by his papal patron when it became clear that he had no influence to bring to bear, and although his official depriva-tion and condemnation did not come until 1478, it was merely the recognition of a long established fact.

James III's reputation for taking the counsel of lowborn favourites rather than relying on the advice and service of his nobility has been greatly exaggerated by later writers. However, there were individuals who had constant access to the king and enjoyed advancement to the undoubted irritation of some members of the royal council. Chief among these were William Scheves and Thomas Cochrane who achieved positions far in advance of their normal expec-tations. Scheves began his career in the 1470's as a court servant whose work included sewing the king's shirts, but the dispute over the archbishopric of St Andrews led to the king grooming his favourite for the position, securing his promotion to the archdeaconry of St Andrews by 1474. Scheves was appointed coadjutor of the see of St Andrews on 13 July 1476, on the grounds of Graham's excommunication and insanity, and secured the archbishopric officially on 11 February 1478; no more popular a choice from the point of view of the Scottish Church, but completely subservient to the wishes of his royal master. Thomas Cochrane, a southern laird, managed, with the king's backing, to trample on vested interests in the north-east, building a stronghold at Auchindoun in Moray and acquiring the revenues of the earldom of Mar.

A robust attitude to the extension of royal control was not limited to church affairs. In October 1475, James III decided to tackle the problem posed by John Macdonald, earl of Ross and lord of the Isles, summoning Ross to appear in parliament on 1 December to answer charges of treason. The list of these unpunished treasons stretched back to 1452 and encompassed the usurpation of royal authority in the west, treasonable dealings with Edward IV of England and James, 9th earl of Douglas, and depredations in Bute and at Rothesay. James appears to have enjoyed popular backing for this showdown, not least from Ross's rivals such as Colin Campbell, earl of Argyll, Robert Colquhoun, bishop of Argyll, and John Stewart, earl of Atholl. Ross's non-appearance at the December parliament led to a swift sentence of forfeiture being pronounced against him and Argyll was given a commission of lieutenancy on 4 December to execute the forfeiture. The king may himself have taken part in the campaign during the following spring and George, earl of Huntly, certainly gave enthusiastic support in Lochaber, eager to benefit from Ross's disgrace.

On 10 July 1476, John Macdonald appeared before a packed parliament in Edinburgh where he was stripped of his earldom of Ross, which was annexed to the crown to be used by the king's second son. However, he was permitted to become a lord of parliament as lord of the Isles, a concession apparently granted at the request of Queen Margaret. John Macdonald was left in the difficult position of attempting to exercise limited authority in the areas under his control, essentially as a crown agent, notwithstanding the undoubted damage to his prestige and the contempt with which his illegitimate son, Angus Og of Islay, appears to have regarded him. The lord of the Isles was summoned again before parliament to answer charges of treason on 7 April 1478, but it became clear that continued resistance to crown authority in the west was almost certainly led by Angus Og at this stage. The king's attempts to subdue the west met with qualified success, as they brought financial benefits to the crown and effectively ensured no further trouble from Macdonald, although there would be repercussions from the shift of royal authority in the west highlands into the increasingly powerful hands of Colin Campbell, earl of Argyll.

Unlike his father, James III had to contend with adult brothers and other family members who were far from supportive of their royal kinsman. Such was James' ability to alienate those closest in blood to him that Alexander, duke of Albany, and John, earl of Mar, both strongly criticized their brother, and Mar was killed in suspicious circumstances in 1480, suffering forfeiture in the process, while Albany fled into exile to avoid treason charges. His elder sister, Mary, was married forcibly to Lord Hamilton, and her resentment was sufficient to lead her to join the rebellion against James in 1482, involving also the king's half-uncles, John, earl of Atholl, James, earl of Buchan, and Andrew, bishop of Moray, and his own queen, Margaret of Denmark. His younger sister, Margaret, evaded her brother's marriage plans for her by bearing a child as a result of an affair with William, 3rd Lord Crichton, for which the latter was exiled to Tain! Ultimate censure was to come when the king's son and

111. Auchindoun Castle, Moray, built by James III's favourite Thomas Cochrane.
112. The coat of arms of John Stewart, earl of Atholl, James's half-uncle, who rebelled against the king in 1482.

heir, James, duke of Rothesay, was the nominal leader of the army that defeated and killed the king in 1488.

The cumulative effect of the discontent generated by the nature of James III's personality and policies culminated in a major rebellion in 1482. The exile of Alexander, duke of Albany, to France had not removed the problem posed by his ambitions, and when relations with Edward IV deteriorated by 1480, leaving James III vulnerable, Albany was quick to seize the advantage. In May 1482, he came to England, probably with the encouragement of certain Scottish lords, and concluded the treaty of Fotheringhay with Edward IV in June. The following month, Albany, in company with Edward's brother, Richard, duke of Gloucester, and an English army of 20,000 men, marched north in the first major invasion of Scotland since 1400.

Claims by Albany to be regarded as Alexander IV, backed by his English allies, were unlikely to have been accepted, but a more credible aim was the securing of the lieutenant-generalship at the head of a faction dominated by his three half-uncles (the sons of Joan Beaufort by her second marriage to James Stewart of Lorne). James III was seized at Lauder, while the Scottish army mustered to repel the invasion force headed south, and taken by the leaders of that army, including Colin Campbell, 1st earl of Argyll, and Archibald, earl of Angus, to Edinburgh castle following the summary execution of some of his personal entourage, from which stems the later legends with their embellishments of Archibald 'bell the cat' and the 'low-born' favourites. The Scottish host having dispersed, Albany and Gloucester reached Edinburgh unchallenged, to find the king a prisoner in the hands of his half-uncles and the government occupied with seeking a solution to this crisis. With the apparent collusion of the queen, Albany enjoyed a brief period of influence, but his sponsor, Edward IV, died on 9 April 1483 and James III recovered power after two months, during which he must have feared that he was in danger of suffering the same fate as his grandfather. In fact, his opponents could not countenance regicide, preferring to hope that the shock would lead James to modify his behaviour. Albany appears to have understood his brother better and fled to England.

Previous attempts by the king to have Albany condemned for treason had been refused by parliamentary assizes, but he was finally able to secure his troublesome brother's forfeiture in July. One year later, Albany reappeared in Scotland in company with the exiled James, 9th earl of Douglas, at the head of a small English force who were engaged in a fight at Lochmaben on 22 July, where Douglas was captured and Albany fled back to England. In the spring of 1485, he returned to Scotland for the last time, suffering capture and imprisonment in Edinburgh castle, from which he escaped to France only to be killed in a tournament in Paris in the summer.

James III's elevated concept of his own position seemed to render him incapable of learning from bitter experience, and he showed none of his father's ability to adjust following setbacks to ensure that he courted sufficient support to offset any alienation caused by his actions. Instead, he continued to promote unpopular counsellors, such as John Ramsay, lord Bothwell, a survivor of Lauder, and he interfered with provisions to the dioceses of Glasgow and Dunkeld when these fell vacant. Rather than re-building relations with those who had opposed him at Lauder, James III pursued them vindictively, passing a Treasons Act in 1484. In July 1486, Margaret of Denmark died, and her eldest son, James, duke of Rothesay, may have feared that his own future was at risk from his distant and increasingly arbitrary father. When Colin Campbell, 1st earl of Argyll, James's chancellor and hitherto an apparently committed supporter of the king, was dismissed from his post in February 1488 and replaced by William

Elphinstone, bishop of Aberdeen, dissatisfaction reached a climax and James III faced his final rebellion; this time culminating in a battle against rebel forces with his own son at their head.

The armies met near Stirling on ground close to the historic site of the battle of Bannockburn, and fought an engagement later to be known as the battle of Sauchieburn, on 11 June 1488. Whether in battle or during the subsequent rout, James III was killed, bringing to an end the reign of a deeply unpopular Stewart monarch who was to suffer further vilification at the hands of later chroniclers and historians. Although some of the stories with which later writers were to support their negative views of James III have been proved to be fabrications or exaggerations, there is sufficient evidence to demonstrate his real shortcomings and defects of character, cast into even sharper relief by the fact that history's verdict on the reign of his son was to be so contrastingly positive.

CM

JAMES IV (1488-1513)

James IV was fifteen years old when he succeeded as king, following his father's death at Sauchieburn on 11 June 1488. He was crowned at the traditional site of Scone on 24 June, underlining his legitimacy and seeking to move forward from the difficult circumstances of his open rebellion against his father. The minority of James IV ran from his accession in 1488 until the spring of 1495, and although twenty-two was comparatively late to assume personal rule, he spent the years acquiring an impressive education and learning about the nature of royal government. Sir David Lindsay of the Mount had been at court as a young man, and knew James IV, therefore his description of the king as 'the glory of all princely governing' may reflect a genuine contemporary perception.

Problems with the post-Sauchieburn administration emerged almost immediately with a rebellion led by Robert, 2nd Lord Lyle, and John Stewart, earl of Lennox, disillusioned and embittered by their exclusion from a government dominated by the Hepburns, and frustrated by their failure to win the power and offices to which they felt entitled after their efforts in 1488. On 11 October 1489 the rebels were defeated in an engagement at the Field of the Moss, near the source of the river Forth, but the three estates pressed for political reconciliation and the parliament held in February 1490 annulled the forfeitures passed the previous summer. With the placating of Lyle and the Lennox Stewarts, James IV's government appears then to have enjoyed general support, and in stark contrast to his father's reign, his royal council represented the whole of the country, involving the most powerful men in the kingdom, such as Hume, Hepburn, Argyll, Angus and Huntly, giving a sense of consultative government. Consultative government, certainly after 1496, did not depend on the summoning of regular parliaments, as only three were held after James IV had assumed personal control. Given that parliament had become an established feature of late fifteenth century government, summoned at least once a year and sometimes more often, James IV's departure from this practice seems surprising, although one reason for his disinclination for parliaments was his personal experience of them as forums for dissent and squabbling factions. Provided that the king's councils were sufficiently representative of the political community to avoid the kind of alienation seen under James III, James IV could achieve most of his objectives without formally summoning the three estates. Parliamentary approval was deemed necessary for certain functions, such as pronouncing forfeitures, framing statutes and obtaining sanction for taxation, although this latter role was not exclusive to parliament as James managed to raise taxes in 1501, 1502 and 1512-13 without recourse to the three estates.

Conscious of the unpopularity of regular taxation, and his disinclination to summon regular parliaments, James IV strove to increase royal income largely by other means. At the beginning of the reign, royal income stood at approximately £13,000 Scots, but by 1513, this had increased to around £40,000 Scots. Crown lands and customs still brought in regular income, but it was the casual sources that proved particularly lucrative. These included 'apprising' which was the practice of valuing lands for sale to pay off debts; 'recognition' which allowed for the repossession of lands that had been dubiously or improperly alienated; the exaction of 'compositions' which were fees and fines for royal charters of confirmation. Not all of James IV's financial schemes evaded censure, however, and the practice of feu-farming of crown lands was condemned particularly on the basis that poor tenants could afford neither the new entry payment ('grassum') nor the increased rents produced by feu-farming, rendering them liable to eviction.

The parliaments that James IV did summon were concerned, principally, with the king's problematic Highland policies. Sporadic attempts to bring the Highlands and Islands under Crown control had only ever resulted in temporary success, for the simple reason that the chief men of the area, particularly the lord of the Isles, had been used to exercising power with effective autonomy, and the geographical distances involved in enforcing hard-won royal authority made it impossible to maintain. Law and order and the payment of royal rents depended on local co-operation, and when appeasement turned to coercion James IV found that royal intervention was met with determined resistance. There is an argument that it was the insensitive nature of royal demands, prompted largely by Archibald, 2nd earl of Argyll, who had a vested interest in the area, which created the backlash and ensured the failure of all attempts to bring the Highlands under firm control. Threats gave way to direct action with the hanging, in July 1499, of John MacDonald of Islay and his sons, but Argyll's royal commission to exercise Crown authority in the north-west met with such strong opposition – including the rebellion of Donald Dubh in the aftermath of the death of the lord of the Isles – that it was left unworkable. The situation did not improve immediately with the appointment of Alexander, 3rd earl of Huntly, as royal lieutenant and a parliament was summoned in 1504 to lay plans for a concerted Highland campaign involving a royal fleet. Another campaign in 1506 focussed on Torquil MacLeod of Lewis's continued defiance, with Huntly's force besieging MacLeod's castle of Stornoway. By early September MacLeod had fled and Donald Dubh was captured and held prisoner, thus ending his aspirations to the lordship of the Isles, but it was not until 1509 that parliament confirmed Huntly's successes in the north and west following a protracted and difficult campaign in which the king himself took little active part.

One of the principal grievances against James III had been the static nature of his government in Edinburgh, and his personal inaccessibility. By contrast, James IV worked energetically at travelling around the country on frequent justice ayres, settling feuds and being seen by his subjects. He took pains to extend the king's writ into distant parts of the kingdom, demonstrating his ability to travel in speed and safety throughout his realm. There was a pious element to some of these journeys, as they were pilgrimages undertaken both as penance for his father's death and at times of personal crisis, such as his wife's illness shortly after the birth of their son. His favoured sites were Whithorn in Galloway and St Duthac's shrine at Tain in Easter Ross. A further self-imposed penance was the wearing of an iron belt, and James also founded four houses of Observantine friars. Such outward demonstrations of piety did not prevent exploitation by the king, who required large subventions from the Church in order to finance his military campaigns, and made dubious nominations to important ecclesiastical offices, such as that of his brother James, duke of Ross, to the archbishopric of St Andrews in 1497 and the more scandalous appointment of his illegitimate son Alexander to the same office, aged eleven, in 1504. The motivation behind these nominations was the desire simultaneously to neutralize the potential political rivalry of his brother (as he would have been well aware of the problems caused by tensions between his father and his uncles) and to gain direct access to the rich revenues of the archbishopric.

James IV embodied those characteristics of medieval kingship most likely to appeal to contemporaries. He embraced the traditional noble sporting pursuits of hawking and hunting and organized a number of lavish tournaments, including the one held in Holyrood palace courtyard in August 1503 to celebrate his wedding, which lasted for three days. These tournaments attracted important competitors from the great courts of northern Europe, and James himself took an active part in the jousting, demonstrating skill in warrior-like pursuits and a willingness to lead from the front which drew the nervous observation from Don Pedro de Ayala, Spanish ambassador to the Scottish court, that the king frequently placed himself in danger. Such actions, however, were well calculated to endear him to his aristocracy and underline his fitness for leadership.

By far the greatest military investment made by James IV was the establishment, from 1502, of a royal navy, upon which he expended particular energy and resources. Apart from the prestige that an impressive naval force demonstrated, it had the practical purpose of offering a measure of protection to Scottish merchant shipping and allowing a response to attacks by English ships. Wooden keels were imported for the building of some of James IV's ships, including the *Margaret*, named after his queen, which was completed at Leith in 1505 at an estimated cost of £8,000. Deeming Leith to be inadequate for the purpose of constructing very large ships, the king established royal dockyards at Newhaven and Airth on the river Forth, the former being chosen for the construction of the famous *Great Michael*, completed in 1511, one of the largest wooden-walled ships ever built. The amount of timber needed was such that the oak forests of Fife were severely depleted, Norwegian wood having to be imported, and lavish spending on her artillery and fittings brought the eventual cost after four years of building to approximately £30,000. The staggering expense involved in building ships on this scale was such that the king had to turn to purchase, hire or joint-ownership of vessels to augment his navy, seconding ships for royal duties when necessary.

James IV was highly conscious of the importance of image and the necessity of enhancing royal prestige by emulating the style and fashions of the European Renaissance. Patronage of the Arts brought the king reflected glory in the quality of paintings, carvings, textiles and music associated with the court, and even some vessels of the king's navy, built for military purposes, were embellished by painters such as Alexander Chalmers. Ships also brought trade, and with well established diplomatic links, the Low Countries were an important source of many pieces of Renaissance art, and the Book of Hours made for James IV and Margaret Tudor is a particularly fine example of Flemish illumination. Literature also flourished during the reign of James IV, especially in the field of poetry; two of the best known poets of the period were William Dunbar and Gavin Douglas. Scotland's first printers, Walter Chapman and Andrew Myllar established their press in 1508 on the present site of Edinburgh's Cowgate, producing Bishop Elphinstone's Aberdeen Breviary in 1509-10, which was a new liturgy for Scotland, further emphasizing the importance and autonomy of the Scottish Church.

113. Tain Collegiate Church, Highland, the objective of James IV's marathon two-day ride from Stirling to visit the shrine of St Duthac.

114. Whithorn Priory, Dumfries and Galloway. James IV was a regular visitor to the shrine of St Ninian here.

115. The restored Great Hall of James IV's palace at Stirling Castle.

Considerable building work was undertaken at James IV's favoured palace of Holyrood, and at Linlithgow, where inspiration for many features was drawn from French and Italian models. The most extensive programme of spending and construction was the continuation of the work initiated by his father at Stirling, where James IV was responsible for the King's House, the Chapel Royal and the completion of the hugely impressive Great Hall. In terms of music, the great liturgical masses and motets by Robert Carver could rival those being composed in mainland Europe at the time, and the more vernacular native music was not overlooked, with James offering patronage to some of the great Gaelic harpists of his day.

Another facet of James IV's character that set him apart from his predecessors was his impressive knowledge, to a greater or lesser extent, of foreign languages. His long education, assisted by a number of learned tutors including Archibald Whitelaw, royal secretary, and John Ireland, royal confessor, who presented the king with his manual of kingship, 'The Meroure of Wyssdome' in 1490, would have contributed to the erudition described by Ayala. Allowances should be made for a certain amount of exaggeration in the list of languages given by Ayala in which James IV was supposedly proficient, some of which may have involved little more than a selection of words and phrases, but he almost certainly knew Latin and French, and his upbringing by his mother, Margaret of Denmark, until her death in 1486 would have given him considerable exposure to Danish. Although unlikely to have been fluent, James seems to have sought to acquire at least a smattering of Gaelic on his northern trips, and perhaps also from the Gaelic musicians to whom he was patron.

The reputation of James IV as a womanizer is not undeserved. He managed to devote some of his formidable energy to keeping a considerable string of mistresses, the first recorded being Marion Boyd, niece to Archibald, 5th earl of Angus, who bore him two illegitimate children, Alexander (later archbishop of St Andrews) and Catherine. Margaret Drummond appears to have succeeded Marion Boyd as royal mistress in 1496, bearing the king a daughter, also called Margaret. Although the liaison was over by 1497 and James had embarked on a long-running affair with Janet Kennedy in 1498, he continued to make payments to her and had his daughter brought from Drummond castle to Stirling following her mother's death in 1502. Janet Kennedy had been the mistress of Archibald, earl of Angus, but her affair with James IV lasted for some years, even following his marriage, and produced a son, James, earl of Moray, born around 1500. The king's pilgrimages to Tain in the early 1500's generally involved stops at Darnaway castle where Janet Kennedy was installed, and she was even brought to Bothwell in Lanarkshire to brighten the king's journey to Whithorn in 1503. A later liaison with Isabel Stewart, daughter of James, earl of Buchan, produced a daughter, Janet, while Bessie Bertram and the picturesquely named Janet 'bare-ars' both received royal gifts, recorded in the Treasurer's Accounts, for services not hard to presume! James IV's exuberant sex-life was a matter for comment by contemporaries, the Spanish ambassador, Ayala, alluding to the king's affairs with Marion Boyd and Margaret Drummond and expressing the somewhat forlorn hope that James, aware of his moral obligations, had given up scandalous liaisons. Dunbar's poem 'The Wowing of the King quhen He was in Dunfermeling' is based on the king's amorous activities, but the monarch appears to have had sufficient popularity to carry him through any serious censure.

In the exercise of foreign diplomacy, the minority government renewed the French alliance, Anglo-Scottish diplomacy having broken down by the end of James III's reign. Attempts to secure a French bride for James IV proved unsuccessful, and rapprochement with Henry VII brought about hopes that his daughter Margaret Tudor might be a suitable match. The reluctance of the English king to agree to this led to James IV taking measures between 1495-7 intended to bring pressure on Henry, particularly the adoption of Perkin Warbeck (styling himself Richard, duke of York), a pretender to the English throne. In September 1496, James and Warbeck led an invasion force into Northumberland, attacking and destroying tower houses in the Tweed and Till valleys, prompting Henry VII to plan a great Scottish expedition in 1497 to punish these incursions. He was forced to abandon these plans after taxation caused the Cornish rising and his resources had to be diverted to fight the battle of Blackheath, Surrey, on 17 June. James IV was quick to take advantage of Henry's problems by launching an attack on Norham castle in July, although he failed to take it.

With neither side able to press home an advantage and tiring of the struggle, Henry VII agreed to his daughter Margaret's marriage to the Scottish king, and in the Treaty of Perpetual Peace, signed in January 1502, an alliance between the two monarchs was arranged with elaborate rules laid down to deal with breaches of the peace both on land and at sea. A further stipulation was that all future English and Scottish kings were to renew the treaty within six months of their accession and papal confirmation of the treaty was to be sought to the extent that excommunication would follow for either king breaking the treaty. The marriage of James IV and Margaret Tudor took place on 8 August 1503 at Holyrood, although the bride's dowry of £10,000 sterling (approximately £35,000 Scots) was a comparatively paltry amount, possibly denoting Henry's lack of enthusiasm for the match. The 'Union of the Thistle and Rose' was to produce the Union of the Crowns in 1603, but at the time the English were uneasily aware that it brought James IV very close to the English throne if the Tudor line should fail.

In fact, the treaty did not lead to a marked improvement in Anglo-Scottish relations, and James IV refused to abandon the French alliance, receiving assistance from France in the form of shipwrights, timber and money in the construction of a royal navy – a project undertaken in 1502, the very year of the treaty! Disputes and breaches of the truce on the borders and at sea continued, one notable example of which was the murder of the Scottish march warden, Sir Robert Ker of Ferniehurst, by John Heron, styled Bastard Heron in the records. This happened on one of the 'days of truce' designated for both sides to hold courts which dealt with frontier offences, and such a serious violation rankled deeply with James IV, who was still demanding redress from the English as late as 1513.

Another incident involved Andrew Barton who, with his brothers John and Robert, was an experienced captain and ship owner, combining service to the king in his naval ambitions with a family career as privateers, preying on English and Continental shipping. The Bartons placed their privately owned vessels at the king's service, as did other Scottish ship owners, in order to augment the navy, and they enjoyed a degree of intimacy with the king which offered considerable protection against prosecution by their victims. Andrew Barton was mortally wounded in a sea fight with the English admiral, Sir Edward Howard, in 1511, prompting protests from James IV who chose to portray the incident in the light of an English violation of the truce, although the point was not laboured due to Barton's undoubtedly dubious piratical activities. The king did very little to disguise his growing preference for good relations with the French, and English nervousness increased when Henry VIII succeeded his father in April 1509, because until Henry produced a son (which was not until 1516), James IV, as his brother-in-law, was also his heir. If James was insensitive to the terms of the English treaty, then Henry VIII soon demonstrated his willingness to brush aside Scottish sensibilities in his desire to invade France.

116. James IV of Scotland, from a Low Countries heraldic roll.

117. Margaret Tudor, daughter of Henry VII of England, who married James in 1503.

118. The arms of Queen Margaret and Mary of Guise, drawn on lozenge shaped shields with crowns above.

James IV's expressed desire to go on crusade has led to charges of political naïveté and the harbouring of grandiose schemes reminiscent of James III's imperial ambitions. However, there is ample evidence that the king was seeking only to act as mediator for a reconciliation between his European allies, Pope Julius II and King Louis XII, in which context his enthusiasm for a crusade was a conventional diplomatic strategy to unite the forces of western Christendom against the Turks. In addition to this, the proffered possibility that his ships might be put to use in pursuing the pope's desire for a crusade was almost certainly a ploy to seek additional finance for the setting up of his navy. James used similar tactics with Louis XII when he was under pressure in 1511 after the formation by Pope Julius II of the so-called Holy League, including Emperor Maximilian, Venice, Ferdinand and Isabella of Spain and Henry VIII. When the League's war against France began in 1512, James IV formally renewed his alliance with France, seeking to build up an alternative league comprising France, Scotland, Denmark and the Irish lords, but was careful to capitalize on Louis XII's vulnerability to the extent that he secured an agreement in May 1513 that the French would equip and victual the Scottish fleet, grant 50,000 francs (about £22,500 Scots) and give James IV the services of seven war galleys commanded by his best admiral, Gaston Pregent de Bidoux.

The war got under way when Henry invaded northern France on 30 June 1513, last-minute efforts by the English ambassador, Nicholas West, to keep the Scots neutral having failed. Papal sentence of excommunication was to be delivered by Christopher Bainbridge, Cardinal-archbishop of York, an aggressive English nationalist and fierce Francophobe, but the Scots' attitude to their king's excommunication was probably to regard it as little more than an English political device which could soon be reversed. Henry VIII soon realized that in reality, his fellow league members were content to let him finance the campaign rather than offer much themselves in terms of practical support. In fact, the campaign consisted of one significant engagement, the 'battle of the Spurs', which was fought on 16 August, before the arrival of Henry VIII in person, and the taking of the towns of Therouanne and Tournai.

Intervention from the Scots came in the summer of 1513. A fleet consisting of thirteen ships, headed by the *Great Michael* and carrying an army of around 4,000 men under the command of James Hamilton, earl of Arran, sailed from the Forth, the king himself travelling on board the *Great Michael* as far as the Isle of May. James IV's naval ambitions never led to his undertaking long sea voyages himself, and he returned to shore in order to organize and lead the land-based phase of the operation. The fleet sailed north in order to avoid the English ships lying in the Downs to intercept them on their way to France, through the Pentland Firth and down past the Hebrides, pausing only to attack Carrickfergus, the main English stronghold in Ulster, on the way. Various delays, including those caused by bad weather, meant that the plan of a concerted attack on Henry VIII's ships by a combined force of Norman, Breton and Scottish fleets failed to materialize; the subsequent running aground of the *Great Michael* was only another blow to a Scottish nation already numbed by disaster.

The Scottish host had been summoned towards the end of July to be led by the king in person into Northumberland, prompting an impressive turnout of earls and lords of parliament, both in the army and with the fleet. At the outset, this was one of the largest armies ever to invade England, probably numbering between 30,000 and 40,000, indicating how popular this campaign was with the Scots, who would have anticipated rich pickings in plunder. James IV's impressive collection of artillery, comprising at least seventeen guns, dragged south by oxen, was put to use immediately, as the campaign got off to a good start with the storming of the Bishop of Durham's castle at Norham, just

119. Norham Castle, Northumberland, taken by James IV in his English campaign of 1513.
120. James IV with his queen, Margaret Tudor, sister of Henry VIII.
121. Sculpture of Mons Meg, Edinburgh Castle. Mons Meg was part of James IV's impressive artillery train.

122. The standard of the Earl Marischal of Scotland, carried at the battle of Flodden 1513 by Black John Skirving of Plewland Hill, his standard bearer. Skirving, having been taken prisoner, concealed the banner about his person. The relic was preserved in the Skirving family until the beginning of the nineteenth century when it was presented to the Faculty of Advocates. The banner bears three harts' heads erased, and the motto 'Veritas vincit'
123. Flodden battlefield, Northumberland, looking from Surrey's position towards Branxton Hill.

south of the Tweed, on 28-9 August. Having thus laid to rest the ghosts of past failures to take Norham, the Scots' army moved south up the Till valley taking the castles of Etal and Ford, the latter belonging to John Heron, who had killed the Scottish March warden around 1504.

The campaign succeeded in diverting some of Henry VIII's forces from waging war in France, and Thomas, earl of Surrey, commanded the English army mustered to do battle with the Scots. Bad weather and the problem of maintaining an army in the field were not sufficient to daunt James, who occupied a superior strategic position on Flodden Hill on the edge of the Cheviots, but the Scots were out-manoeuvred, leaving their positions in driving wind and rain to join battle with Surrey's forces on the rough and, in places, marshy terrain of the slopes of Branxton Hill on 9 September 1513. The conditions were completely unfavourable for the tactics chosen by the king and his commanders: namely the Swiss technique of organizing large phalanxes in close formation, and the tactic of sending forward lines of pikemen – the latter were unable to wield their weapons to good effect in close quarter fighting. Theories of military strategy were all very well, but were no substitute for skill and experience. The resulting carnage meant that the whole campaign, so promising at the outset, could scarcely have ended more disastrously, with the death of King James IV, the archbishop of St Andrews, one bishop, two abbots, nine earls, fourteen lords of parliament and thousands of rank and file.

CM

JAMES V (1513-1542)

The reign of James V, ushered in with yet another royal minority, was rendered still more unstable by the disastrous depletion of the adult males in the upper ranks of Scottish society at the battle of Flodden. James IV's widow, Margaret Tudor, became Queen Regent, in charge of her eighteen-month-old son's interests until he could rule in person, but as the sister of the English king Margaret was not universally popular in Scotland, and it was possibly to strengthen her position that she married the young Archibald Douglas, 6th earl of Angus, in 1514. Angus's pro-English policies were resented, and the minority of James V was characterized by power struggles, principally between the families of Hamilton, earl of Arran, and Douglas, earl of Angus. Some order was imposed under the governorship of John, duke of Albany, (the French son of James III's troublesome brother Alexander) between 1515 and 1524, one notable achievement being the negotiation of the Franco-Scottish treaty of Rouen in 1517. Indeed, the subsequent pro-French slant to James V's diplomacy stemmed from the influence brought to bear on the young king by his tutor, Gavin Dunbar, archbishop of Glasgow, and by Albany himself. However, Albany's governorship was punctuated with frequent absences in France, and efforts to satisfy competing interests in the struggle between Hamilton and Angus for control of the government were doomed to failure.

In 1525, a scheme was devised in the July parliament that allowed for four groups of magnates to keep custody of the young king in three-month rotations, at the end of which they would hand over to the next group. This scheme foundered when, at the end of the first quarter, Angus refused to relinquish control, fearing that his rival, James Hamilton, 1st earl of Arran, would destroy his influence. This led to a period of Douglas ascendancy based on control of the adolescent king, and it is hardly surprising that James, trapped as a pawn in this cynical game of power politics, resented Angus, chafing under his control and establishing the deep hatred which he harboured towards Angus for the rest of his life. Nor had his mother, Queen Margaret, remained enamoured of her second husband for long, and although her efforts to end Albany's authority as governor of Scotland and the Franco-Scottish amity espoused by him served the purposes of her brother, Henry VIII, her antipathy to Angus greatly hindered English plans to re-introduce him into a position of political influence. She was repeatedly exhorted to live with her husband once more and patch up their differences, this sensitive diplomacy being entrusted by Cardinal Wolsey to Thomas Magnus in 1524. When she subsequently divorced Angus and took as her third husband Henry Stewart, Lord Methven, she received a rebuke redolent of stones and glass houses when Henry warned his sister that her shifts in affection were harming her reputation!

In early June 1528, the sixteen-year-old James V effected a dramatic escape from Douglas-controlled Edinburgh Castle, choosing a time when Angus, by this time chancellor, and his uncle, Archibald Douglas of Kilspindie, were both absent from court (Kilspindie was allegedly visiting his mistress in Dundee) and making for Stirling, where he declared his minority to be at an end. Angus and his faction were forced out of government for more than a year, although the Douglases' rivals were not initially strong enough to destroy them, a royal siege of the great Douglas stronghold of Tantallon in the autumn of 1528 failing to remove the Douglas threat. Angus still retained powerful English support, and Thomas Magnus was sent to Scotland with the mission of reconciling James with Angus, impetus being given to his efforts by the fear that the king would contract a foreign marriage alliance. The inability of Angus to deal effectively with border lawlessness provided the perfect excuse for James V to challenge the authority of his erstwhile chancellor, and Angus was replaced as warden of the east march by George, 4th Lord Hume. Douglas of Kilspindie, styled 'Greysteil' by later writers after the eponymous hero of a late fifteenth-century epic poem, had reputedly been close to the young king and admired by him, but he too found himself ousted from his offices, ceding the position of keeper of the privy seal to George Crichton, bishop of Dunkeld, and the provostship of Edinburgh to Robert, Lord Maxwell. A long period of exile in England followed.

In common with most Stewart kings at the beginning of their personal rule, shortage of revenue was a major problem, and James V sought to solve it by emulating his father's exploitation of various sources of casual royal income, particularly the Scottish Church. James found himself in a uniquely strong position to do this, as Scotland was situated strategically north of a schismatic England, Henry VIII having broken with Rome at the outset of the 1530s over the matter of his divorce from Catherine of Aragon and subsequent marriage to Anne Boleyn. The prospect of the Scots maintaining their allegiance to the Catholic Church at a time when Protestant heresies were taking hold in various parts of Europe was sufficient for the papacy to give in to James V's demands. The lucrative nature of this mild blackmail brought the enormous windfall payment of £72,000 Scots, payable over four years, from the Scottish Church hierarchy, but the king's exploitation of the Church did not end there. The huge wealth of the abbeys of Kelso, Melrose and Holyrood and the priories of Pittenweem, St Andrews and Coldingham were made available to James V by the expedient of granting them to royal bastard infants (he had at least seven illegitimate children by six mistresses), making his father's peccadilloes and appointments of child bishops pale by comparison.

Another strong bargaining position was the matter of the king's marriage, with possible brides ranging from Danish, Italian and French candidates to his English cousin Mary Tudor. The diplomatic courting of James V led to his acquiring several honours, including the English Order of the Garter, the French Order of St Michael and the Imperial Order of the Golden Fleece, although he ultimately followed his inclination towards an alliance with Catholic France. James took the unusual step of personally sailing for France to meet his projected bride, Mary of Bourbon, daughter of the duke of Vendome, whose offered dowry was 100,000 crowns (in excess of £100,000 Scots). Once he arrived at the duke's court, apparently incognito, he decided against Mary on the less-than-gallant grounds that she was a 'misshapen hunch-back'. Finding Madeleine, the daughter of the French king, François I, more attractive – both physically and in terms of prestige – James secured her hand and the couple were married in Paris, in the cathedral of Nôtre Dame, on 1 January 1537. Sadly, her charms clearly masked a sickly constitution, and she died at Holyrood shortly after their return to Scotland.

Still determined to make a French marriage, James despatched David Beaton (soon to become Archbishop of St Andrews) to negotiate a second match, and the result of his diplomacy was the marriage of James V to Mary of Guise-Lorraine. She was the sister of François, duke of Guise, and Charles, cardinal of Lorraine, and such was her importance in the marriage market that she had also attracted the attention of Henry VIII, his third wife, Jane Seymour, having died bearing him a son. Her preference for the Scottish king (an element of self-preservation perhaps affecting her choice!) and the consequent strengthening of the 'Auld Alliance' infuriated the rejected Henry. For the Scots, the whole enterprise had been very lucrative, with the dowries for James's two French marriages amounting to a total of £168,750 Scots; a sum five times the amount received by James IV on his marriage to Margaret Tudor in 1503.

The image of James V as a ruthless character stems largely from the notorious executions of John, Master of Forbes, and Janet, lady Glamis, in 1537. In addition to this, the king launched attacks of varying severity on certain border families such as the Maxwells, Johnstons, Scotts, Humes and Armstrongs, but most of this was to do with his determination to purge all those with Douglas connections, possessed as he was with an immoderate hatred of his former chancellor, Angus. The burning at the stake on Castle Hill in Edinburgh of Janet, lady Glamis, aroused public sympathy and censure of the king, but although she was accused of trying to poison him, her real crime in his eyes was the support she extended to her brother Archibald, earl of Angus. The king was certainly not above exploiting certain vulnerable members of the nobility, compelling the 3rd earl of Morton to make over his earldom to the Crown and forcing the Master of Crawford to renounce his succession to the Crawford earldom.

A similarly cynical motive may have lain behind the execution of Sir James Hamilton of Finnart, Master of Works, in August 1540. Finnart had been in charge of the substantial building work undertaken to extend and improve Falkland palace, but his services to the king were not sufficient to prevent his downfall. In 1540, charges brought against Hamilton included the accusation that he had entered into a plot to kill the king with members of the disgraced Douglas family. In 1529, Finnart had been involved in tentative negotiations with Archibald Douglas of Kilspindie, uncle of the earl of Angus, aimed at seeking the latter's political rehabilitation, and this may have been sufficient to condemn him in the eyes of the king, who consequently secured Finnart's considerable wealth.

124. James V, by an unknown artist.
125. Princess Madeleine of France, James's first wife.
126. James's second wife, Mary of Guise.
127. Illustration from the Seton Armorial showing James and Mary.

Fear of treason and conspiracy, a common factor in the charges brought against most of those attacked by the king, has been viewed as evidence of James' extreme unpopularity, but this was heavily exaggerated by later writers. It was clearly not sufficient to prevent James V leaving his realm for nine months in 1536-7, a strong indication that he did not feel seriously threatened or lacking control over his kingdom.

James spent lavishly on building projects, continuing his predecessors' work on the showcase palace at Linlithgow which drew praise even from Mary of Guise, accustomed as she was to the great châteaux of the Loire. He also, in line with the imperial pretensions first exhibited by his grandfather, issued the gold 'bonnet piece' of 1539 which carried the king's portrait on one side and an imperial crown on the other. The Scottish crown was itself remodelled and enriched under the king's direction in time for its use by him at the queen's coronation at Holyrood in 1540.

In the spring of 1540, James V launched an impressive naval expedition to the northern and western Isles, returning to Edinburgh by 6 July. A number of Highland men were taken to the castles of Dunbar and Tantallon and to the Bass Rock, probably as hostages for the good rule of their chieftains, and it seems that James's principal objective was to repeat the strategy exercised over the border lords in order to curb their lawlessness. On that occasion, in May 1530, the king had ridden to the borders to dispense justice personally, during which time the chief border magnates remained in ward – effectively a voluntary imprisonment to demonstrate loyalty. The aim, of course, was to underline his authority over all parts of his kingdom, sending the message that disloyalty would be punished and that he was a force to be reckoned with. Robert, Lord Maxwell, one of the warded border magnates, does not appear to have suffered from this, appreciating that he would do well to demonstrate his loyalty to the king and securing his monarch's good graces to the extent that he was appointed as one of the vice-regents of the realm in 1536-37 when the king was in France.

The succession seemed secure when the queen fulfilled her duty as consort by giving birth to two sons, James in 1540 and Arthur in 1541. Unfortunately, both princes died in 1541 in a chilling echo of the deaths of James IV's first two sons bearing the same names, but by the spring of 1542, Mary was pregnant again, giving birth on 8 December at Linlithgow to a daughter – the future Mary Queen of Scots.

In the autumn of 1542, Henry VIII renewed his claim to English overlordship of Scotland, and although it was late in the campaigning season, a Scottish army was put into the field, the earl of Huntly achieving initial success at Hadden Rig, near Berwick, following which the duke of Norfolk abandoned his invasion in October. This defensive action was followed by a Scottish offensive that ended in the defeat of a Scottish force under the command of Robert Lord Maxwell on 24 November at Solway Moss by an English force under Sir Thomas Wharton. This encounter was little more than a skirmish, the Scots finding themselves strategically wrong-footed between a river and a bog, apparently fighting as valiantly as possible before surrendering. Seven Scots were killed in the engagement and Maxwell was taken prisoner, but later English rumours that he preferred capture to returning to face the wrath of James V have no apparent basis in fact. Plans to renew the war in the spring were cut short by the death of James V at Falkland Palace from either cholera or dysentery on 14 December, six days after the birth of his daughter, at the age of only thirty.

Many of the colourful stories which have grown up around the character of James V, in common with several of his Stewart predecessors, are embellishments or, in some cases,

128. Palace of Holyroodhouse, Edinburgh. A modern facsimile of a seventeenth-century engraving showing the palace as remodelled by James V.

129. The statue of James V adorning the north-east angle of the renaissance palace block at Stirling Castle.

130. 'Bonnet Piece' of James V, with the imperial crown on the reverse.

131. Falkland Palace, Fife, extensively remodelled in French style for James V and the scene of his death in December 1542.

fabrications by later writers. John Knox's recounting of the famous deathbed scene at Falkland when the king is reputed to have responded to the news of the birth of his daughter with the words 'it cam wi' a lass and it'l gang wi' a lass' comes under this heading, as does Walter Scott's enduring legend of the king roaming incognito among his subjects as 'the guidman of Ballengeich'. Instances of James V's cruelty and arbitrary brutality were also exaggerated by later writers with a Protestant axe to grind against the defender of orthodoxy in the face of the forces of reformation: although James did act ruthlessly on occasion, it was within the sphere of practical politics and not notably with greater severity than his predecessors. In fact, James V seems to have enjoyed a considerable degree of support from the political community during his reign and, but for yet another untimely Stewart death, there is no reason to suppose that he would not have continued to do so.

CM

MARY (1542-1567)

Mary Queen of Scots was the only surviving child of James V and Queen Mary of Guise, born on 8 December 1542 at Linlithgow Palace just before her father's untimely demise on 14 December. James V was disappointed at the birth of a daughter and apparently, according to John Knox, indicated that the Stewart dynasty would pass as it had begun – 'wi' a lass'. This was premature, for the official Stewart line would not die out until the death of Queen Anne in 1714, while James's six-day-old daughter was to become the most famous queen of Scotland.

Mary's early childhood was spent in the sheltered environment of the royal court. Her baptism, coming soon after her father's funeral, was an unfussy ceremony that no one bothered to comment upon. She would have known little of the political tensions that emerged during her minority government. Neither would she have known much about the terrible Anglo-Scottish warfare and English occupation of southern Scotland, brought about by her very existence. Although only a baby, England's Henry VIII had determined that Mary should be betrothed to his heir, the sickly Prince Edward. Although this was initially agreed to, the Scots reneged on the deal within months of Mary's coronation at Stirling Castle on 9 September 1543. The 'Rough Wooing' then began that would devastate much of the Borders and eastern Scotland during the mid-1540s. There was a real threat that the occupying English forces would attempt to kidnap the young queen, so she was kept at Stirling during these troubled years. It was only during Scotland's darkest hour after the defeat at Pinkie in September 1547, that Mary was secreted away to remote Inchmahome Priory.

After Stirling, where Mary had many young friends and the personal attention of her mother, Inchmahome would have been rather austere. During her stay here, help from France arrived in Scotland to start repelling the English forces. The 'Auld Alliance' between Scotland and France appeared to be functioning once more, but there were some who muttered that French help had come late. France's intervention complicated Mary's life even more for they demanded that she become betrothed to King Henri II's heir, the Dauphin François. Her mother favoured a French alliance and the government agreed to send Mary to France in the summer of 1548. The five-year-old queen was sent to Dumbarton Castle to await her passage to France by the western sea route. It was feared that English ships might have tried to seize her if she travelled by the East Coast. Mary of Guise chose to remain in Scotland, putting duty before family. Mary was accompanied by many of her early childhood

132. Linlithgow Palace, Lothian. Mary was born in the Queen's Apartments in the north quarter of the palace.

133. Inchmahome Priory, Lake of Menteith, Stirlingshire. Mary was taken for safety to the island monastery after Henry VIII launched his 'Rough Wooing' of Scotland.

134. The château of Blois, where Mary spent time in 1551 and 1559.
135. The château of Amboise, Indre-et-Loire, where Mary may have watched the hanging of
Protestants from the castle walls.

household, but the most noted of these would be the faithful 'Four Maries' (i.e., the Marys Beaton, Fleming, Livingston and Seton).

Mary arrived at Roscoff in France on 13 August 1548. She would not return to her native Scotland for thirteen years. Her party joined the household of the French royal children and Mary met her future husband, the four-year-old Dauphin François, for the first time. They became good friends thereafter and François's young sister, Princess Elisabeth, became Mary's closest friend during this period of her life. Mary spoke only Scots at this time, so she hurriedly learnt French to please both her hosts and her Guise relations. This transformation to Francophile culture was so successful that when Mary returned to Scotland as an adult, she had forgotten much of her native Scots tongue and preferred using French for the rest of her life.

Mary of Guise visited her in 1550 and noted that her daughter was progressing with her linguistic studies, as well as learning the social graces expected of an elite lady. Mary's governess, Madame de Parois, made sure that her charge could write in the fashionable Italianate hand of the European elite. Mary also dabbed with Latin and Greek, but her scholarship was not on a par with that of Princess Elizabeth of England, who was one of the ablest female scholars of her age. Elizabeth, though not intended to be a future ruler, read Machiavelli's *The Prince*. Mary, despite already being a queen, was not schooled in the politics of government by the French court. They assumed she would be their Dauphiness, rather than an independent ruler, and thus denied Mary the full education she needed for what would be a troubled future. Mary was, however, an accomplished musician and poet who had a higher appreciation of culture than most women of her age.

Despite Mary's hurried exit from Scotland to France in 1548, Henri II's ambitions for Mary's throne were not settled until 1558. Some French politicians complained about the high costs involved with helping the Scots, which delayed a final decision on the marriage of Mary and the Dauphin. It was only when France needed to utilize her traditional alliance with the Scots once more, as a bolster to their 'Auld Enemy' of England, that serious negotiations began. The Catholic Mary Tudor of England had died and was succeeded by her Protestant sister Elizabeth. Mary had no part in these discussions, leaving everything to her Scottish commissioners. They represented the Scots Parliament and naturally wanted the best agreement for both Scotland and her queen. Mary and the Dauphin were formally betrothed on 11 April 1558 amidst much public rejoicing in Paris. Their official marriage contract recognized the rights of the Scottish nation and noted that the Scots and French people were to have dual nationality. If François died Mary could stay in France or return to Scotland. If Mary died then the succession of the nearest heir to the throne, the earl of Arran, was recognized. This was acceptable to the Scots' negotiators, but unbeknown to them a secret treaty had been signed by their queen that promised Scotland to François if Mary should die without issue.

Skulduggery was clearly at work here for half of the Scottish commissioners would die in mysterious circumstances before they landed back in Scotland. Henri II had insisted that the wedding would not proceed until secret papers were signed. Mary was so obsessed with getting married that she knowingly signed away her kingdom without bothering to consult any Scots. Her detachment from political reality in this instance does her no credit for she had lived for a decade in one of the most corrupt and powerful royal courts of Europe. Mary knew of manipulation and intrigues, yet fell in with French ambition in her haste to show off her finery at what would be truly magnificent nuptials. What she failed to appreciate was that Scotland was not hers to give away. Only parliament could pronounce on the future of the Scottish nation, since Mary was queen of Scots, not queen of Scotland.

136. Mary Queen of Scots at the age of nine.
137. The queen mother, Mary of Guise, who acted as Mary's regent.
138. François II of France, who married the young queen in 1558.
139. Palace of Holyroodhouse, Edinburgh. Mary established her court in the palace in 1561.

The marriage was solemnized on 24 April 1558 at Notre Dame Cathedral. Mary's Guise relations basked in the triumph of their niece marrying the heir to the French throne. Behind the scenes the marriage changed little in the relationship between the sickly François and Mary. They continued as good friends rather than passionate lovers. Henri II urged Mary to press her claim to the English throne by quartering the arms of England in her new coat of arms. Much of Europe did not recognize Elizabeth's monarchy, preferring to see Mary as rightful heir as the granddaughter of Margaret Tudor and great-granddaughter of Henry VII. However, English reaction and the tripartite Anglo-Franco-Spanish peace treaty of Câteau-Cambrésis in 1559 temporarily halted Henri's support for Mary's claim.

The health of the sickly Dauphin continued to cause alarm, yet it was not François but Henri II's untimely death, in June 1559, that would upset Mary's plans. Henri died as a result of an accident during a jousting tournament. This had been planned as part of the marriage festivities for Mary's childhood friend Princess Elisabeth, who married Philip II of Spain as a result of the Câteau-Cambrésis agreement. Whilst the French court mourned, plans were made for the coronation of François and Mary at Rheims in September 1559.

Mary was now queen of two nations facing challenges from Calvinists. Instead of the strong leadership of her father-in-law she witnessed François making an inept attempt as French king. He was more interested in hunting than affairs of state and did little to stop religious strife. To make matters worse Mary's mother was finding it very difficult to control Scotland. This was followed by a troubled 1560 as Mary's mother died in June with civil war underway in Scotland and François died from a brain abscess in December. Mary was inconsolable at first, but then realized that she had power back in her own hands and could manipulate her situation. Ambassadors flocked to her chambers with offers of royal marriage. Mary apparently wanted to marry the Spanish infanta Don Carlos, but this was unacceptable to France. In the end Mary decided that her best option was to return to Scotland.

Mary's entourage left Calais on 14 August, playing 'cat and mouse' with aggressive English warships in the Channel. Despite a North Sea fog they made good time, so that when the galleys docked at Leith early in the morning of 19 August no one was ready to welcome their queen. No one had expected her to arrive so soon. Local dignitaries hurriedly gathered to greet Mary and they could not have failed to be impressed by her appearance. With Stewart, Tudor and Guise blood in her veins Mary was now six feet tall and a great beauty of her age. In fact she would have towered over the majority of Scottish people, reinforcing her regal superiority. They escorted Mary to a nearby house for refreshments and word quickly spread that the queen had returned. Crowds gathered to welcome Mary and escort her to Holyroodhouse, where the hastily gathered nobility awaited their queen. Mary's welcome lasted for several days with general music and merrymaking. Most were delighted to have their young, vivacious queen back to rule in person. However, a minority of leading religious reformers including John Knox demurred from this welcome. Knox's greatest fear was that her return would upset the progress of the Scottish Reformation, which had been underway for two years.

Knox made his point a few days after Mary's return when she went to Mass in Holyrood Chapel. An angry crowd gathered to protest about the service and a riot was only prevented by the intervention of Mary's half-brother, Lord James Stewart. The reality of being a resident monarch in a religiously divided nation now hit Mary. Her insistence in maintaining her faith had to be explained, but she also had to concede to the wishes of those Scots who now worshipped in the Protestant manner. She declared that Scots could now worship as they pleased, which was a wise move in the circumstances but did not placate the intransigent Knox and his followers. Mary's entry into Edinburgh was outwardly joyous, yet there were oppositional religious undertones in some of the festivities. For the queen there was only one way to resolve this situation; she must confront John Knox.

At this infamous meeting, for which we only have Knox's point of view, there was plain speaking by both sides. Mary saw his challenge to her authority as treasonable and argued sternly that subjects must obey their princes. Knox saw her faith as the major obstacle and put forward academic arguments that Mary did not have the ability to answer. Mary was never going to change her faith, so she and Knox were destined never to agree. Knox was certainly in the habit of upsetting queens, whom he regarded as a 'monstrous regiment' unless they were good Protestants who put their duty to God before their kingdoms. It was perhaps fortunate for Knox that he was dealing with Mary, rather than her mother-in-law, Catherine de Medici, who would order the massacre of French Calvinists in 1572. It is also worth noting that Knox's monstrous regiment was not intended to be womenkind in general, whom he admired and loved just as long as they were dutiful Protestant wives and mothers. His argument was with Catholic rulers whom he regarded as oppressors.

Religion would continue to cause trouble during Mary's personal rule, but she never let it curtail her activities. Mary, like her Stewart forebears, wanted to see more of her kingdom and travelled extensively during 1561-67 visiting Lowlands, Highlands and Borders. She never reached the Isles, but stands out as the last Stewart monarch to traverse much of the kingdom of the Scots. None of her successors' progresses compare with her itineraries. Many castles and houses can justly boast that 'Mary Queen of Scots slept here'. For instance in the late summer and autumn of 1562 Mary went from Holyrood to Angus, Aberdeenshire, Banff and Inverness, returning by a different East Coast route. This was rather longer than intended as Mary had been forced to face the first noble insurrection of her personal rule. The earl of Huntly's forces faced up to those of the queen, led by Lord James Stewart (now the earl of Moray), at Corrichie on 28 October 1562. Huntly was defeated and disgraced, but died before his trial for treason. Mary had triumphed with the help of her half-brother and was not deterred from further journeys. In the summer of 1563 her progress went from Edinburgh to Inveraray Castle, then to Whithorn and by way of Peebles back to Holyrood. The reaction of the Scots to Mary's travels was enthusiastic. Those who lived in remoter parts of the realm were struck by Mary's poise and beauty.

With the exception of Corrichie and simmering religious tensions, Mary's first years back in Scotland appear idyllic. She had a fairly laid back approach to affairs of state, letting her councillors discuss and administer royal policy whilst she did her needlework. Mary had a tendency to be overly-emotional if events did not turn out the way she hoped. Her bouts of crying are well documented and tended to be quite prolonged. This, added to her hands off approach to government, made her look very much like the 'weaker vessel' of early modern society. Mary never really understood that to succeed as a female monarch you had to display supposedly masculine attributes such as bravery, confidence and political astuteness. Mary did persist with her claim to the English throne, but Elizabeth was always reluctant to name any successors. A meeting between the two queens was scheduled but never materialized. They were destined never to meet in person but corresponded with each other on a regular basis.

It is ironic that Mary wanted to remarry to cement her claims to England, yet the smart Elizabeth refused all offers of marriage to hold on to her wealth and power. The possibility of Mary remarrying was common gossip in Scotland. Mary was not short of suitors including Don Carlos who was once more proposed as her husband. This would have caused religious ructions in Scotland, so it was as well that Don Carlos was declared unfit to marry after a tragic accident. Elizabeth now pitched in her candidates, Lord Robert Dudley and Henry, Lord Darnley, a second cousin of Mary's. Elizabeth's intentions were mischievous, for she planned to veto any marriage with an English subject. However all this scheming backfired spectacularly when Mary fell in love with the nineteen-year-old Darnley and refused to send him back to England.

Mary's choice was disliked by the Scottish nobility, particularly her long-time supporter Moray, who feared that Darnley's blood relationship to the queen would reduce their powers. Mary married Darnley on 29 July 1565 at Holyrood. Their ceremony was at the unusually early hour of six o'clock to prevent any rioting about the ceremony's Catholic rites. Celebrations were held later that day with feasting and dancing. The next day Mary declared Darnley as King of Scots, but this did not amount to the granting of the crown matrimonial which would have to be discussed by parliament. The title of king had not been discussed with the nobility so it was little wonder that this announcement was greeted with stony silence. Mary's marriage was really the start of her fall from grace since Darnley would prove an unsuitable consort – childish, arrogant and selfish. If Mary hoped that he could be moulded into kingship she was mistaken.

Resentment of Darnley's position caused another serious challenge to Mary's reign, when Moray, who had been her right-hand man, rebelled against her in the so-called Chaseabout Raid of 1565. Mary played a personal part in putting down this insurrection, showing signs of good leadership in adversity, but more dangers lay ahead that would not be so easily quashed. Moray fled to England to rally support for his cause. Darnley became bored with playing king and chose to boycott vital meetings. He was little support to Mary when she discovered that she was pregnant that autumn. Darnley then became jealous of any men who had the confidence of the queen and singled out David Riccio, Mary's Italian secretary, for revenge. He also planned to use sympathetic nobles to gain the crown matrimonial from parliament and reduce Mary's role in government. These were treasonable intentions that disgraced the nation.

On 9 March 1566 the infamous murder of Riccio at Holyrood was perpetrated by Darnley, Lord Ruthven, Lord Lindsay, the earl of Morton and others. That Mary did not miscarry after witnessing this horrible murder is miraculous. She determined to shut out Darnley from her affections, but had to deal with the more immediate problem of large scale political opposition to her rule. Mary tried to handle this by pardoning those lords involved with the Chaseabout Raid, but not those involved with Riccio's murder. This was a stop-gap measure that allowed her to have her baby in relative peace. Prince James was born in Edinburgh castle on 19 June. There was widespread rejoicing that Scotland had a male heir to the throne once more, but James's arrival signalled another decline in his mother's fortunes. Renegades could now place their hopes in the future king of Scots and sideline his mother, just as other factions had done throughout the Stewart dynasty in Scotland.

James was placed in the care of Lord Mar at Stirling castle for his own protection. In doing this she confined her infant son to a solitary and cruel upbringing, but Mary hoped this would pre-empt any coups from using her son against her. Once again Mary's political judgement was poor, for within a year she would be forced into a humiliating surrender to rebel lords at Carberry Hill, near Musselburgh. Scottish government was now out of control and it would have taken a monarch with considerable political skill to handle this situation. Unfortunately Mary lacked experience in crisis management and it cost her the throne of Scotland.

140. Henry Stewart, Lord Darnley, Mary's second husband, with his young brother Charles.
141. The queen and Darnley as depicted in the Seton Armorial.
142. The queen's musician, David Riccio, who was killed by Lord Darnley and his
co-conspirators in 1566.

143. Colour sketch of the scene of Darnley's assassination in Kirk o' Fields, by an unknown artist (nineteenth-century facsimile of sixteenth-century original).

144. Portrait miniature and signature of the earl of Bothwell, the prime suspect in the murder of Lord Darnley.

145. Lochleven castle, where Mary was imprisoned after her scandalous liaison with Bothwell.

Mary's downfall was due to exceptional circumstances and her own poor judgement. Her marriage to Darnley had irretrievably broken down. Attempts at reconciliation were futile and it was just too convenient for Mary when Darnley was murdered at Kirk O' Field during the early hours of 10 February 1567. The explosion that demolished the house at Kirk O' Field woke the entire town, yet this was not the cause of Darnley's death. His corpse mysteriously appeared lying on the lawn of a nearby garden without a scratch on it. This was one of the most notorious murders in the annals of Scottish history and remains unsolved to this day. The finger of suspicion pointed at James Hepburn, earl of Bothwell, and his henchmen, though many others were probably in on the plot to kill Darnley. Mary was also suspected as she had formed an attachment to this roguish earl well before Darnley's murder.

Falling for Bothwell's devilish charm was Mary's greatest *faux pas*. Her reputation never recovered from the events of 1567. Apologists maintain that she turned to the earl in desperation and that he took full advantage. There is no doubting that Bothwell's ambition to marry Mary was paramount, but Mary's willingness to wed him on 15 May is beyond dispute. Just to make matters worse she allowed this ceremony to be held by Protestant rites, making her look hypocritical. Scotland descended into civil war with those who supported Mary being known as the 'Queen's Men' and those who espoused the cause of young Prince James, the 'King's Men'. During Mary's surrender at Carberry on 15 June, Bothwell was nowhere to be seen. Even he had deserted the queen, and would end his days in 1578 as a royal prisoner in Dragsholm Castle in Denmark. Mary was incarcerated at Lochleven Castle. There she suffered a miscarriage of twins around 23 July, while under pressure to abdicate in favour of her infant son. She signed papers to this effect on 24 July.

Mary could not be written off as queen of Scots at this point, for her supporters liberated her from Lochleven in May 1568. These Queen's Men lost the subsequent battle at Langside, however, forcing Mary to flee into England on 16 May. An even longer incarceration now awaited Mary, as her cousin Elizabeth could not let Mary roam freely in a kingdom she counter-claimed. Mary did herself no favours by getting involved in various intrigues to gain the English throne. That she was not charged with treason until the autumn of 1586 was probably due to Elizabeth's reluctance to prosecute a fellow royal. Nonetheless Mary's execution at Fotheringhay castle on 8 February 1587 shocked Europe. Regardless of the threat Mary posed to Elizabeth, regicide was still a rare event. Martyrdom has kept Mary at the forefront of interest in Scottish history, but most forget that the most tragic figure of all was the orphaned King James, who lacked the presence of any close family in his formative years. After the Union of the Crowns in 1603 James VI ordered Fotheringhay to be demolished and moved his mother's remains from Peterborough Cathedral to Westminster Abbey. They were re-interred in a splendid tomb that outshines the nearby tomb of Queen Elizabeth I. James had finally been allowed to honour his mother's memory, just as any dutiful son would.

MM

JAMES VI (1567-1625)

James VI was the only child of Mary Queen of Scots and her second husband, Henry, Lord Darnley. He was born at Edinburgh castle on 19 June 1566, during a very troubled period of Scottish history. His baptism by Catholic rite at Stirling in December 1566 was a magnificent occasion. However, the euphoria of this event was quickly dissipated by

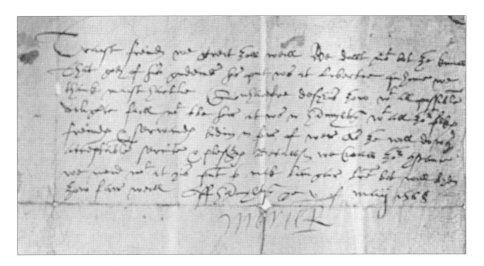

146. Letter from Mary to Maxwell of Pollock, commanding him to join her forces at
Hamilton prior to the battle of Langside.
147. Dundrennan Abbey, Dumfries and Galloway, where Mary spent her last night on Scottish soil.
148. Tapestry attributed to Mary during her long years of captivity in England.

the murder of James's father in February 1567. This was followed by his mother's hasty remarriage, capitulation to rebel lords and incarceration at Lochleven, during which she abdicated in favour of her son. Thus, at the age of one, James was crowned King of Scots at Scone on 29 July 1567. Apart from this visit to Scone, the young king was kept at Stirling castle for his own protection. Here James was looked after by the earl and countess of Mar, whose strictness ensured that his childhood was a miserable experience. He was given a thorough education but one of his tutors, George Buchanan, never failed to remind his young pupil that his mother was little better than a whore. He terrified the young king and made sure that his tutee would become a rigorous defender of Protestantism. Religion did play a central part in James's adult life and he was an able scholar, but his early years were devoid of the emotional support that children need. He was, in his own words, 'without father or mother, brother or sister'.

Scotland was governed by a succession of regents during the minority of James VI. Their turnover is symbolic of the political turbulence that beset the nation during this time. The first regent was his half-uncle, the earl of Moray, who was murdered in January 1570. Power then passed to James's grandfather, the earl of Lennox, but he was shot in September 1571. The next regent was the king's guardian, the earl of Mar. He died of natural causes in October 1572 to be succeeded by the infamous earl of Morton. Morton was not deposed until 1580 and was subsequently executed in 1581 for his part in Riccio's murder. James was still too young to rule in person, so control rested with whoever had custody of his person. In 1580 this was Esmé Stewart, soon to become duke of Lennox, who had recently returned from France. Lennox was a cousin of the king's father and was thus warmly welcomed by him. Others were less than pleased by Lennox's influence over the king and this led to another scarring episode in the young king's life known as the 'Ruthven Raid'. A band of nobles led by the Lord Ruthven, newly created as earl of Gowrie, kidnapped the king in August 1582 and held him captive for ten months.

James liberated himself from the clutches of the Ruthven family in June 1583. He was still not old enough to rule in person, however, and factions continued to battle for the control of Scottish government. This time it was James Stewart, earl of Arran, who rose to prominence, but he fell from grace in November 1585 leaving James to govern his own kingdom at last. The nineteen-year-old monarch inherited the same factional turmoil that most of his Stewart ancestors had to cope with. Nevertheless, from the outset James determined to be a peacemaker rather than warmonger. This was a creditable stance for a young ruler, and accounts for the nobility being made to walk hand in hand to a royal banquet in May 1586. Sadly this harmony would not last, for within weeks some of the nobility were at loggerheads again. Noble feuding would continue for much of James' reign, but the king continued to attempt pacification between feuding parties during his Scottish residency. The only thing he did not tolerate were noble challenges to his right to rule the Scots.

The first international challenge to James's monarchy came in February 1587 when his mother was executed by Elizabeth I of England. He sensibly did not avenge this action and left it to diplomats to publicly express his sorrow about Mary's death. By this time he was receiving a handsome annuity from Queen Elizabeth, so he could hardly bite the hand that fed him. In private he was upset by the turn of events, regardless of the anti-Mary vitriol he had been force fed by George Buchanan. He hoped that he would

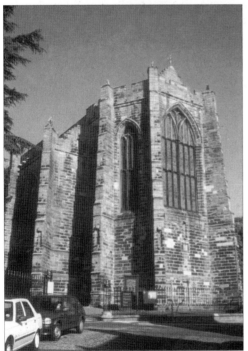

149. Edinburgh Castle, birthplace of James VI on 19 June 1566.
150. Church of the Holy Rude, Stirling, scene of the infant king's coronation.
151. The first of James's many regents, his half-uncle James Stewart, earl of Moray.

152. A youthful portrait of King James VI of Scotland (aged around 14 years) seated on a throne.
153. Thistle Merk piece of James VI.

succeed to the English throne and fulfill his mother's ambition for a Stewart to be monarch of both realms. Elizabeth would, however, never publicly acknowledge James as her heir, so Anglo-Scottish relations had to remain friendly until her death in 1603. James would, nevertheless, order a splendid tomb to be made for his mother's remains in Westminster Abbey after 1603.

Now that James was an orphan, his thoughts naturally turned to the future of the Stewart dynasty. He was expected to marry and brides were sought from European royal houses. Scotland was not a rich country, but the prospect of James becoming king of England made him an eligible royal batchelor. The final choice was between two Protestant princesses; the older Katherine of Navarre and the younger Anna of Denmark. James apparently prayed and meditated about this before opting to marry Anna, the daughter of Frederick II. Some felt that he should have opted for the thirty-year-old Katherine, but it was the fourteen-year-old Anna who won his heart. Preparations were made for the marriage which took place by proxy, on 20 August 1589, at the stately Kronborg castle in Denmark. Anna should then have set sail for Scotland, but bad weather in the North Sea forced her flotilla back to Norway (which was then part of Denmark). James grew impatient with her delay and eventually sailed to Norway to meet his bride for the first time. They duly met on 19 November 1589 and were married again in person. They used French as a medium as neither could speak each other's language at first. As the winter was setting in the couple accepted the invitation of Anna's mother, Queen Sophia, to stay in Denmark until the spring. James and Anna therefore had a longer than usual honeymoon at the Danish Court, during which time there were many celebrations. This also bonded the lonely James to a large loving family, whom he got to know well. In return Anna's family stayed in touch with the couple, visiting whenever opportunity allowed. They were especially close to King Christian IV, Anna's younger brother, who would rule Denmark until 1648. Anna never really lost her Danish roots, nor wanted to, unlike the more usual acclimatization expected of a Scottish queen of foreign birth.

The Scottish mercantile communities were delighted by the wedding as it promised them special favour when trading to the Baltic countries through Danish-controlled Øresund. Lavish wedding gifts were forthcoming from the burghs and the Scottish elite. This was just as well for Scotland was not really ready for the extra expense that the marriage would incur. There had not been separate king's and queen's households since the days of James V and Mary of Guise and each household had its own budgets to meet. None of the royal palaces were really prepared for Anna's arrival either as little had been spent on them in decades. James knew that he would be embarrassed by the relative poverty of Scottish monarchy compared to the opulence of Danish royalty upon their return.

James and Anna landed at Leith on 1 May 1590. The new queen consort was crowned on 17 May and made a magnificent entry into Edinburgh on the same day. There had not been such a grand occasion for a queen of Scots since the joint coronation and entry of Margaret Tudor in 1503. Everything looked rosy for the young king and his even younger bride, but it would prove to be a rather stormy relationship on occasion. Their family backgrounds could not have been more diverse, with James' parents both having been murdered, whilst Anna's father died naturally and her mother outlived her. Anna was used to the company of brothers and sisters, whilst James had no siblings. James was

154. A portrait of the young James VI.

155. James and his queen, Anna of Denmark, from the Seton Armorial.

156. The arms of Queen Anna after 1603.

157. Henry, Prince of Wales, the eldest son of James VI. He died of typhoid aged 18 leaving his
less gifted brother Charles as heir to the throne.

a stern scholar, whilst Anna was an artistic patroness who loved banquets and merry-making. They did not agree about their children's upbringing and both overspent their allowances, leading to fiscal friction. When James pawned Anna's jewels for rather a long period, she naturally objected. Also, in an age when women were supposed to show unquestioned deference to their husbands Anna was not inclined to do this until James gave her jewellery.

Many propose that James was homosexual, but there can be no disputing that in the first years of their marriage he really did love Anna. He was a most uxorious husband and nothing should be made of the fact that there was no heir to the throne until 1594. Anna had an unfortunate miscarriage in the summer of 1590 that probably made conception more difficult as a result. She had other miscarriages before the full term birth of Prince Henry on 19 February 1594 (who died 6 November 1612). This was followed by the arrival of Princess Elizabeth on 19 August 1596. Both were very obvious named to flatter Queen Elizabeth I. The other children of this marriage to be born in Scotland were Margaret, on 24 December 1598 (died 1599), Charles, on 19 November 1600 (the future King Charles I), and Robert, on 18 January 1602 (died 27 May 1602). It was only after the Union of the Crowns in 1603 that James and Anna dared to name daughters after their own mothers, hence Mary, born 8 April 1605 (died 16 December 1607), and Sophia, born on 22 June 1610 (died the next day). The death of any of the royal children hurt James and Anna deeply. Neither could bear to attend a funeral as a consequence. They loved all their children, but the greatest bond of all was between husband and wife. It was James who wrote to Anna after they were temporarily parted by the 1603 Union of the Crowns, that 'I ever preferred you to all my bairns.'

Even though James had taken the reins of power into his own hands in 1585, he still had several important advisors to turn to. One of them, Sir John Maitland of Thirlestane, became Chancellor in 1587. This made him the head of the royal government and a trusted friend. Unfortunately Maitland fell foul of Queen Anna, who found his wife rude and his power over the king autocratic. Anna and others campaigned against him and he was deposed in 1593. From then on James was his own man in political terms and ruled without a chancellor for several years. It was during this time that James had to face one of his most difficult situations. The maverick Francis Stewart, earl of Bothwell, a nephew of the earl who had caused so much trouble for Mary Queen of Scots, challenged James's authority on several occasions. This peaked in the summer of 1593 when Bothwell gained entry to the king's bedchamber. It was said that the earl sought reconciliation yet James, who was paranoid about his personal security, assumed that he was going to be assassinated. This was just one of several occasions in his life when the king tended to jump to the wrong conclusions if he felt hemmed in. This time he triumphed against Bothwell when there were sufficient armed men to see the earl banished and forfeited.

Even before his marriage, James had faced up to a challenge from the earl of Huntly's supporters at the Brig O'Dee near Aberdeen in April 1589. This was a military challenge by known Catholic lords fighting for the counter-Reformation and against their political enemy Maitland of Thirlestane. The king must have felt himself falling between two court factions, but this had a happier outcome as Huntly never appeared at the battle in person and was quickly forgiven. Huntly was, after all, married to Henrietta Stewart, the king's close kinswoman, who was very important in Queen Anna's household. In his

158. Huntingtower Castle, Perth and Kinross, where the young James VI was held captive during 1582-83.
159. The north quarter of Linlithgow Palace, (left) rebuilt for James VI.

heart James could not banish a friend overseas, so he simply sent Huntly home for a few months in the north-east. This infuriated the kirk, who vehemently opposed any Catholic noblemen in Scotland.

The king's willingness to forgive his Catholic friends was a wise move politically as it kept the peace in remoter areas of Scotland. In post-Reformation Scotland he could never publicly back these men, yet in private he supported them against their accusers. The known Catholic earls of Huntly, Errol and Crawford controlled vast areas of the Highlands, as did Lord Maxwell in the Western Borders. The 'Spanish Blanks' episode could have ended the fortunes of these Northern earls and their families, but James chose to be lenient after their cipher letters to the king of Spain were intercepted. James was being pragmatic. He did not want to isolate Scotland from powerful European monarchs in the way that Elizabeth of England had. He wanted to be able to communicate with both Catholic and Protestant powers, whilst keeping on peaceable terms. It is therefore not surprising that one of his first initiatives after becoming king of England was to make peace with Spain. James even exploited Queen Anna's conversion to Catholicism in the early 1590s for political purposes. He could not contact major Catholics directly, but was able to use Anna and the earl and countess of Huntly as intermediaries. It was only when the Northern earls pushed their policies too far and allied themselves to the infamous Bothwell in 1594 that the king was forced to mount an armed expedition against them. Forfeiture and exile followed, but not for long as they all returned to Scotland within a short while.

The kirk was infuriated by royal leniency towards elite Catholics. Their austere anti-Catholic views were well known and some attacked the royal family directly for having Catholic friends. James and Anna were also reprimanded for feasting, drinking and dancing. An academic disputation between the king and Scottish theologians was acceptable, but to publicly criticize the royal family was unforgivable. Several ministers found themselves under house arrest for their bluntness and relations between king and kirk deteriorated. In 1596 leading Presbyterian Andrew Melville called the king 'God's sillie vassal' to his face, when they were arguing about who was the head of the church. Presbyterians put God at the head of the kirk with everyone else, including monarchs, as his subjects. James demurred from this opinion and would soon advance his theories about the divine right of monarchy.

James had tolerated the advance of the Presbyterians in the 1580s and 1590s until they criticized his family. From then on he took exception to any churchman questioning his actions and reinstated bishops to Scotland as a form of controlling the kirk. After 1603 this became much more noticeable as the king found the English church structure much more to his liking. James liked being the unquestioned head of the Church of England and would have liked the same reverence from the Scots. This is why he advanced the cause of Episcopalians against the Presbyterians which culminated in the 'Five Articles' of Perth from the General Assembly of the kirk held in this burgh in 1618. These articles attempted to set Scottish faith back into the Episcopalian mould. The Presbyterians were outwitted on this occasion and many refused to comply with these orders. Although this was primarily a dispute amongst Protestants it was similar in intensity to the early days of the Scottish Reformation. James's meddling only led to prolonged angst in the kirk that stirred up incalculable religious strife for his heir, Charles I, and would not be settled finally until 1690.

160. James VI of Scotland and I of England, with Queen Anna. Note that the arms of Scotland halved with his wife's arms on the Seton Armorial (p.194) has now been replaced by a shield bearing the Scottish lion rampant quartered with the arms of England (top left) and Ireland (bottom right).

James's ultimately forgiving attitude to leading Catholics contrasts markedly with the treatment meted out to Bothwell and the Ruthvens in August 1600. This was the time of the so-called 'Gowrie Conspiracy', when the earl of Gowrie and his brother allegedly entrapped James at their Perth townhouse. They had asked the king to dine with them as he had been hunting in the Perth area. Later when the king cried out for help, his courtiers rushed in and murdered the earl and his brother. Whether this was a genuine murder plot or a revenge attack by the king has never been proved. Certainly James had no pleasant memories of the time the Ruthvens had held him hostage in 1582 and the angry crowd that gathered outside the house blamed the king, not the Ruthvens. Like the earl of Bothwell, the Ruthvens were now banished and forfeited.

In the political arena James's actions could be more subtle. In the areas of Scotland where he could not trust the nobility to keep order and support him, he took a deliberate interest in the local lairds. The lairds were open to political gestures from central government and could likewise take advantage of their monarch's interest in them. Prior to the 1603 Union, many younger sons of substantial lairds found their way to the royal court and gained offices and other privileges. So there was a comforting safety net of lairds in Jacobean Scotland that the king could count upon. This was often reinforced by the progresses made by James in Lowland Scotland, where he cultivated laird and noble alike. Where he thought it was appropriate he elevated lairds to the peerage to further their loyalty. This slightly muddled the honours' system in Scotland, but was nothing like the wholesale inflation of the honours that James instigated in England after 1603 that devalued titles.

James never travelled as far as his mother and grandfather had, for he did not visit the Highlands or Isles. In fact James's attitudes towards to Gaels were less than respectful. He wanted to civilize them, as if they were savages. This showed his lamentable ignorance of gaelic custom and culture that proved very damaging to gaelic heritage. He tried to impose order through measures such as the Statutes of Iona, that attempted to give chiefs a Lowland education and outlook. He ruthlessly suppressed anyone who opposed his will through his lieutenants in the North. The MacGregors, for example, learned this to their great cost when they were outlawed by 'fire and sword'. Many were thereafter hunted like game, forfeited and executed without mercy leaving their families destitute. That the MacGregors survived is due to the sympathy of other highlanders who disliked such direct interference in their domain.

In the Borders James instigated a similar policies against recalcitrant thieves after the Union of the Crowns. Some were exiled to Ireland, where their mischief was deemed less of a threat to authority. No one bothered to consult the native Irish about this and it set a precedent for transporting one nation's problems to another. So confident was the king that the problem of the Borders had been solved that he renamed them his 'Middle Shires'. Technically the former Border Marches did straddle the two kingdoms of what James preferred to call Greater Britain. However the Borderers never took to the name change which lapsed with the death of James in 1625. By then they were arguably more peaceful than they had been in three centuries, so this was a success for Jacobean peace-making. The same could not be said for the Highlands though, which remained troubled for another two centuries.

The dynastic union for which James and Anna longed came about in the spring of 1603. Elizabeth I died on 24 March 1603 and Sir Robert Carey then made his record-breaking ride north to reach Holyrood on the evening of 26 March. James was delighted by the news. He had attained the throne his mother had longed for and could not wait to get his hands on it. The new James VI and I prepared to leave Scotland with an almost indecent haste. New clothes and travelling equipment were hurriedly made for the journey south, with little expense spared. James wanted to make a magnificent progress southwards, but it was only as the day of departure drew near that he gave cognisance to the feelings of the Scottish people. He attended a service in St Giles and noted the sadness of the crowd who had gathered to see him. He promised them that he would return every three years, but reneged on this as he would only come back in 1617 for a short stay.

On 5 April the king's procession left Holyrood with cannons blazing from the castle. There were many Scottish and English nobles in the vanguard with all their servants and baggage as well. It must have been quite a sight for the onlookers. They headed to Lord Home's house at Dunglass and crossed the border into the bounds of Berwick the next day. The journey went onwards like a magnificent progress with much feasting and merrymaking along the way. The English put aside their reservations about the Scots to welcome their new king in great style. Queen Anna, accompanied by Prince Henry and Princess Elizabeth left Edinburgh on 1 June to make their progress southwards. Only 'Baby Charles' was left at Dunfermline, as they thought he was too weak to travel, but even he had left Scotland by 1604.

Scotland lost far more than her resident monarchy in 1603. The unique Scottish court culture vanished overnight and the creeping anglicization of the elite became more pronounced. For example the famous poet William Drummond of Hawthornden, though he remained in Scotland, switched from writing in Scots to composing in English. Other poets tried to write in English as well, even though they still spoke Scots. This left ordinary Scots as the guardians of Scottish culture. Though the Scottish Privy Council and Parliament remained, the loss of a resident monarch was deeply felt by the people. James became obsessed with uniting his kingdoms, but neither the Scots nor the English were in favour of this. The idea lingered during the first decade of the joint monarchy, but it was ahead of its time. Full parliamentary union would not come about until 1707 and even then it was controversial.

James adopted a policy of 'government by pen' for the Scots. In other words he issued instructions by letter to his privy councillors in Edinburgh, knowing they would carry them out. He also established the first proper mail service between Edinburgh and London, shortly after the union. James was confident that this was a workable system for major politicians such as George Home, earl of Dunbar, traversed the Great North Road to visit him. This made the king's need to return to Scotland less likely. In fact so many Scots travelled south that the English began to complain about their presence. James was therefore forced to curb this activity by banning Scots unless they had been issued with one of his passports. The typical clannishness of the Scots at the new 'British' court was misunderstood by English courtiers who resented any favours bestowed upon them. James's gentlemen of the bedchamber were almost entirely Scottish after he arrived in England and this only slowly changed in balance of Englishmen. James saw no problem with this as he surrounded himself with men he could trust. He had yet to get to know the English elite.

James's penchant for having favourites was apparent in Scotland, long before this was commented upon in England. Too much innuendo has been made from these friendships. James had a paternal attitude to young men at court. Those whose company he enjoyed were favoured, just as a reigning queen would favour her ladies-in-waiting. Unscrupulous individuals exploited this for their own political advantage, as was the case with Robert Ker who rose from being a younger son of a Border laird to become earl of Somerset in 1613. Somerset fell from grace to be replaced by James's best known favourite George Villiers, later duke of Buckingham, who was also a good friend of Prince Charles. Those who had the confidence of a monarch were always destined not the die in poverty and Buckingham is no exception.

James should be remembered more for his scholarship and writings than his favourites. He was certainly not the 'wisest fool' that history has labelled him. This is probably a misquote as James, had he not been a king from the cradle, would surely have become a university professor. His scholarship was legendary in Europe and his writings, such as *Basilikon Doron* (1598), *Trew Lawe of Free Monarchies* (1598), *Daemonologie* (1598) and the *Counterblast to Tobacco* (1604), were well read. He also translated texts as well as writing and appreciating poetry for many years. He patronized poets and dramatists, just as his wife Anna did during her Scottish and English years. However James was not the lover of architecture that his grandfather and great-grandfather had been, though this was compensated for in his wife Anna's enthusiastic building programmes at her royal palaces in both Scotland and England. Anna even renamed Somerset House in London as 'Denmark' House.

The king's only return visit to Scotland was not undertaken until 14 March 1617. He was accompanied by a very large retinue that wound its way northwards, reaching Edinburgh on 16 May. The Scots were thrilled to have their monarch back and many orations were made in his honour as he revisited favoured locations. After years in a wealthier nation he found the Scots badly dressed, but still made the most of their hospitality when it was offered. Some of the Englishmen who accompanied him were less than civil about the Scots and appeared most ungracious guests of their northern neighbours. Nobility who had kept to their own localities after the union now flocked back to the temporarily rejuvenated Scottish court. Amidst all the hunting and feasting, James found time to attend the Scottish Parliament; just like the old days. Barely three months after he had returned, James was heading south again by the west coast route. He was back at Windsor by 12 September.

Anna did not return to Scotland with her husband in 1617. Her health was not good by then and she died on 2 March 1619. James nearly died of gastric illness just after this, perhaps as a result of his grief, but he would live on for another six years. His relationship with his heir, Prince Charles, was strained. Charles had always been closer to his mother than his father and the fact that he had not been destined to inherit the crowns of Scotland and England did not help. It was his elder brother Prince Henry who had been schooled for kingship, but Henry died tragically of typhoid in 1612.

By 1625 James was a tired old man who had been king of Scots for nearly fifty-eight years. He was the last Stewart monarch to really know and understand the Scots. His middle way had paid the dividends of peace both domestically and internationally, but the storm clouds were gathering for his successors. His failure to bring about full incorporating union between his united monarchies was long forgotten by 1625. Scotland and England continued to be governed separately by the same monarch and his respective Scots and English politicians.

The king died on 27 March 1625. His state funeral took place on 7 May at Westminster Abbey, after which his remains were interred in the vault containing the bones of his great-great-grandfather Henry VII. It is interesting that he chose to lie beside the founder of the Tudor dynasty, rather than near his wife or mother. There is no stone-carved memorial to either James or Anna at Westminster as the days of funereal ostentation had passed by the time of their deaths.

MM

FIVE

THE BRITISH STEWARTS
MONARCHS OF THREE REALMS
1625 – 1714

CHARLES I (1625-1649)

Prince Charles, duke of Albany, was not destined to be king of Scots at his birth. He was the second son of King James VI and Queen Anna and was born at Dunfermline Abbey on 19 November 1600. His older brother Prince Henry, duke of Ross, was bred for kingship. By contrast Charles was so sickly that his parents did not expect him to survive. His baptism at Holyroodhouse on 23 December was therefore a modest event with none of the elaborate celebrations that had accompanied his older brother's ceremony. Charles's early days were spent at Dunfermline Abbey where he was well cared for. His guardian was Alexander Seton, Lord Fyvie, a high-ranking courtier. Charles however remained weak and developed rickets, much to the anxiety of his carers. When his parents and siblings departed for England in 1603, 'Baby Charles' was left behind as he was deemed too weak to undertake the journey. His only consolation was 'play babies' given to him by his parents before they left.

'Duke Charles' was fitter the following year and travelled to Windsor to be reunited with his parents in the summer of 1604. Fyvie was honourably discharged of his duties as guardian of the prince and returned to Scotland, where he was then Chancellor. The care of the prince was then given to Sir Robert and Lady Carey. It would be Lady Carey's careful nurturing that led to Charles emerging as a well-educated and confident, if physically small, royal prince. He could never escape being in the shadow of his older brother Henry, but attended the British Royal Court and took part in its many festivities. He was created duke of York in 1605 and was made a knight of the garter in 1611.

When Prince Henry died of typhoid on 6 November 1612, Charles's life changed forever. He was now heir to the thrones of Scotland, England and Wales, and Ireland; an awesome responsibility. His only surviving sibling, Princess Elizabeth, married Frederick, the Elector Palatine, in 1613 and left for Europe. Charles probably felt lonely, but regarded his new brother-in-law as a lifelong friend. With King James ageing and Queen Anna in poor health, Charles knew that he would have to take on more responsibilities. He therefore left the care of the Careys to establish his own household.

Henry had been bold and daring, with a court to rival that of his fathers. Charles by contrast was quiet, shy and scholarly, showing due respect to both his parents. He was closest to his mother and was devastated when Queen Anna died in 1619. They had shared a love of art, music, masquing and architecture. Charles would continue to be a well-informed royal collector of art. James made him Prince of Wales in 1616, but refused to take his son back to Scotland in 1617. This was a very unwise move in retrospect for Charles had forgotten what being a Scot was and had no empathy for the country of his birth. The strained relationship between father and son was alleviated by the go-between role of George Villiers, duke of Buckingham, a favourite of James and companion to Charles.

Charles's marriage had been the subject of diplomatic gossip for many years. A Spanish match for the heir to the throne had been mooted since 1608. James VI, being even handed as ever, wanted his son to marry a Catholic princess to balance Princess Elizabeth's wedding to a Protestant prince. Charles went to Spain during 1622-23, accompanied by Buckingham, in an abortive attempt to gain the hand of the Spanish Infanta Donna Maria, daughter of Philip IV. Charles was said to be very much in love with the Infanta, but his trip to Spain cost a fortune, with no result to show for it. Charles was disappointed, humiliated and angry at the turn of events, but a Spanish marriage would not have been popular with either the Scots or English people.

It was not until after the death of his father that Charles married Princess Henrietta Maria, daughter of the late Henri IV of France and sister to Louis XIII. The negotiations had taken place before James's death and he had given the match his blessing at their formal betrothal in November 1624. Reactions were muted, but much less hostile than the proposed Spanish match. The Scots may not have been enamoured with Henrietta Maria's vehement Catholicism and the concessions granted to her to practice her faith, but she was a French princess. The spirit of the 'Auld Alliance' between Scotland and France appeared to be temporarily revived with the public celebrations that welcomed the marriage and arrival of the new queen in 1625. Henrietta was styled 'queen of England' yet she was equally the queen consort of Scots.

The marriage was a success after a rather rocky start. The queen was only fifteen and very strong headed. To the English she was uncompromisingly French and took a very long time to adapt to her adopted country's language and culture. Henrietta's petiteness nevertheless complimented Charles's lack of stature and their relationship produced

162. Dunfermline Palace, birthplace of Charles I, engraving by John Slezer.
163. Portrait of Charles I by Sir Anthony Van Dyck.

164. Portrait of Charles I and Henrietta Maria.
165. Twelve shilling piece of Charles I.
166. Portrait of Henrietta Maria by Sir Anthony Van Dyck.

many children once they had matured as a couple. Prince Charles, later King Charles II, was born on 29 May 1630. Princess Mary arrived on 4 December 1631, married the Prince of Orange in 1641 and died in 1660. Prince James, later King James VII, was born on 14 October 1633. Princess Elizabeth arrived on 28 December 1635 and died on 8 September 1650, a year after her father's execution. Prince Henry was born on 8 July 1639 and died on 13 September 1660, just after the Restoration of the Monarchy. A gap of five years followed before the birth of their last child Henrietta Maria on 16 June 1644, during the British Civil Wars. She married Philip, duke of Orleans, in 1661 and died in 1670.

Like his father, Charles was a family-oriented king who remained uxorious after marriage. He became even closer to Henrietta Maria after the assassination of Buckingham in 1628. He also cared for his nieces and nephews after Elizabeth and Frederick were forced into exile in Holland as a result of the Thirty Years' War. His nephew, Prince Rupert, would later return to help him fight the civil wars. In the pre-war years, Charles frequently commissioned portraits of himself and his family by artists such as Van Dyck. Although intended to flatter, these show happy family groupings with their dogs and horses nearby. This happiness would be relatively short-lived, though, for war would severely interrupt royal family life in the 1640s.

Like his father, Charles governed Scotland from a distance. Unlike James VI, however, he was lamentably out of touch with the feelings of the Scottish people and ruled them nonchalantly through his privy council. He rarely bothered to write in person to these councillors, leaving his ministers to govern in his place. Fortunately, these office-holders were very competent and smoothed over any cracks in the chain of command. Charles even refused the offer of improved intelligence from Scotland. It was as if Scotland (and Ireland) were of little importance to him, but when he made a return visit to Scotland in 1633 this was only a simmering tension. Charles was welcomed back to Scotland and the visit culminated in his coronation at Holyrood on 18 June. He visited the Lowlands, attended parliament and feasted with the nobility, but this was not the happy visit the Scots had in 1617 when King James returned. Charles had meddled too much and upset the equilibrium of absentee royal government.

He instituted several changes in government during this visit that were very unpopular with the kirk, the privy council, the law courts, the nobility and the lairds. So, in short, his meddling upset everyone holding authority in Scotland. He also taxed the Scots more heavily than his father had done. Resentment that had been subdued before 1633 now came to the surface and this was particularly apparent in matters of religion. This was destined to be a major area of contention between Charles and the Scots. When he ordered an English-style prayer book to be used in Scottish kirks from 1637 onwards riots broke out. Instead of sensibly backing down on this issue Charles became more and more belligerent in his defence of the divine right of kings. The Scots became equally intransigent about their right to worship without his interference. This confrontation of beliefs culminated in the signing of the National Covenant in 1638 and the Anglo-Scottish Bishop's Wars of 1639-41 in defence of Scottish Presbyterianism.

Charles briefly returned to Scotland in 1641 to appease the Covenanters, who were named thus after the signing of the National Covenant. Although a temporary peace was agreed, Charles had handled this situation very badly and paid a very heavy price for his religious arrogance towards the Scots. The prayer book in effect cost Charles his head in

1649 as it triggered a disastrous series of events. He was forced to summon his English parliament in 1640 to pay for the Bishop's Wars, after a personal rule lasting eleven years, and this led to civil war in his British Kingdoms. The Covenanters fought against Charles in the English and Scottish Civil Wars of 1642-46. They even held him as their prisoner at Newcastle in 1646, before handing him over to parliamentary forces. Other non-covenanting Scots fought for the king, though loyalties often shifted according to political expediency. For instance, the 1647-48 Engagers included moderate Covenanters who fought against English parliamentary forces to restore the king's freedom. Charles appeared ready to do anything to regain power after being imprisoned by his enemies, but these plans came to nought.

Queen Henrietta Maria left England for France with her new daughter in July 1644. Princess Mary was by then married and living in Holland. Prince Charles escaped to France in 1646, followed by Prince James in 1648. This left in England only Princess Elizabeth and Prince Henry, who shared their father's captivity and witnessed his last speeches. It was with good reason, therefore, that Charles wrote to his queen saying that 'there was never man so alone as I.'

In his final days Charles showed remarkable dignity and composure. He refused to recognise the kangaroo court that put him on trial in January 1649. His subsequent execution outside the magnificent Banqueting Hall in Whitehall on 30 January stunned onlookers. He went from 'a corruptible to an incorruptible crown', leaving England as a republic. The Scots were shocked by this blatant regicide by a handful of Englishmen and quickly hailed the absentee Prince Charles as their new King Charles II. This act brought a ferocious reaction from the English government that led to further warfare and bloodshed in Scotland. Charles, for all his faults, was never as cruel to the Scottish people as Oliver Cromwell's forces were to be.

MM

CHARLES II (1649-1685)

Prince Charles was born on 29 May 1630 at St James's Palace, the eldest son and first child of Charles I and Queen Henrietta Maria. He was styled Prince of Great Britain and held both Scottish and English titles. His childhood was secure and affluent. Charles was physically large for his years and kept robust health in contrast to his father's sickly childhood physique. He was an assertive child who enjoyed attention and became a Knight of the Garter at the age of only eight. His parents delighted in his progress, but they also created a religious divide in the mind of the young prince. Charles was drawn by his mother's Catholicism, but knew that he had to be a Protestant adult to succeed to the throne. It was a dilemma that Charles never really resolved throughout his life.

The outbreak of war ended the idyllic childhood of the royal children. Charles joined his father in the English military campaigns of 1642-44. In 1642 he was sent to Wales to gather support for the royalist cause and led similar campaigns in the south-west of England. This put Charles out of immediate danger, but when the war swung in favour of the parliamentary forces he was exiled first to the Isles of Scilly, then Jersey and finally France. His exile was far from threadbare, as the young Prince Charles had a retinue of over 300 people and still lived an opulent lifestyle. He went to live with his mother at St

167. Engraved portrait of Charles II by Samuel Cooper.

168. New Parliament House, Edinburgh, late seventeenth-century engraving by Captain John Elphinstone.
169. Dunnottar Castle, Aberdeenshire, the last fortress to hold out for the cause of Charles II.
170. Oliver Cromwell in a portrait engraving by Samuel Cooper.

Germain for a while and their combined court became a centre of intrigue and diplomacy. It was certainly preferable to the parliamentary house arrest his siblings were enduring at St James's Palace at this time.

In May 1648 the Scottish Parliament urged Charles to come to Scotland and launch an invasion of England. He liked the idea, though his mother urged caution. Charles moved to Holland to be nearer suitable shipping should this plan go ahead. As the brother of Princess Mary, then married to the Prince of Orange, Charles was welcome in the Hague. He was now free of guardians and could behave as he liked. He therefore began indulging what would become his lifelong passion for women by making Lucy Walter his first mistress. She bore him the most famous of his illegitimate progeny, a son named James, later created duke of Monmouth.

A royalist fleet set sail for Britain that summer, intending to rendezvous with the Scottish Engagers, who wanted to liberate King Charles I. However, all they achieved was a little piracy off the Kent coast. The Scottish army of the Engagement moved south, only to be rebuffed by parliamentary forces. Charles returned to the Hague deeply disappointed at the turn of events, but put in place more plans to go to Scotland, or Ireland, with another fleet. His loyalty was first and foremost to his father's liberation so when a news-sheet arrived on 4 February 1649 declaring that his father had been executed, Charles's world was turned upside down. The eighteen-year-old prince burst into tears as he realised that a mighty burden had just landed upon his young shoulders.

The Scots Parliament proclaimed him King Charles II as soon as they learned about the execution of his father. It was natural for the eldest son of a monarch to succeed, but the circumstances surrounding Charles's accession to the Scottish throne were exceptional. The Scots were indignant that English regicides had not consulted them, for Charles was still king of Scots, as well as king of England. Charles II, however, was still in exile and the remnants of the English Parliament had declared England and Wales to be a republic. Scots' dignitaries went to the Hague to urge Charles to come home with them, though they were still divided between Covenanters and non-Presbyterian royalists. Charles had to be pragmatic and consider which Scottish faction could yield him the most support. He preferred the Covenanters, but had no love for their Presbyterianism. Negotiations for Charles's visit to Scotland were lengthy and complex, but in the end a compromise treaty was agreed that allowed him to come in the summer of 1650.

Charles's fleet evaded republican ships and was anchored in the Moray Firth by midsummer. After landing the Scots made their 'covenanted' king very welcome. He was feted wherever he went on his journey to the Lowlands. Bonfires, bells and loyal toasts were the order of the day. This euphoria only lasted until the royal entourage reached Edinburgh, as tensions arose when it was known that Charles had reluctantly agreed to sign the Covenants of faith. The Covenanters tried to oust die-hard royalists from the king's household, with limited success. This appeared a trivial issue, though, in comparison with military reality. In supporting the new king, Scotland showed blatant defiance of England's republic, who now sought savage retribution in the form of Oliver Cromwell's New Model Army.

Cromwell was recalled from his vindictive Irish campaigns to fight the Scots with 11,000 men. The 23,000 strong Covenanting army opposing him would be no walk over for they had cut their teeth as mercenaries in the Thirty Years' Wars and proved a ferocious fighting force in the earlier civil wars. Cromwell's army marched towards Edinburgh, but found the Scots' defences too good to penetrate. Finally he met the Covenanters at the Battle of Dunbar on 3 September 1650. As the forces were not evenly matched the Scots should have won outright, but they were over confident. Cromwell struck at dawn, taking them by surprise, and the result was a complete Scottish rout. This was a disaster for the Scottish nation on the scale of defeat at Flodden in 1513. They lost 14,000 men and all their artillery. Cromwell proceeded to take Edinburgh and thereafter put the nation into a terrifying military subjection that would last until 1660.

Charles should have been avenging his father's death, but instead of triumphantly marching into England he was forced into an undignified retreat. Charles's crisis management was poor and his rages only complicated things further. Though the king attended parliament on a regular basis, the military actions he sanctioned after Dunbar were little better than a farce. Cromwell gradually garrisoned Southern Scotland and amidst this chaos Charles had a rather rushed coronation at Scone on 1 January 1651. The Covenanters took charge of the ceremony and they chose to break with tradition by not including anointing. They also forced the king to subscribe to the Covenants once more, just before placing the crown on his head. Charles did this willingly as there was a crowd watching, but in private he must have had his doubts about the Covenant.

After the coronation Charles II took a more direct hand in military strategy. He inspected Covenanting garrisons in the Lowlands and tried to raise support from the more religiously conservative North East. His kingdom was rapidly shrinking however, despite his best efforts. Cromwell's army and navy battered the Covenanters' defences, and his troops marched through to Glasgow in May 1651. A bridgehead was established in Fife during July 1651 and the highly strategic burgh of Perth surrendered on 2 August. Charles and the Covenanters had lost the battle to save Scotland from total Cromwellian occupation, but they were not finished yet. Whilst Cromwell was occupied in taking Perth, they wrong-footed him by forming a renegade force of 12,000 and marching into England. This force reached Merseyside before encountering any opposition and proceeded to the Worcester area where they assumed royalist support was still strong. However few turned out and their forces were roundly defeated on 3 September. Many loyal Scots were killed or taken prisoner during this final battle of the British civil wars.

The king now had no option but to flee and one of the most hazardous episodes in his life ensued as he played cat and mouse with the Cromwellian forces. Charles hid in barns, houses, gardens and oak trees, variously disguising himself as a labourer and then a tenant farmer. He travelled dangerously as there were spies everywhere, but finally made his way to France through the relatively unguarded port of Shoreham in Sussex on 14 October 1651.

Charles would never return to Scotland and his unpleasant memories of his brief sojourn there dominated his later kingship. He believed that the Scots had failed him and he never forgave them, which was uncharitable considering those Scots who lost their lives fighting for him in Scotland and at Worcester. His egotism was as much to blame as anything else for the failure of the Scottish campaign. Charles thereafter remained in exile in France, Germany and the Low Countries until the English monarchy was restored in May 1660. After nine years of occupation, and several years of enforced unifi-

171. Carbisdale, Sutherland, scene of the final defeat of the Royalist Marquis of Montrose in 1650. His defeat opened the way for Charles II to come to terms with the Covenanters in Scotland.
172. Kinneff Church, Aberdeenshire, where the Scottish regalia was buried under the floor for safekeeping during the Cromwellian occupation.

173. Charles II by Samuel Cooper.
174. Portrait of Catherine of Braganza, queen consort of Charles II, in the Portuguese dress
which she wore on her arrival in England in May 1662.
175. Holyroodhouse, Edinburgh, remodelled for Charles II but only visited by James, duke of
York, and Princess Anne.

cation with England, Scotland was now free to run her own affairs. Charles slowly restored the government of Scotland, putting the clocks back to 1651. He was lenient to most former supporters of the Cromwellian regime as he wanted to keep the loyalty of the Scots people.

The most pressing issue for the Scots was, not surprisingly, religion. Charles was slow to respond to the Presbyterians after his many years in an increasingly absolutist Western Europe. He admired the way the French handled religious tensions and believed that the kirk should obey him. He therefore began to meddle with kirk affairs, just like his father and grandfather, with similarly disastrous consequences for Scotland. In 1662 he took his revenge on Presbyterian church government by restoring the Scottish Episcopalian church and demanding that ministers obey bishops. In a provocative move he also outlawed the Covenants. 270 ministers refused to conform and lost their livings. Many simply took to the fields to preach at open air conventicles that were well attended by their former parishioners. Charles banned these conventicles, but this made the Presbyterians even more resolute to in their defiance of his authority. The Covenanters' Pentland Rising of 1666 was quashed, but gave Charles a reminder that they could not be lightly dismissed. In 1672 Charles tried conciliation, but this brought back few to the kirk. By 1679 the Covenanters had taken up arms against the king once more. A band of Covenanters assassinated James Sharp, archbishop of St Andrews, the head of Charles's religious establishment in Scotland, dragging him from his carriage as he returned to his cathedral city. On 1 June, a government force was severly mauled as it tried to disperse an armed conventicle in what became known as the Battle of Drumclog. The rebels lost the next battle at Bothwell Brig in Lanarkshire on 22 June when the king's illegitimate son, the duke of Monmouth, took command.

The result of this victory was that open Covenanting opposition to Charles diminished as many Covenanters were now in prison, or were being transported as indentured labour to the American and Caribbean colonies. This left a hard core of die-hards, known as Cameronians after their first leader, Richard Cameron, to continue the defence of Presbyterianism during the last five years of Charles's reign. This was a black period of Scottish history known as 'the killing times' when a hundred Presbyterians were martyred. Such savage retribution alarmed even moderate Episcopalian Scots and Charles's sending of his brother James, duke of York, to Scotland during 1681-82 did not placate them.

Rumours that Charles secretly favoured Catholicism in his later years alarmed the Scots. Added to this was general distaste for his debauched behaviour at a highly immoral royal court that shocked Presbyterian and Episcopalian alike. The Scots' concern was aggravated by Charles's childless marriage to Catherine of Braganza, who despite marrying on 21 May 1662 produced no heirs to the British throne. Charles had countless progeny by his many mistresses and lovers, but singularly failed to make his queen into a mother. Their marriage can only be described as a miserable one, as Charles let Catherine down on numerous occasions. This left his younger brother James to succeed as James VII & II and he was openly Catholic. So despite having crowned him in person over thirty years earlier, the Scots were left with bittersweet memories of the kingship of Charles II. Few lamented his death on 6 February 1685, but the Scots were probably then more alarmed at the prospect of a having a Catholic James VII as their new monarch.

MM

JAMES VII (1685-1688)

James, duke of Albany (and York), was born at St James's Palace in London on 14 October 1633. He was the third child and second son of King Charles I and Queen Henrietta Maria. He was named after his late grandfather, James VI, and had a fairly tranquil childhood until the outbreak of civil war in the 1640s. As a younger son, James's upbringing would take a different path to that of his elder brother's. His education was not in statesmanship, but practicality. He was a skilled linguist and had a great interest in the developing scientific world of the seventeenth century. He spent three years at Oxford during the first civil wars, but became more proficient in military arts than fine arts in this seat of learning. He was taken prisoner when the town surrendered to parliamentary forces on 25 June 1646 and remained under house arrest in and around London until 1648.

There were plans to replace Charles I with James, so an escape was planned to prevent a usurpation of the throne. The fourteen-year-old prince showed resourcefulness and initiative by dressing in drag to evade the guards. He was assisted by Colonel Bampfield, who arranged that a barge would take them down the Thames to a waiting Dutch ship on the night of 21 April 1648. The escape succeeded and James was in the Low Countries by the 23 April. He was reunited with his sister Mary, whom he had not seen since her wedding to the Prince of Orange in 1641. The euphoria of this meeting soon faded, however, when the reality of exile dawned upon him. James would spend the next twelve years in Western Europe in the relative poverty of the exiled court, though he always hoped to return earlier than this. This troubled period in his life left James with a permanent dislike of politics and republicanism in particular.

James was pleased to return to Britain in May 1660, even if it was in the shadow of his brother Charles II. Holding many offices such as that of Lord Admiral gave James a good income. He therefore established his own household and requested that Charles let him marry one of his sister's ladies-in-waiting, Anne Hyde. James had first met Anne in 1655 and had promised to marry her in 1659, though he rescinded the offer when faced with the opposition of his mother and brother. When James left for Britain she was already four months' pregnant, so Charles reluctantly agreed to their marriage, in secret, on 3 September 1660. This only made matters worse for Anne, as senior courtiers vilified her as little better than a whore. Their son was born in October, but died in 1661. Henrietta Maria lobbied to have the marriage declared invalid, which hardly endeared her to her new daughter-in-law. It took until December for James to publicly declare that Anne was his wife, after which Henrietta Maria reluctantly acknowledged her and sped back to France in disgust.

With the departure of his mother, the marriage of James and Anne was finally allowed to work and they gained public acceptance. Their union would produce seven children, though only two daughters survived into adulthood. They were Princess Mary, born 30 April 1662 and Princess Anne, born 6 February 1665, both of who would become queens of the British kingdoms in due course. The loss of four sons and one daughter in infancy was very distressing to James and Anne. James also had many illegitimate children by his various mistresses for, like his brother Charles II, he had an overactive libido. After Anne's death on 31 March 1671, James chose a wife with the open consent of the court. He married Princess Mary of Modena on 30 September 1673. They had two more

176. James VII was created duke of York and Albany at his baptism. New York is named after him.
177. Royal banner of Scotland carried at the battle of Worcester in 1651.

178. James VII of Scotland and II of England took Stewart arrogance to an
extreme in this portrait.

children, Prince James on 28 June 1688 (later the 'Old Pretender who died in 1766) and Princess Louisa Maria Theresa on 28 June 1692 (died 1712).

James had an active naval career in the 1660s and 1670s that involved service at sea fighting against the Dutch. He was an able admiral and insisted on commanding the fleet in person, regardless of protests from his family about the dangers this involved. He probably preferred life at sea to the political intrigues of the court. He could also escape from heated anti-Catholicism, which was already threatening to mar his future kingship. James had been a high church Anglican until he openly converted to Catholicism in 1672. This led to several attempts to exclude him from the English throne, as Charles II was still childless. When the sea offered no longer offered refuge from his protagonists, Charles sent his brother to Brussels in the summer of 1679 and Scotland during 1679-82.

In Scotland, James used his military skills to batter the remainder of the Covenanters, but it should also be remembered that he revived the Scottish Court after a very long gap. Holyroodhouse and Falkland were rebuilt to house his entourage. Elite Scots flocked to meet him and his charming wife and many stayed near the rejuvenated court. True to his interest in science, he established the Royal College of Physicians in Edinburgh. James also summoned parliament and tried to enforce a new 'Test Act' to bolster loyalty to King Charles and diminish Presbyterianism. One victim of this policy was the duke of Argyll, who was forced into exile in Holland rather than take an oath of loyalty that denied the Covenants. Throughout his stay in Scotland James made no effort to hide his Catholicism and this led to open opposition to his accession to the throne upon the death of his brother Charles II in February 1685.

There had not been a King James since 1625, but the new James VII had the rockiest of regal inductions. In the spring of 1685 there were simultaneous uprisings in Scotland and England against James VII and II. Argyll had returned to lead a Scottish rebellion, whilst Charles II's senior illegitimate son, James, duke of Monmouth, rose up in the English West Country to claim the throne for himself as a true Protestant. Worst still, they were assisted by James's son-in-law Prince William of Orange. Such family disloyalty proved how unpopular James's Catholicism was, but both rebellions were savagely put down and the leaders executed. James also stationed professional armies in both locations to ensure future loyalty.

His kingship was dominated by religion, for in order to help his fellow Catholics, James was forced to offer toleration to Presbyterians as well. The killing times were now over and Scots were allowed freedom of worship. Few converted to Catholicism as the king wished and Scots began to resent his open favouritism of Catholic nobility in government. Many Scots looked beyond James to see the potential succession of his Protestant daughter Princess Mary and her husband Prince William, who both had direct claims to the British thrones. However, this was thwarted by the birth of a son, James, to King James and Queen Mary in 1688. This was an entirely natural pregnancy and delivery, despite subsequent Protestant assertions that it was faked. Britain had a new heir to the throne, the only snag was that he was bound to be Catholic. This was too much for the people, who were predominantly Protestant in Scotland, England and Wales. When William of Orange landed at Torbay in November 1688 a chain of events began that led to the deposition of King James and the start of Jacobitism in British History. Jacobitism took its name from 'Jacobus', being the Latin form of James, and this would cause problems to successive Scottish and British governments (after the 1707 Union) until their defeat at Culloden in 1746.

Whether James VII was pushed or fell from the monarchy is hotly debated by historians, even today. What is clear is that James fled from London in advance of William's arrival there, defiantly throwing the Great Seal of England into the Thames as he left. No one could therefore use the seal to forge a document of abdication. James was deemed to have abdicated by the English Parliament, who had notionally 'invited' William and Mary to Britain even though they were coming anyway. During 1688, all the Scots could do was observe events in England. Their parliament was divided about the flight of James VII until the Jacobites walked out. Parliament then decided that the Catholic James had forfeited the Scottish crown, so the era of William and Mary began.

MM

WILLIAM II AND MARY II (1688-1702)

Prince William of Orange and his wife Princess Mary both had strong claims to the British kingdoms. William, despite his Dutch roots as son of William II of Orange, was also the son of Princess Mary Stuart, daughter of King Charles I. He married his much younger first cousin Mary, the daughter of Anne Hyde and James, duke of Albany, in 1677. Their wedding had been discussed as early as 1674 when an Anglo-Dutch peace was concluded. James opposed the match then as he hoped Mary might marry the Dauphin of France, but this was highly unlikely. By 1677, both Charles II and James saw the advantages of alliance with Holland so the marriage went ahead. As James's wife, Mary of Modena, was almost constantly pregnant, the likelihood of William and Mary succeeding to the British kingdoms was remote at this stage. Moreover, the fifteen-year-old Mary was apparently unhappy about marrying someone twelve years' her senior and four inches shorter, but their political alliance did grow into a very loving relationship.

The childhood of both William and Mary was similar amidst comfortable court life, but the level of their education differed. Whereas William had been well educated in Calvinism, languages, fine arts and military tactics, Mary's education was more feminine and artistic but equally Protestant. William was a frail child, whilst Mary was tall and beautiful throughout her life. Mary had been born on 30 April 1662 and grew up with both parents until her mother's death in 1671. She was fond of her stepmother, Mary, and missed her family when she departed for Holland in 1677.

William was born on 13 November 1650, just one week after his father's untimely demise from smallpox. He had to endure anti-Orangist government in Holland until he achieved power in his own right during the popular revolution of 1672. He was now head of state and lost no time in expelling French forces from his country and making peace with his uncle Charles II. This marked him as a major European power in his own right, despite his youth. By 1679 he had regained all the territory lost to France by the previous regime and these countries resumed trading which was vital to the Dutch economy. In 1685 he welcomed refugee French Huguenots into Holland and this enhanced the Dutch economy even further. He was, therefore, a very successful statesman by the time of the so-called 'Glorious Revolution' that led William and Mary to the English throne. William undoubtedly wanted English wealth and power to bolster Holland against the might of France, whereas Mary was probably just glad to return to her homeland and took no active role in either Scottish or English politics.

179. William II of Scotland and III of England.
180. Mary II as Princess of Orange, painted by Gaspar Netscher.
181. Portrait of King William with a view of the 1690 Irish Battle of the Boyne in the background.

Reaction to William and Mary's arrival was much more muted in Scotland. They observed the events that led to the overthrow of James VII and quietly noted that at least William and Mary were Protestant successors. When the Scottish parliament met in May 1689 they eventually announced a claim of right that created William II and Mary II as king and queen of Scots. Only south of the border was William regarded as 'the Third' of England. If James VII had not addressed a letter to the Scottish parliament asserting his powers over it in such arrogant tones and his supporters had not walked out of the proceedings, their conclusions might have been different. William was indignant at the Scot's delay as his English parliament had quickly declared his rights to the throne. However, this served as a lesson in Anglo-Scottish legal differences and he just had to be patient. Technically James VII had never taken a coronation oath in Scotland, unlike his brother Charles II. He was, therefore, deemed to have forfeited the Scottish crown by being an unconstitutional Catholic, or so parliament stated. As in England, where his flight was depicted as *de facto* abdication, the legal arguments for a change in monarchy were rather weak.

Opposition to William in Scotland was a potent force, despite his Stewart wife. However, the immediate concern of the Scots was the threat of counter-rebellion by James VII, who was gathering his forces in Ireland. This was uncomfortably close to Scotland where James still had open support. Indeed, Viscount Dundee led the first of several Jacobite risings in the summer of 1689, during which government forces were humiliated at the Battle of Killiecrankie on 27 July. Unfortunately, 'Bonnie Dundee' died as a result of injuries sustained at this battle and his rising collapsed. Former Cameronians now zealously hounded the renegade Jacobites and expected William to note their efforts in the form of a proper and lasting kirk settlement in Scotland.

William was distracted by crushing the rebellion in Ireland, but when the Scots parliament met in April 1690 the church of Scotland was finally settled as a Presbyterian kirk after a century of religious strife. The Presbyterians had expected a Calvinist king to accede to all their demands sooner than this, but William was a shrewd tactician. He refused to accept the Covenants and made public his views about maintaining patronage, which the Presbyterians abhorred. However, the kirk was now settled and the General Assembly could meet annually - which it had not done for many decades. Inevitably, William's concessions to Presbyterians upset the Episcopalians who were numerically strong in the North East. Support for Jacobitism was also strong amongst the Episcopalians and anyone not praying for William and Mary in their pulpits could be ousted from their parishes. Many were caught by this and replaced by Presbyterian ministers, making William unpopular in the North.

The Highlands were always a problem area, yet William spent most of his money on sending troops to Europe to fight Louis XIV and could not keep a standing army in Scotland to address lawlessness there. To maintain law and order he used local clan chiefs instead and tried to woo the allegiance of Jacobite chiefs with bribes. This scheme backfired disastrously on 13 February 1692 with the massacre at Glencoe. This was one of the most disgraceful episodes in Scottish history and the blame for it lay squarely at the top, with King William and his Scottish politicians. It drove a wedge between William and the Scots and enhanced support for the Jacobite cause, which was the last thing the king wanted. The deliberate slaughter of Glencoe Macdonalds was severe retribution for being only a few days late to take an oath of loyalty to the new king and queen. Scots were shocked at the brutality of this and by the subsequent deaths of the Macdonald men, women and children who had managed to escape the sword of the Campbells, only to die of exposure in frozen hills nearby. An official enquiry was a typical whitewash that never revealed the truth behind the order for the massacre.

The death of Queen Mary on 28 December 1694 left William distraught for months afterwards. This meant that William was sole monarch of the Scots, though in practice he had always been the major power behind the throne as Mary had never participated in government. To placate the Scots for Glencoe and enhance his personal standing, the king willingly agreed to let the Scots have their own Company of Scotland in 1695 to trade with Africa, the Indies and the Americas. This also allowed Scots to establish their own trading post at the Isthmus of Darien in Central America. Previously, Scottish merchants had not been allowed to trade directly with English colonies because of the draconian English Navigation Acts. These only allowed English ships to carry goods in and out of their ports and had been designed to thwart Dutch mercantile expansion into the English sphere of influence. The Acts had the knock on effect of stalling Scottish trade in developing colonial markets. What seemed like a good idea turned into yet another disaster for the Scots that further distanced them from King William. The Darien venture swallowed a quarter of Scotland's liquid capital, yet failed miserably as Darien was ill suited to settlement. William did nothing to help the settlers of this colony when they encountered severe difficulties such as disease, Spanish attacks and poor soils. The English colonies in the Caribbean could have helped them, but King William forbade them to do so for fear of antagonising Spain who had a competing claim to Darien. William did not want Spain to ally with his great enemy France and cared little for the 2,000 Scots who died as a result of the failed venture and the thousands of Scots who lost their life savings. Anti-English feeling in Scotland boiled over and resulted in riots against the king and his ministers.

The Scottish economy was not as advanced as that of England and the failure of Darien led to discussions about a full parliamentary union between the realms. However this would not be accomplished until the reign of William's successor and sister-in-law, Queen Anne. Even the establishment of the Bank of Scotland in 1695 did little to bolster the Scottish economy as it merely acted as a clearing bank for many years, rather than accrue deposits. Few Scots lamented the death of William on 8 March 1702 at Kensington Palace. He had been a true European who had little interest in Scotland other than using her taxes to fund his perpetual warfare against the expansionism of Louis XIV of France. The link between Scotland and the Stuart monarchy was now tenuous, so it is not surprising that some maintained their loyalty to James VII. In comparison to William, James now appeared an honourable statesman who had at least visited Scotland. The seeds of lasting support for Jacobitism in Scotland had therefore germinated.

MM

ANNE (1702-1714)

Queen Anne succeeded her brother-in-law, William II, on 8 March 1702. To her it was a 'sunshine day', yet at her birth on 6 February 1665 few could have predicted that the second daughter of James VII and his first wife Anne Hyde would become the last Stuart

182. Anne gives her assent to the Act of Union, 1707, mezzotint by Valentine Green.
183. The pavilion at Moray House, Edinburgh, where the Scottish ministers hid from the mob
after the signing of the Articles of Union.

monarch of Scotland and England. There was talk of her marrying the Prince of Hanover, but negotiations fell through. On 28 July 1683, Anne married Prince George of Denmark, the second son of Frederick III, after which she was known as Princess Anne of Denmark. They were distantly related as Anne was the great-great-grand-daughter of Frederick II of Denmark, the father of James VI's consort Anna. George was Frederick II's great-grandson. Theirs was a Protestant alliance for, like her elder sister Mary, Anne had received a Protestant education. Anne remained a devout Anglican throughout her life and wisely chose not to meddle with the religion of either her Scottish or English subjects, unlike her Stuart predecessors. She had, after all, deserted the cause of her father during the 1688 crisis to preserve her religion. However, the open betrayal of her father left her with feelings of guilt for the rest of her life.

After their wedding, Anne and George lived in a grace and favour apartment in the palace of Whitehall given to them by her uncle, Charles II. This palace was their main London home until 1702 and their favourite country house was at Richmond until 1688 and Windsor thereafter. Anne briefly visited Scotland in 1681, when her father was holding court there as duke of York. Rent free houses did not stop Anna and George from getting into debt by overspending. Anne had a royal income and George still had estates in Denmark, but payments due to them were always slow to materialise. On top of their monetary problems, relations between Anne and her sister Mary became difficult after Anne's marriage. There was an undeniable rivalry between their husbands over who had precedence at royal ceremonials, which appears petty yet was deadly serious in its day. If either was offered preferential treatment the other took offence all too easily. As Anne and George were resident in Britain, they were more readily available for royal events. However, George had married the younger sister and was a younger son himself, unlike William of Orange, who was a European ruler married to the eldest sister.

Life under the rule of her father, James VII, was awkward for Anne as she refused to acknowledge his favouritism of Catholics and openly declined to change her faith. This alienated Anne even further from her father and stepmother. Protestant courtiers rallied to her household, in defiance of James VII. Anne wrote secretly to her sister, discussing matters that could be defined as treasonable. They certainly would have discussed the birth of their stepbrother James, whose existence now put their succession to the throne in doubt. What they agreed about this is unrecorded, but Anne's rejection of James VII and her flight to Nottingham at the start of the 1688 rebellion were clearly planned. When William and Mary assumed joint power, Anne's right to the succession was upheld, for she and her heirs would take precedence over any child born to King William by a second marriage. James VII, now in exile in France, never forgave either of his daughters for their treachery in taking his throne from him.

Surviving under William and Mary's rule was difficult for Anne and George. They bickered about money and dabbled with oppositional politics. William resented the warmth of the public towards Anne as a mother and queen in waiting. Anne's friendship with her sister waned once more and William behaved spitefully towards his brother-in-law, Prince George. All their old rivalries now came flooding back, leaving the monarchy at an impasse until the death of Queen Mary in 1694. This forced a grief-stricken reconciliation between Anne and William, during which he gave Anne 'most of her sister's jewels.' They now had the shared responsibility of protecting the throne for the young Duke of Gloucester against the threats of the Jacobites. In public, at least, they buried their differences.

It would be seven years before Anne inherited the throne, but this was a relatively quiet period in her life. Anne's greatest tragedy was then her ultimate inability to give birth to a child who survived into adulthood. She tried desperately to produce healthy heirs, yet by 1700 she had endured no less than eighteen pregnancies. Of these only five were live births - the others being miscarriages or stillbirths. All these pregnancies had a detrimental effect upon the health of Anne, who was left a semi-invalid as a result. Moreover she insisted upon personally nursing any of her children who were sickly, rather than assigning this to servants and courtiers. The loss of each surviving child hurt Anne and George deeply. Lady Mary and Lady Anne for example died of smallpox, a scourge of the seventeenth century. Despite there being great hopes for William, Duke of Gloucester, he also died of this disease aged eleven, on 30 July 1700. He had never been strong, but he was popular and his death was greatly mourned, even by his uncle, William II.

From her accession in 1702 until her death in 1714, Anne was not as active a monarch as her predecessor. She preferred to leave affairs of state to her chief ministers, yet was not an ineffectual queen. This was a period of intense political party activity at both the Scottish and English parliaments and Anne had opinions on political matters that were listened to. She never visited Scotland, nor did she intend to, but her ministers kept her informed of political affairs there. These came to a head early in her reign during the succession crisis of 1702-03. England had accepted that there would be a Hanoverian succession to their throne upon Anne's death through the descendants of Elizabeth, daughter of James VI. The Scots parliament refused to follow suit, insisting that they had the right to determine their own successor to the Scottish crown, as long as they were Protestant. This brought about renewed calls from England for parliamentary union to stop Scots divergence from accepted English practice. The Scots' reaction was to condemn the interference of English ministers in their internal affairs. Punitive laws were passed in England against Scots and their goods. This eventually led to commissioners for union being appointed by the queen in February 1706.

Anne avidly supported the idea of union and this helped with its acceptance in England. Her commissioners from both Scotland and England were hand picked to sway the balance of their discussions in favour of full, incorporating union. They met at Westminster and negotiated for several months. The articles of the Treaty of Union were agreed and put to the respective parliaments of Scotland and England. These were comprehensive measures relating to trade, the law, taxation, coinage, weights and measures, compensation for Darien and parliamentary representation, amongst other issues. For the monarchy there was now tacit acceptance by the Scots of the Hanoverian succession.

The Scots parliament was hardly a representative body when it convened in November 1706, but they painstakingly went through every article of union. Bribery and suspicious new peerages were the order of the day amongst the landowners, so many of them now switched to favour union. The burgesses were also for union as they were promised trading advantages. Once the rights of the kirk were inserted into the act, the majority of the clergy were satisfied with it. However, the mobs were not as easily persuaded as the politicians were and they barracked the pro-unionists on a nightly basis. Popular opinion now registered with the queen for all the wrong reasons. She promptly sent an English army northwards to muster on the border in case rebellion broke out in Scotland.

Anne saw the completion of union on 1 May 1707 as the highlight of her reign. Scottish anti-unionists felt nothing but betrayal. The debate about the union is as heated today as it was in 1706-07, though Scotland has her own parliament once more. Union distracts from other aspects of Anne's reign, which gave its name to a period of genteel arts, culture and architecture in Britain. One year after the Act of Union, the death of Prince George from asthma 28 October 1708 left Anne in 'an unspeakable grief'. Their marriage, unlike her father's and uncle Charles II's, had been solid and without scandal. It was reminiscent of the marriages of James VI and Charles I where arranged matches turned to lasting love, fidelity and friendship. Anne lived on as a widow until 1 August 1714.

As the last of the Stuarts, she had kept both Hanoverian and Jacobite from prematurely snatching her throne. This was no mean achievement for a female ruler in the early-eighteenth century, but the problem of the Jacobites would come back to haunt her Hanoverian successors George I and George II. In reality few English politicians really understood the problems of Scotland after 1707 and the monarchy preferred to ignore this part of their new United Kingdom. None of the royal family had visited the country since the stay of James VII as duke of York during 1679-82 and none would return there until the nineteenth century.

MM

FURTHER READING

GENERAL BACKGROUND

Barrow, G.W.S., *Kingship and Unity: Scotland 1000-1306* (London, 1981).

Duncan, A.A.M., *Scotland: the Making of the Kingdom* (Edinburgh, 1975).

Grant, A., *Independence and Nationhood: Scotland 1306-1469* (London, 1984).

Grant, A., and Stringer, K.J. (eds), *Medieval Scotland: Crown, Lordship and Community* (Edinburgh, 1993).

Mitchison, R., *From Lordship to Patronage: Scotland 1603-1746* (London, 1983).

Oram, R.D., *Scotland's Kings and Queens: Royalty and the Realm* (Edinburgh, 1997).

Smyth, A.P., *Warlords and Holy Men: Scotland AD 80-1000* (London, 1984).

Watson, F., *Scotland: A History 8000 BC – AD 2000* (Stroud, 2000).

Wormald, J., Court, *Kirk and Community: Scotland 1469-1625* (London, 1981).

THE EARLIEST KINGS

Aitchison, N., *Macbeth* (Stroud, 1999).

Anderson, M.O., *Kings and Kingship in Early Scotland*, 2nd edition (Edinburgh, 1980).

Chadwick, H.M., *Early Scotland: the Picts, the Scots and the Welsh of Southern Scotland* (Cambridge, 1949).

Foster, S., *Picts, Gaels and Scots* (Edinburgh, 1996).

Henderson, I., *The Picts* (London, 1967).

Hudson, B.T., *Kings of Celtic Scotland* (Westport, Connecticut, 1994).

Laing, L. and Laing, J., *The Picts and the Scots* (Stroud, 1993).

Small, A. (ed.), *The Picts: a New Look at Old Problems* (Dundee, 1987).

THE HOUSE OF CANMORE

Barrow, G.W.S., *David I of Scotland (1124-1153): the Balance of New and Old* (Reading, 1984).

Oram, R.D. (ed.), *Scotland in the Reign of Alexander II* (Forthcoming, Glasgow, 2002).

Owen, D.D.R., *William the Lion. Kingship and Culture 1143-1214* (East Linton, 1997).

Reid, N. (ed.), *Scotland in the Reign of Alexander III* (Edinburgh, 1990).

Stringer, K.J., *The Reign of Stephen: Kingship, Warfare and Government in Twelfth-Century England* (London, 1993) [This gives a detailed account of David I's campaigns in northern England.]

Wilson, A.J., *St Margaret, Queen of Scotland* (Edinburgh, 1993).

THE HOUSE OF BRUCE & THE HOUSE OF BALLIOL

Balfour-Melville, E.W.M., *Edward III and David II* (1954).

Barron, E.M., *The Scottish Wars of Independence* (1934, 2nd edition 2000).

Barrow, G.W.S., *Robert the Bruce and the Community of the Realm of Scotland* (1965, 3rd edition 1988).

Barrow, G.W.S., 'A Kingdom in Crisis: Scotland and the Maid of Norway', *Scottish Historical Review*, lxix (1990).

Boardman, S., *The Early Stewarts: Robert II and Robert III, 1371-1406* (1996).

Brereton, G. (ed.), *Froissart's Chronicles* (1968).

Brown, M., *The Black Douglases: War and Lordship in Late Medieval Scotland 1300-1455* (1998).

Child, F.J., *The English and Scottish Popular Ballads* (5 volumes, Boston 1882-98).

Donaldson, G., *Scottish Kings* (1969).

Duncan, A.A.M., *The Nation of Scots and the Declaration of Arbroath* (1970).

Duncan, A.A.M., '"Honi soit qui mal y pense": David II and Edward III, 1346-52', *Scottish Historical Review*, lxvii (1988).

Duncan, A.A.M. (ed.), *John Barbour's The Bruce* (1998).

MacDonald, A., *Border Bloodshed; Scotland, England and France at War, 1369-1406* (2000).

McNamee, C., *The Wars of the Bruces: Scotland, England and Ireland 1306-28* (1997).

Nicholson, R., 'David II, the historians and the chroniclers', *Scottish Historical Review*, xlv (1966).

Nicholson, R., *Scotland – the Later Middle Ages* (1974).

Penman, M., 'Christian Days and Knights: the Religious Devotions and Court of David II of Scotland, 1329-71', *Historical Research*, October 2001.

Penman, M., *The Bruce Dynasty in Scotland: David II, 1329-71* (forthcoming).

Reid, R.C., 'Edward de Balliol', *Transactions of the Dumfriess-shire and Galloway Antiquarian and Natural History Society*, 35 (1956-57).

Simpson, G.G., 'The Heart of King Robert I: Pious Crusade or Marketing Gambit?', in B.E. Crawford ed., *Church, Chronicle and Learning: Essays in Medieval and Early Renaissance Scotland* (2000).

Skene, W.F., *John of Fordun's Chronicle of the Scottish Nation* (2 volumes, 1872, reprint 1993).

Stones, E.J.G. (ed.), *Anglo-Scottish Relations 1174-1328* (1965).

Watson, F., *Under the Hammer: Edward I and Scotland, 1286-1307* (1998).

Watt, D.E.R. *et al* (eds), *Scotichronicon of Walter Bower* (9 volumes, 1987-99), volumes 6 and 7.

Webster, B., 'David II and the Government of Fourteenth Century Scotland', *Transactions of the Royal Historical Society,* 5th series, xvi (1966).

Young, A. and Stead, M., *In the Footsteps of Robert Bruce* (1999).

THE STEWART DYNASTY IN SCOTLAND

Brown, Michael, *James I* (East Linton, 1994).

Cameron, J., *James V: the Personal Rule 1528-1542* (East Linton, 1998).

Fraser, A., *Mary, Queen of Scots* (London, 1969).

Lee, M., *Government By Pen. Scotland under James VI & I* (Urbana, 1980).

Lynch, M. (ed.), *Mary Stewart: Queen in Three Kingdoms* (Oxford, 1988).

Lynch, M. and Goodare, J. (eds), *The Reign of James VI* (East Linton, 1999).

Macdougall, N.T., *James III: a Political Study* (Edinburgh, 1982).

Macdougall, N.T., *James IV* (Edinburgh, 1989).

McGladdery, C., *James II* (East Linton, 1990).

Smith, A. G. R., ed., *The Reign of James VI & I,* (London, 1973).

Willson, D. H., *King James VI & I* (London, 1959).

Wormald, J., 'James VI & I: Two Kings or One?', *History*, 68 (1983).

Wormald, J., *Mary Queen of Scots: a Study in Failure* (London, 1988).

THE BRITISH STEWARTS

Armitage, D., 'Making the Empire British: Scotland and the Atlantic World 1542-1717', *Past and Present,* 155 (1997).

Brown, K. M., *Kingdom or Province? Scotland and the Regal Union 1603-1715* (Basingstoke, 1992).

Carlton, C., *Charles I. The personal monarch* (London, 1995).

Cowan, E. J., *Montrose: For Covenant and King* (London, 1977).

Cowan, E. J., 'The solemn League and Covenant', in R. A. Mason, ed., *Scotland and England, 1286-1815* (Edinburgh, 1987).

Cowan, I. B., 'The reluctant revolutionaries: Scotland in 1688', in E. Cruickshanks, ed., *By Force or Default? The Revolution of 1688-89* (Edinburgh, 1989).

Cruickshanks, E., *The Glorious Revolution* (Basingstoke, 2000).

Donald, P., *An Uncounselled King. Charles I and the Scottish Troubles* (Cambridge, 1990)

Dow, F., *Cromwellian Scotland. 1651-1660* (Edinburgh, 1979).

Furgol, E., *A Regimental History of the Covenanting Armies. 1639-51* (Edinburgh, 1990).

Furgol, E., 'The Civil Wars in Scotland', in J. Kenyon & J. Ohlmeyer, eds. *The Civil Wars* (Oxford, 1998).

Fissell, M., *The Bishop's War* (Cambridge, 1994).

Gentles, I., *The New Model Army in England, Ireland and Scotland, 1645-53* (Oxford, 1991).

Glassey, L. J. K, *Charles II and James VII & II* (Basingstoke, 1997).

Gregg, E., *Queen Anne* (London, 1984).

Harris, T., 'Reluctant Revolutionaries? The Scots and the Revolution of 1688-89', in H. Nenner, ed. *Politics and the Political Imagination in Later Stuart Britain* (Rochester, 1997).

Hodge, P., ed., *Scotland and the Union* (Edinburgh, 1994).

Kidd, C., 'Protestantism, constitutionalism and British identity under the later Stuarts', in B. Bradshaw & P. Roberts, eds., *British consciousness and identity, the making of Britain 1533-1707* (Cambridge, 1998).

Hopkins, P., *Glencoe and the End of the Highland War* (Edinburgh, 1998).

Hutton, R., *Charles II: King of Scotland, Ireland and England* (Oxford, 1991).

Lee, M., *The Road to Revolution: Scotland under Charles I, 1625-37* (Urbana, 1985).

Lenman, B., *The Jacobite Risings in Britain, 1689-1746* (Edinburgh, 1995).

Levack, B., *The Formation of the British State: England, Scotland and the Union 1603-1707* (Oxford, 1987).

Macinnes, A., *Charles I and the Covenanting Movement, 1625-41* (Edinburgh, 1991).

MacInnes, A. I., *Clanship, Commerce and the House of Stuart, 1603-1788* (East Linton, 1996).

Miller, J., *James II. A study in kingship* (London, 1991).

Moorhouse, R., 'Disaster. Scotland's brave, brief empire', *BBC History Magazine,* 2/7 (2001).

Morrill, J., ed., *The Scottish National Covenant in its British Context, 1638-51* (Edinburgh, 1990).

Morrill, J., 'The Wars(s) of the Three Kingdoms', in G. Burgess, ed., *The New British History* (London, 1999).

Ouston, H., '"From Thames to Tweed Departed": The Court of James, Duke of York in Scotland, 1679-82', in E. Cruickshanks, ed. *The Stuart Courts* (Stroud, 2000).

Riley, P. W. J., *King William and the Scottish Politicians* (Edinburgh, 1979).

Riley, *The Union of England and Scotland* (Manchester, 1978).

Robertson, J., ed., *A Union for Empire. Political Thought and the British Union of 1707* (Cambridge, 1995).

Russell, C., *The Fall of the British Monarchies 1637-1642* (Oxford, 1992).

Russell, C., 'The Anglo-Scottish Union 1603-1643', in A. Fletcher & P. Roberts, eds., *Religion, Culture and Society in Early Modern Britain* (Cambridge, 1994).

Scott, P. H., *'The Boasted Advantages' The Consequences of the Union of 1707* (Edinburgh, 1999).

Sharpe, K., *The Personal Rule of Charles I* (New Haven, 1992).

Stevenson, D., *King or Covenant? Voices from Civil War* (East Linton, 1996).

Stevenson, D., *Union, Revolution & Religion in 17th Century Scotland* (Aldershot, 1997).

Whatley, C., *Bought and Sold for English Gold* (Edinburgh, 1994).

Young, J. R., ed., *Celtic Dimensions of the British Civil Wars* (Edinburgh, 1997).

LIST OF ILLUSTRATIONS

Colour Section

Index

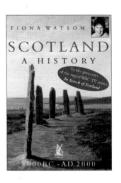
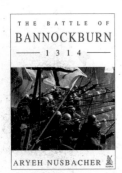